John Richard Green

Stray studies from England and Italy

John Richard Green

Stray studies from England and Italy

ISBN/EAN: 9783337277048

Printed in Europe, USA, Canada, Australia, Japan

Cover: Foto ©Andreas Hilbeck / pixelio.de

More available books at **www.hansebooks.com**

STRAY STUDIES

FROM

ENGLAND AND ITALY

BY

JOHN RICHARD GREEN

London
MACMILLAN AND CO.
AND NEW YORK
1892

All rights reserved

PREFACE

I HAVE to thank the Editors of *Macmillan's Magazine* and the *Saturday Review* for allowing me to reprint most of the papers in this series. In many cases however I have greatly changed their original form. A few pages will be found to repeat what I have already said in my 'Short History.'

CONTENTS

	PAGE
A BROTHER OF THE POOR	1
SKETCHES IN SUNSHINE:—	
I. CANNES AND ST. HONORAT	27
II. CARNIVAL ON THE CORNICE	38
III. TWO PIRATE TOWNS OF THE RIVIERA	50
IV. THE WINTER RETREAT	60
V. SAN REMO	67
THE POETRY OF WEALTH	77
LAMBETH AND THE ARCHBISHOPS	91
CHILDREN BY THE SEA	141
THE FLORENCE OF DANTE	153
BUTTERCUPS	169
ABBOT AND TOWN	181
HOTELS IN THE CLOUDS	207
ÆNEAS: A VERGILIAN STUDY	221
TWO VENETIAN STUDIES:—	
I. VENICE AND ROME	249
II. VENICE AND TINTORETTO	258

CONTENTS

	PAGE
THE DISTRICT VISITOR	269
THE EARLY HISTORY OF OXFORD	283
THE HOME OF OUR ANGEVIN KINGS	309
CAPRI	329
CAPRI AND ITS ROMAN REMAINS	339
THE FEAST OF THE CORAL-FISHERS	353

A BROTHER OF THE POOR

A BROTHER OF THE POOR

There are few stiller things than the stillness of a summer's noon such as this, a summer's noon in a broken woodland, with the deer asleep in the bracken, and the twitter of birds silent in the coppice, and hardly a leaf astir in the huge beeches that fling their cool shade over the grass. Afar off a gilded vane flares out above the grey Jacobean gables of Knoll, the chime of a village clock falls faintly on the ear, but there is no voice or footfall of living thing to break the silence as I turn over leaf after leaf of the little book I have brought with me from the bustle of town to this still retreat, a book that is the record of a broken life, of a life "broken off," as he who lived it says of another, "with a ragged edge."

It is a book that carries one far from the woodland stillness around into the din and turmoil of cities and men, into the misery and degradation of "the East-end,"—that "London without London," as some one called it the other day. Few regions are more unknown than the Tower Hamlets. Not even Mrs. Riddell has ventured as yet to cross the border which parts the City from their weltering mass of busy life, their million of hard workers packed together in endless rows of monotonous streets, broken only by ship-yard or factory or huge breweries, streets that stretch away eastward from Aldgate to the Essex marshes. And yet, setting aside the poetry of life which is everywhere, there is poetry enough in East London; poetry in the great river which washes it on the south, in the fretted tangle of cordage and mast that peeps over the roofs of Shadwell or in the great hulls moored along the wharves of Wapping; poetry in the "Forest" that fringes it to the east, in the few glades that remain of Epping and Hainault,—glades ringing with the shouts of school-children out for their holiday and half mad with delight at the sight of a flower or a butterfly; poetry of the present in the work and toil of these acres of dull bricks and mortar where everybody, man woman and child, is a worker, this England without a "leisure class"; poetry in the thud of the steam-engine and the white trail of steam from the tall sugar refinery, in the blear eyes of the Spitalfields weaver, or the hungering faces of the group of labourers clustered from morning till night round the gates of the docks and watching for the wind that brings the ships up the river: poetry in its past, in strange old-fashioned squares, in quaint gabled houses, in grey village churches, that have been caught and overlapped and lost, as it were, in the great human advance that has carried London forward from Whitechapel, its limit in the age of the Georges, to Stratford, its bound in that of Victoria.

Stepney is a belated village of this sort; its grey old church of St. Dunstan, buried as it is now in the very heart of East London, stood hardly a century ago among the fields. All round it lie tracts of human life without a past; but memories cluster thickly round "Old Stepney," as the people call it with a certain fond reverence, memories of men like Erasmus and Colet and the group of scholars in whom the Reformation began. It was to the country house of the Dean of St. Paul's, hard by the old church of St. Dunstan, that Erasmus betook him when tired of the smoke and din of town. "I come to drink your fresh air, my Colet," he writes, "to drink yet deeper of your rural peace." The fields and hedges through which Erasmus loved to ride remained fields and hedges within living memory; only forty years ago a Londoner took his Sunday outing along the field path which led past the London Hospital to what was still the suburban village church of Stepney. But the fields through which the path led have their own church now, with its parish of dull straight streets of monotonous houses already marked with premature decay, and here and there alleys haunted by poverty and disease and crime.

There is nothing marked about either church or district; their character and that of their people are of the commonest East-end type. If I ask my readers to follow me to this parish of St. Philip, it is simply because these dull streets and alleys were chosen by a brave and earnest man as the scene of his work among the poor. It was here that Edward Denison settled in the autumn of 1867, in the second year of the great "East London Distress." In the October of 1869 he left England on a fatal voyage from which he was never to return. The collection of his letters which has been recently printed by Sir Baldwyn Leighton has drawn so much attention to the work which lay within the narrow bounds of those two years that I may perhaps be pardoned for recalling my own memories of one whom it is hard to forget.

A few words are enough to tell the tale of his earlier days. Born in 1840, the son of a bishop, and nephew of the late Speaker of the House of Commons, Edward Denison passed from Eton to Christchurch, and was forced after quitting the University to spend some time in foreign travel by the delicacy of his health. His letters give an interesting picture of his mind during this pause in an active life, a pause which must have been especially distasteful to one whose whole bent lay from the first in the direction of practical energy. "I believe," he says in his later days, "that abstract political speculation is my *métier*;" but few minds were in reality less inclined to abstract speculation. From the very first one sees in him what one may venture to call the best kind of "Whig" mind, that peculiar temper of fairness and moderation which declines to push conclusions to extremes, and recoils instinctively when opinion is extended beyond its proper bound His comment on Newman's "Apologia" paints his real intellectual temper with remarkable precision. "I left off reading Newman's 'Apologia' before I got to the end, tired of the ceaseless changes of the writer's mind, and vexed with his morbid scruples—perhaps, too, having got a little out of harmony myself with the feelings of the author, whereas I began by being in harmony with them. I don't quite know whether to esteem it a blessing or a curse; but whenever an opinion to which I am a recent convert, or which I do not hold with the entire force of my intellect, is forced too strongly upon me, or driven home to its logical conclusion, or over-praised, or extended beyond its proper limits, I recoil instinctively and begin to gravitate towards the other extreme, sure to be in turn repelled by it also."

I dwell on this temper of his mind because it is this practical and moderate character of the man which gives such weight to the very sweeping conclusions on social subjects to which he was driven in his later days. A judgment which condemns the whole system of Poor Laws, for instance, falls with very different weight from a mere speculative theorist and from a practical observer whose mind is constitutionally averse from extreme conclusions. Throughout however we see this intellectual moderation jostling with a moral fervour which feels restlessly about for a fitting sphere of action. "Real life," he writes from Madeira, "is not dinner-parties and small talk, nor even croquet and dancing." There is a touch of exaggeration in phrases like these which need not blind us to the depth and reality of the feeling which they imperfectly express, a feeling which prompted the question which embodies the spirit of all these earlier letters,—the question, "What is my work?"

The answer to this question was found both within and without the questioner. Those who were young in the weary days of Palmerstonian rule will remember the disgust at purely political life which was produced by the bureaucratic inaction of the time, and we can hardly wonder that, like many of the finer minds among his contemporaries, Edward Denison turned from the political field which was naturally open to him to the field of social effort. His tendency in this direction was aided, no doubt, partly by the intensity of his religious feeling and of his consciousness of the duty he owed to the poor, and partly by that closer sympathy with the physical suffering around us which is one of the most encouraging characteristics of the day. Even in the midst of his outburst of delight at a hard frost ("I like," he says, "the bright sunshine that generally accompanies it, the silver landscape, and the ringing distinctness of sounds in the frozen air"), we see him haunted by a sense of the way in which his pleasure contrasts with the winter misery of the poor. "I would rather give up all the pleasures of the frost than indulge them, poisoned as they are by the misery of so many of our brothers. What a monstrous thing it is that in the richest country in the world large masses of the population should be condemned annually to starvation and death!" It is easy to utter protests like these in the spirit of a mere sentimentalist; it is less easy to carry them out into practical effort, as Edward Denison resolved to do. After an unsatisfactory attempt to act as Almoner for the Society for the Relief of Distress, he resolved to fix himself personally in the East-end of London, and study the great problem of pauperism face to face.

His resolve sprang from no fit of transient enthusiasm, but from a sober conviction of the need of such a step. "There are hardly any residents in the East rich enough to give much money, or with enough leisure to give much time," he says. "This is the evil. Even the best disposed in the West don't like coming so far off, and, indeed, few have the time to spare, and when they do there is great waste of time and energy on the journey. My plan is the only really practicable one, and as I have both means, time, and inclination, I should be a thief and a murderer if I withheld what I so evidently owe." In the autumn of 1867 he carried out his resolve, and took lodgings in the heart of the parish which I sketched in the opening of this paper. If any romantic dreams had mixed with his resolution they at once faded away before the dull, commonplace reality. "I saw nothing very striking at Stepney," is his first comment on the sphere he had chosen. But he was soon satisfied with his choice. He took up in a quiet, practical way the work he found closest at hand. "All is yet in embryo, but it will grow. Just now I only teach in a night school, and do what in me lies in looking after the sick, keeping an eye upon nuisances and the like, seeing that the local authorities keep up to their work. I go to-morrow before the Board at the workhouse to compel the removal to the infirmary of a man who ought to have been there already. I shall drive the sanitary inspector to put the Act against overcrowding in force." Homely work of this sort grows on him; we see him in these letters getting boys out to sea, keeping school with little urchins,—"demons of misrule" who tried his temper,—gathering round him a class of working men, organizing an evening club for boys. All this, too, quietly and unostentatiously and with as little resort as possible to "cheap charity," as he used to call it, to the "doles of bread and meat which only do the work of poor-rates."

So quiet and simple indeed was his work that though it went on in the parish of which I then had the charge it was some little time before I came to know personally the doer of it. It is amusing even now to recollect my first interview with Edward Denison. A vicar's Monday morning is never the pleasantest of awakenings, but the Monday morning of an East-end vicar brings worries that far eclipse the mere headache and dyspepsia of his rural brother. It is the "parish morning." All the complicated machinery of a great ecclesiastical, charitable, and educational organization has got to be wound up afresh, and set going again for another week. The superintendent of the Women's Mission is waiting with a bundle of accounts, complicated as only ladies' accounts can be. The churchwarden has come with a face full of gloom to consult on the falling off in the offertory. The Scripture-reader has brought his "visiting book" to be inspected, and a special report on the character of a doubtful family in the parish. The organist drops in to report something wrong in the pedals. There is a letter to be written to the inspector of nuisances, directing his attention to certain odoriferous drains in Pig-and-Whistle Alley. The nurse brings her sick-list and her little bill for the sick-kitchen. The schoolmaster wants a fresh pupil-teacher, and discusses nervously the prospects

of his scholars in the coming inspection. There is
the interest on the penny bank to be calculated, a
squabble in the choir to be adjusted, a district visitor
to be replaced, reports to be drawn up for the Bishop's
Fund and a great charitable society, the curate's sick-
list to be inspected, and a preacher to be found for the
next church festival.

It was in the midst of a host of worries such as
these that a card was laid on my table with a name
which I recognized as that of a young layman from
the West-end, who had for two or three months past
been working in the mission district attached to the
parish. Now, whatever shame is implied in the
confession, I had a certain horror of "laymen from
the West-end." Lay co-operation is an excellent
thing in itself, and one of my best assistants was a
letter-sorter in the post-office close by; but the
"layman from the West-end," with a bishop's letter
of recommendation in his pocket and a head full of
theories about "heathen masses," was an unmitigated
nuisance. I had a pretty large experience of these
gentlemen, and my one wish in life was to have no
more. Some had a firm belief in their own eloquence,
and were zealous for a big room and a big congregation.
I got them the big room, but I was obliged to leave
the big congregation to their own exertions, and in
a month or two their voices faded away. Then
there was the charitable layman, who pounced down
on the parish from time to time and threw about

meat and blankets till half of the poor were demoralized. Or there was the statistical layman, who went about with a note-book and did spiritual and economical sums in the way of dividing the number of "people in the free seats" by the number of bread tickets annually distributed. There was the layman with a passion for homœopathy, the ritualistic layman, the layman with a mania for preaching down trades' unions, the layman with an educational mania. All however agreed in one point, much as they differed in others, and the one point was that of a perfect belief in their individual nostrums and perfect contempt for all that was already doing in the neighbourhood.

It was with no peculiar pleasure therefore that I rose to receive this fresh "layman from the West"; but a single glance was enough to show me that my visitor was a man of very different stamp from his predecessors. There was something in the tall, manly figure, the bright smile, the frank winning address of Edward Denison that inspired confidence in a moment. "I come to learn, and not to teach," he laughed, as I hinted at "theories" and their danger; and our talk soon fell on a certain "John's Place," where he thought there was a great deal to be learned. In five minutes more we stood in the spot which interested him, an alley running between two mean streets, and narrowing at one end till we crept out of it as if through the neck of a bottle. It was by no means the choicest part of the parish: the drainage was imperfect, the houses miserable; but wretched as it was it was a favourite haunt of the poor, and it swarmed with inhabitants of very various degrees of respectability. Costermongers abounded, strings of barrows were drawn up on the pavement, and the refuse of their stock lay rotting in the gutter. Drunken sailors and Lascars from the docks rolled along shouting to its houses of ill-fame. There was little crime, though one of the "ladies" of the alley was a well-known receiver of stolen goods, but there was a good deal of drunkenness and vice. Now and then a wife came plumping on to the pavement from a window overhead; sometimes a couple of viragoes fought out their quarrel "on the stones"; boys idled about in the sunshine in training to be pickpockets; miserable girls flaunted in dirty ribbons at nightfall at half-a-dozen doors.

But with all this the place was popular with even respectable working people in consequence of the small size and cheapness of the houses—for there is nothing the poor like so much as a house to themselves; and the bulk of its population consisted of casual labourers, who gathered every morning round the great gates of the docks, waiting to be "called in" as the ships came up to unload. The place was naturally unhealthy, constantly haunted by fever, and had furnished some hundred cases in the last visitation of cholera. The work done among them in the "cholera time" had never been forgotten by the people, and, ill-famed as the place was, I visited it at all times of the day and night with perfect security. The apostle however of John's Place was my friend the letter-sorter. He had fixed on it as his special domain, and with a little aid from others had opened a Sunday-school and simple Sunday services in the heart of it. A branch of the Women's Mission was established in the same spot, and soon women were "putting by" their pence and sewing quietly round the lady superintendent as she read to them the stories of the Gospels.

It was this John's Place which Edward Denison chose as the centre of his operations. There was very little in his manner to show his sense of the sacrifice he was making, though the sacrifice was in reality a great one. No one enjoyed more keenly the pleasures of life and society: he was a good oarsman, he delighted in outdoor exercise, and skating was to him "a pleasure only rivalled in my affection by a ride across country on a good horse." But month after month these pleasures were quietly put aside for his work in the East-end. "I have come to this," he says, laughingly, "that a walk along Piccadilly is a most exhilarating and delightful treat. I don't enjoy it above once in ten days, but therefore with double zest." What told on him most was the physical depression induced by the very look of these vast, monotonous masses of sheer poverty.

"My wits are getting blunted," he says, "by the monotony and *ugliness* of this place. I can almost imagine, difficult as it is, the awful effect upon a human mind of never seeing anything but the meanest and vilest of men and men's works, and of complete exclusion from the sight of God and His works,—a position in which the villager never is." But there was worse than physical degradation. "This summer there is not so very much actual suffering for want of food, nor from sickness. What is so bad is the habitual condition of this mass of humanity—its uniform mean level, the absence of anything more civilizing than a grinding organ to raise the ideas beyond the daily bread and beer, the utter want of education, the complete indifference to religion, with the fruits of all this—improvidence, dirt, and their secondaries, crime and disease."

Terrible however as these evils were, he believed they could be met; and the quiet good sense of his character was shown in the way in which he met them. His own residence in the East-end was the most effective of protests against that severance of class from class in which so many of its evils take their rise. When speaking of the overcrowding and the official ill-treatment of the poor, he says truly: "These are the sort of evils which, where there are no resident gentry, grow to a height almost incredible, and on which the remedial influence of the mere presence of a gentleman known to be on the alert is inestimable." But nothing, as I often had occasion to remark, could be more judicious than his interference on behalf of the poor, or more unlike the fussy impertinence of the philanthropists who think themselves born "to expose" Boards of Guardians. His aim throughout was to co-operate with the Guardians in giving, not less, but greater effect to the Poor Laws, and in resisting the sensational writing and reckless abuse which aim at undoing their work. "The gigantic subscription lists which are regarded as signs of our benevolence," he says truly, "are monuments of our indifference."

The one hope for the poor, he believed, lay not in charity, but in themselves. "Build school-houses, pay teachers, give prizes, frame workmen's clubs, help them to help themselves, lend them your brains; but give them no money, except what you sink in such undertakings as above." This is not the place to describe or discuss the more detailed suggestions with which he faced the great question of poverty and pauperism in the East-end; they are briefly summarized in a remarkable letter which he addressed in 1869 to an East-end newspaper:—
"First we must so discipline and regulate our charities as to cut off the resources of the habitual mendicant. Secondly, all who by begging proclaim themselves destitute, must be taken at their word. They must be taken up and kept at penal work—not for one morning, as now, but for a

month or two; a proportion of their earnings being handed over to them on dismissal, as capital on which to begin a life of honest industry. Thirdly, we must promote the circulation of labour, and obviate morbid congestions of the great industrial centres. Fourthly, we must improve the condition of the agricultural poor." Stern as such suggestions may seem, there are few who have really thought as well as worked for the poor without feeling that sternness of this sort is, in the highest sense, mercy. Ten years in the East of London had brought me to the same conclusions; and my Utopia, like Edward Denison's, lay wholly in a future to be worked out by the growing intelligence and thrift of the labouring classes themselves.

But, stern as were his theories, there is hardly a home within his district that has not some memory left of the love and tenderness of his personal charity. I hardly like to tell how often I have seen the face of the sick and dying brighten as he drew near, or how the little children, as they flocked out of school, would run to him, shouting his name for very glee. For the Sunday-school was soon transformed by his efforts into a day-school for children, whose parents were really unable to pay school-fees; and a large school-room, erected near John's Place, was filled with dirty little scholars. Here too he gathered round him a class of working men, to whom he lectured on the Bible every Wednesday evening; and here he delivered addresses to the dock-labourers whom he had induced to attend, of a nature somewhat startling to those who talk of "preaching down to the intelligence of the poor." I give the sketch of one of these sermons (on "Not forsaking the assembling of yourselves together") in his own words:—"I presented Christianity as a society; investigated the origin of societies, the family, the tribe, the nation, with the attendant expanded ideas of rights and duties; the common weal, the bond of union; rising from the family dinner-table to the sacrificial rites of the national gods; drew parallels with trades' unions and benefit clubs, and told them flatly they would not be Christians till they were communicants." No doubt this will seem to most sensible people extravagant enough, even without the quotations from "Wordsworth, Tennyson, and even Pope," with which his addresses were enlivened; but I must confess that my own experience among the poor agrees pretty much with Edward Denison's, and that I believe "high thinking" put into plain English to be more likely to tell on a dockyard-labourer than all the "simple Gospel sermons" in the world.

His real power however for good among the poor lay not so much in what he did as in what he was. It is in no spirit of class self-sufficiency that he dwells again and again throughout these letters on the advantages to such a neighbourhood of the presence of a "gentleman" in the midst of it. He lost little, in the end he gained much, by the resolute stand he made against the indiscriminate almsgiving which has done so much to create and encourage pauperism in the East of London. The poor soon came to understand the man who was as liberal with his sympathy as he was chary of meat and coal tickets, who only aimed at being their friend, at listening to their troubles, and aiding them with counsel, as if he were one of themselves, at putting them in the way of honest work, at teaching their children, at protecting them with a perfect courage and chivalry against oppression and wrong. He instinctively appealed in fact to their higher nature, and such an appeal seldom remains unanswered. In the roughest costermonger there is a vein of real nobleness, often even of poetry, in which lies the whole chance of his rising to a better life. I remember, as an instance of the way in which such a vein can be touched, the visit of a lady, well known for her work in the poorer districts of London, to a low alley in this very parish. She entered the little mission-room with a huge basket, filled not with groceries or petticoats, but with roses. There was hardly one pale face among the women bending over their sewing that did not flush with delight as she distributed her gifts. Soon, as the news spread down the alley, rougher faces peered in at window and door, and great "navvies" and dock-labourers put out their hard fists for a rosebud with the shyness and delight of schoolboys. "She was a *real* lady," was the unanimous verdict of the alley;

like Edward Denison she had somehow discovered that man does not live by bread alone, and that the communion of rich and poor is not to be found in appeals to the material but to the spiritual side of man.

"What do you look on as the greatest boon that has been conferred on the poorer classes in later years?" said a friend to me one day, after expatiating on the rival claims of schools, missions, shoe-black brigades, and a host of other philanthropic efforts for their assistance. I am afraid I sank in his estimation when I answered, "Sixpenny photographs." But any one who knows what the worth of family affection is among the lower classes, and who has seen the array of little portraits stuck over a labourer's fireplace, still gathering together into one the " home " that life is always parting—the boy that has "gone to Canada," the girl "out at service," the little one with the golden hair that sleeps under the daisies, the old grandfather in the country—will perhaps feel with me that in counteracting the tendencies, social and industrial, which every day are sapping the healthier family affections, the sixpenny photograph is doing more for the poor than all the philanthropists in the world.

It is easy indeed to resolve on "helping" the poor; but it is far less easy to see clearly how we can help them, what is real aid, and what is mere degradation.

I know few books where any one who is soberly facing questions like these can find more help than in the "Letters" of Edward Denison. Broken and scattered as his hints necessarily appear, the main lines along which his thought moves are plain enough. He would discriminate between temporary and chronic distress, between the poverty caused by a sudden revolution of trade and permanent destitution such as that of Bethnal Green. The first requires exceptional treatment; the second a rigid and universal administration of the Poor Laws. "Bring back the Poor Law," he repeats again and again, "to the spirit of its institution; organize a sufficiently elastic labour test, without which no outdoor relief to be given; make the few alterations which altered times demand, and impose every possible discouragement on private benevolence." The true cure for pauperism lies in the growth of thrift among the poor. "I am not drawing the least upon my imagination when I say that a young man of twenty could in five years, even as a dock-labourer, which is much the lowest employment and least well paid there is, save about £20. This is not exactly Utopia; it is within the reach of nearly every man, if quite at the bottom of the tree; but if it were of anything like common occurrence the destitution and disease of this life would be within manageable limits."

I know that words like these are in striking contrast with the usual public opinion on the subject, as well as with the mere screeching over poverty in which sentimentalists are in the habit of indulging. But it is fair to say that they entirely coincide with my own experience. The sight which struck me most in Stepney was one which met my eyes when I plunged by sheer accident into the back-yard of a jobbing carpenter, and came suddenly upon a neat greenhouse with fine flowers inside it. The man had built it with his own hands and his own savings; and the sight of it had so told on his next-door neighbour —a cobbler, if I remember rightly—as to induce him to leave off drinking, and build a rival greenhouse with savings of his own. Both had become zealous florists, and thrifty, respectable men; but the thing which surprised both of them most was that they had been able to save at all.

It is in the letters themselves however rather than in these desultory comments of mine that the story of these two years of earnest combat with the great problem of our day must be studied. Short as the time was, it was broken by visits to France, to Scotland, to Guernsey, and by his election as Member of Parliament for the borough of Newark. But even these visits and his new parliamentary position were meant to be parts of an effort for the regeneration of our poorer classes. His careful examination of the thrift of the peasantry of the Channel Islands, his researches into the actual working of the "Assistance Publique" in Paris, the one remarkable speech he delivered in Parliament on the subject of vagrancy, were all contributions to this great end. In the midst of these labours a sudden attack of his old disease forced him to leave England on a long sea-voyage, and within a fortnight of his landing in Australia he died at Melbourne. His portrait hangs in the school which he built, and rough faces as they gaze at it still soften even into tears as they think of Edward Denison.

SKETCHES IN SUNSHINE

I

CANNES AND ST. HONORAT

IN a colloquial sort of way we talk glibly enough of leaving England, but England is by no means an easy country to leave. If it bids us farewell from the cliffs of Dover, it greets us again on the quay of Calais. It would be a curious morning's amusement to take a map of Europe, and mark with a dot of red the settlements of our lesser English colonies. A thousand Englands would crop up along the shores of the Channel or in quiet nooks of Normandy, around mouldering Breton castles or along the banks of the Loire, under the shadow of the Maritime Alps or the Pyrenees, beneath the white walls of Tunis or the Pyramids of the Nile. During the summer indeed England is everywhere—fishing in the fiords of Norway, sketching on the Kremlin, shooting brigands in Albania, yachting among the Cyclades, lion-hunting in the Atlas, crowding every steamer on the Rhine, annexing Switzerland, lounging through Italian galleries, idling in the gondolas of Venice. But even winter is far from driving England home again; what it really does is to concentrate it in a hundred little Britains along the sunny shores of the South. Each winter resort brings home to us the power of the British doctor. It is he who rears pleasant towns at the foot of the Pyrenees, and lines the sunny coasts of the Riviera with villas that gleam white among the olive groves. It is his finger that stirs the camels of Algeria, the donkeys of Palestine, the Nile boats of Egypt. At the first frosts of November the doctor marshals his wild geese for their winter flitting, and the long train streams off, grumbling but obedient, to the little Britains of the South.

Of these little Britains none is more lovely than Cannes. The place is a pure creation of the health-seekers whose gay villas are thrown fancifully about among its sombre fir-woods, though the "Old Town," as it is called nowadays, remains clinging to its original height, street above street leading up to a big bare church of the Renascence period, to fragments of mediæval walls and a great tower which crowns the summit of the hill. At the feet of this height lie the two isles of Lerins, set in the blue waters of the bay; on the east the eye ranges over the porphyry hills of Napoul to the huge masses of the Estrelles; landwards a tumbled country with bright villas dotted over it rises gently to the Alps. As a strictly winter resort Cannes is far too exposed for the more delicate class of invalids; as a spring resort it is without a rival. Nowhere is the air so bright and elastic, the light so wonderfully brilliant and diffused. The very soil, full of micaceous fragments, sparkles at our feet. Colour takes a depth as well as a refinement strange even to the Riviera; nowhere is the sea so darkly purple, nowhere are the tones of the distant hills so delicate and evanescent, nowhere are the sunsets so sublime. The scenery around harmonizes, in its gaiety, its vivacity, its charm, with this brightness of air and light. There is little of grandeur about it, little to compare in magnificence with the huge background of the cliffs behind Mentone or the mountain wall which rises so steeply from its lemon groves. But everywhere there is what Mentone lacks—variety, largeness, picturesqueness of contrast and surprise. Above us is the same unchanging blue as there, but here it overarches gardens fresh with verdure and bright with flowers, and houses gleaming white among the dark fir-clumps; hidden little ravines break the endless tossings of the ground; in the distance white roads rush straight to grey towns hanging strangely against the hill-sides; a thin snow-line glitters along the ridge of the Maritime Alps; dark purple shadows veil the recesses of the Estrelles.

Nor is it only this air of cheerfulness and vivacity which makes Cannes so pleasant a spring resort for invalids; it possesses in addition an advantage of situation which its more sheltered rivals necessarily want. The high mountain walls that give their complete security from cold winds to Mentone or San Remo are simply prison walls to visitors who are too weak to face a steep ascent on foot or even on donkey-back, for drives are out of the question except along one or two monotonous roads. But the country round Cannes is full of easy walks and drives, and it is as varied and beautiful as it is accessible. You step out of your hotel into the midst of wild scenery, rough hills of broken granite screened with firs, or paths winding through a wilderness of white heath. Everywhere in spring the ground is carpeted with a profusion of wild flowers, cistus and brown orchis, narcissus and the scarlet anemone; sometimes the forest scenery sweeps away, and leaves us among olive-grounds and orange-gardens arranged in formal, picturesque rows. And from every little height there are the same distant views of far-off mountains, or the old town flooded with yellow light, or islands lying gem-like in the dark blue sea, or the fiery hue of sunset over the Estrelles.

Nor are these land-trips the only charm of Cannes. No one has seen the coast of Provence in its beauty who has not seen it from the sea. A sail to the isles of Lerins reveals for the first time the full glory of Cannes even to those who have enjoyed most keenly the large picturesqueness of its landscapes, the delicate colouring of its distant hills, the splendour of its sunsets. As one drifts away from the shore the circle of the Maritime Alps rises like the framework of some perfect picture, the broken outline of the mountains to the left contrasting with the cloud-capt heights above Turbia, snow-peaks peeping over the further slopes between them, delicate lights and shadows falling among the broken country of the foreground, Cannes itself stretching its bright line of white along the shore. In the midst of the bay, the centre as it were of this exquisite landscape, lie the two isles of Lerins. With the larger, that of St. Marguerite, romance has more to do than history, and the story of the "Man in the Iron Mask," who was so long a prisoner in its fortress, is fast losing the mystery which made it dear even to romance. The lesser and more distant isle, that of St. Honorat, is one of the great historic sites of the world. It is the starting point of European monasticism, whether in its Latin, its Teutonic, or its Celtic form, for it was by Lerins that the monasticism of Egypt first penetrated into the West.

The devotees whom the fame of Antony and of the Cœnobites of the Nile had drawn in crowds to the East returned at the close of the fourth century to found similar retreats in the isles which line the coasts of the Mediterranean. The sea took the place of the desert, but the type of monastic life which the solitaries had found in Egypt was faithfully preserved. The Abbot of Lerins was simply the chief of some thousands of religious devotees, scattered over the island in solitary cells, and linked together by the common ties of obedience and prayer. By a curious concurrence of events the cœnobitic life of Lerins, so utterly unlike the later monasticism of the Benedictines, was long preserved in a remote corner of Christendom. Patrick, the most famous of its scholars, transmitted its type of monasticism to the Celtic Church which he founded in Ireland, and the vast numbers, the asceticism, the loose organization of such abbeys as those of Bangor or Armagh preserved to the twelfth century the essential characteristics of Lerins. Nor is this all its historical importance. What Iona is to the ecclesiastical history of Northern England, what Fulda and Monte Cassino are to the ecclesiastical history of Germany and Southern Italy, that this Abbey of St. Honorat became to the Church of Southern Gaul. For nearly two centuries, and those centuries of momentous change, when the wreck of the Roman Empire threatened civilization and Christianity with ruin like its own, the civilization and Christianity of the great district between the Loire, the Alps, and the Pyrenees rested mainly on the Abbey of Lerins. Sheltered by its insular position from the ravages of the barbaric invaders who poured down on the Rhône and the Garonne, it exercised over Provence and Aquitaine a supremacy such as Iona till the Synod of Whitby exercised over Northumbria. All the more illustrious sees of Southern Gaul were filled by prelates who had been reared at Lerins; to Arles, for instance, it gave in succession Hilary, Cæsarius, and Virgilius. The voice of the Church was found in that of its doctors; the famous rule of faith, "quod ubique, quod semper, quod ab omnibus," is the rule of Vincent of Lerins; its monk Salvian painted the agony of the dying Empire in his book on the government of God; the long fight of semi-Pelagianism against the sterner doctrines of Augustin was chiefly waged within its bounds.

Little remains to illustrate this earlier and more famous period of the monastic history of Lerins which extends to the massacre of its monks by Saracen pirates at the opening of the eighth century. The very look of the island has been changed by the revolutions of the last hundred years. It is still a mere spit of sand, edged along the coast with sombre pines; but the whole of the interior has been stripped of its woods by the agricultural improvements which are being carried on by the Franciscans who at present possess it, and all trace of solitude and retirement has disappeared. A well in the centre of the island and a palm-tree beside the church are linked to the traditional history of the founders of the abbey. Worked into the later buildings we find marbles and sculptures which may have been brought from the mainland, as at Torcello, by fugitives who had escaped the barbaric storm. A bas-relief of Christ and the Apostles, which is now inserted over the west gate of the church, and a column of red marble which stands beside it, belong probably to the earliest days of the settlement at Lerins. In the little chapels scattered over the island fragments of early sarcophagi, inscriptions, and sculpture have been industriously collected and preserved. But the chapels themselves are far more interesting than their contents. Of the seven which originally lined the shore, two or three only now remain uninjured; in these the building itself is either square or octagonal, pierced with a single rough Romanesque window, and of diminutive size. The walls and vaulting are alike of rough stonework. The chapels served till the Revolution as seven stations which were visited by the pilgrims to the island, but we can hardly doubt that in these, as in the Seven Chapels at Glendalough, we see relics of the earlier cœnobitic establishment.

The cloister of the abbey is certainly of a date later than the massacre of the monks, which took place according to tradition in the little square of wild greensward which lies within it; but the roughness of its masonry, the plain barrel roof, and the rude manner in which the low, gloomy vaulting is carried round its angles, are of the same character as in the usual tenth-century buildings of Southern Gaul. With the exception of the masonry of its side walls there is nothing in the existing remains of the abbey church itself earlier than its reconstruction at the close of the eleventh century. The building has been so utterly wrecked that little architectural detail is left;

but the broad nave, with its narrow side aisles, the
absence, as in the Aquitanian churches, of triforium
and clerestory, and the shortness of the choir space,
give their own individual mark to St. Honorat. Of
the monastic buildings directly connected with the
church only a few rooms remain, and these are destitute of any features of interest. They are at present
used as an orphanage by the Franciscans whom the
Bishop of Frejus, by whom the island was purchased
some fifteen years ago, has settled there as an agricultural colony, and whose reverence for the relics
around them is as notable as their courtesy to the
strangers who visit them. If it is true that the island
narrowly escaped being turned into a tea-garden and
resort for picnics by some English speculators, we
can only feel a certain glow of gratitude to the Bishop
of Frejus. The brown train of the eleven brothers
as we saw them pacing slowly beneath the great
caroub-tree close to the abbey, or the row of boys
blinking in the sunshine as they repeat their lesson
to the lay-brother who acts as schoolmaster, jar less
roughly on the associations of Lerins than the giggle
of happy lovers or the pop of British champagne.

There is little interest in the later story of St.
Honorat, from the days of the Saracen massacre to
its escape from conversion into a tea-garden. The
appearance of the Moslem pirates at once robbed it
of its old security, and the cessation of their attacks
was followed by new dangers from the Genoese and

Catalans who infested the coast in the fourteenth century. The isle was alternately occupied by French and Spaniards in the war between Francis and Charles V.; it passed under the rule of Commendatory abbots, and in 1789, when it was finally secularized, the four thousand monks of its earlier history had shrunk to four. Perhaps the most curious of all the buildings of Lerins is that which took its rise in the insecurity of its mediæval existence. The Castle of Lerins, which lies on the shore to the south of the church, is at once a castle and an abbey. Like many of the great monasteries of the East, its first object was to give security to its inmates against the marauders who surrounded them. Externally its appearance is purely military; the great tower rises from its trench cut deep in the rock, a portcullis protects the gate, the walls are pierced with loopholes and crowned with battlements. But within, the arrangements, so far as it is possible to trace them in the present ruined state of the building, seem to have been purely monastic. The interior of the tower is occupied by a double-arched cloister, with arcades of exquisite first-pointed work, through which one looks down into the little court below. The visitor passes from this into the ruins of the abbot's chapel, to which the relics were transferred for security from the church of St. Honorat, and which was surrounded by the cells, the refectory, and the domestic buildings of the monks. The erection of the castle is dated in the twelfth century, and from this time we may consider the older abbey buildings around the church to have been deserted and left to ruin; but we can hardly grumble at a transfer which has given us so curious a combination of military and monastic architecture in the castle itself.

Something of the feudal spirit which such a residence would be likely to produce appears in the abbot's relations with the little town of Cannes, which formed a part of his extensive lordship on the mainland. Its fishers were harassed by heavy tolls on their fishery, and the rights of first purchase in the market and forced labour were rigorously exacted by the monastic officers. It is curious to compare, as one's boat floats back across the waters of the bay, the fortunes of these serfs and of their lords.

II

CARNIVAL ON THE CORNICE

CARNIVAL in an ordinary little Italian town seems, no doubt, commonplace enough to those who have seen its glories in Rome—the crowded Corso, the rush of the maddened horses, the firefly twinklings of the Maccoletti. A single evening of simple fun, a few peasants laughing in the sunshine, a few children scrambling for bonbons, form an almost ridiculous contrast to the gorgeous outburst of revelry and colour that ushers in Lent at the capital. But there are some people after all who still find a charm in the simple and the commonplace, and to whom the every-day life of Italy is infinitely pleasanter than the stately ceremonial of Rome. At any rate the stranger who has fled from Northern winters to the shelter of the Riviera is ready to greet in the homeliest Carnival the incoming of spring. His first months of exile have probably been months of a little disappointment. He is far from having found the perpetual sunshine which poets and guide-books led him to hope for. He has shivered at Christmas just as he shivered at home, he has had his days of snowfall and his weeks of rain. If he is thoroughly British, he has growled and grumbled, and written to expose "the humbug of the sunny South" in the *Times*; if he is patient, he has jotted down day after day in his diary, and found a cold sort of statistical comfort in the discovery that the sunny days after all outnumbered the gloomy ones. The worst winter of the Riviera, he is willing to admit, would be a very mild winter at home; but still, after each concession to one's diary and common sense, there remains a latent feeling of disappointment and deception.

But Carnival sweeps all this feeling away with the coming of the spring. From the opening of February week follows week in a monotony of warm sunshine. Day after day there is the same cloudless cope of blue overhead, the same marvellous colour in the sea, the same blaze of roses in the gardens, the same scent of violets in every lazy breath of air that wanders down from the hills. Every almond-tree is a mass of white bloom. The narcissus has found a rival along the terraces in the anemone, and already the wild tulip is preparing to dispute the palm of supremacy with both. It is the time for picnics, for excursions, for donkey-rides, for dreams beneath the clump of cypresses that shoot up black into the sky, for siestas beneath the olives. It is wonderful what a prodigious rush of peace and good temper follows on the first rush of spring. The very doctors of the winter resort shake hands with one another, the sermons of the chaplain lose their frost-bitten savour and die down into something like charity, scandal and tittle-tattle go to sleep in the sunshine. The stolid, impassive English nature blooms into a life strangely unlike its own. Papas forget their *Times.* Mammas forget their propriety. The stout British merchant finds himself astride of a donkey, and exchanging good-humoured badinage with the labourers in the olive-terraces. The Dorcas of Exeter Hall leaves her tracts at home, and passes without a groan the pictured Madonna on every wall. Carnival comes, and completes the wreck of the proprieties. The girls secure their window and pelt their black-bearded Professor in the street below without dread of a scolding on the "convenances." The impassive spinster whose voice never rises at home above the most polite whisper screams with delight at the first sugarplum that hits her, and furtively supplies her nieces with ammunition to carry on the war. "It is such fun, isn't it, papa?" shout the boys as they lean breathless over the balcony, laughing and pelting at the crowd that laughs and pelts back again. And papa, who "puts down" fairs in England, and wonders what amusement people can find in peep-shows and merry-go-rounds, finds himself surprised into a "Very jolly indeed!"

It is the same welcome to the spring that gives its charm to the Carnival in the minds of the Italians themselves. To the priest of course Carnival is simply a farewell to worldly junketings and a welcome to Lent, but like every other Church festival it is flinging off its ecclesiastical disguise and donning among the people themselves its old mask as a sheer bit of nature-worship. The women still observe Lent, and their power as housekeepers forces its observance to a certain extent on their husbands and sons. The Italian shrugs his shoulders and submits in a humorous way to what is simply a bit of domestic discipline, revenges himself by a jest on the priesthood, and waits with his quiet "pazienza" till the progress of education shall have secured him a wife who won't grudge him his dinner. But Lent is no reality to him, and spring is a very real thing indeed. The winter is so short that the whole habit of his life and the very fabric of his home is framed on the apparent supposition that there is no such thing as winter at all. His notion of life is life in the open air, life in the sunshine. The peasant of the Cornice looks on with amazement at an Englishman tramping along in the rain. A little rainfall or a little snow keeps every labourer at home with a murmur of "cattivo Dio" between his teeth. A Scotchman or a Yorkshireman wraps his plaid around him and looks with contempt on an idle race who are "afraid of a sprinkle." But the peasant of North Italy is no more of an idler than the peasant of the Lowlands. The truth is, that both he and his home are absolutely unprepared for bad weather. His

clothes are thin and scanty. His diet is low. The
wonder is how he gets through a hard day's work on
food which an English pauper would starve upon.
He has no fireplace at home, and, if he had, he has
no fuel. Wood is very dear, and coal there is none.
If he gets wet through there is no hearth to dry himself or his clothes at. Cold means fever, and fever
with low diet means death. Besides, there is little
loss in staying at home on rainy days. In England
or the Lowlands the peasant farmer who couldn't
"bide a shower" would lose half the year, but a rainy
day along the Cornice is so rare a thing that it makes
little difference in the year's account.

It is much the same with the townsman, the trader,
the professional man. When work in the shop or
office is over his life circles round the café. Society
and home mean for him the chatty, gesticulating
group of friends camped out round their little tables
on the pavement under the huge awning that gives
them shade. When winter breaks up the pleasant
circle, and the dark, chilly evenings drive him, as we
say, "home," he has no home to flee unto. He is
not used to domestic life, or to conversation with his
wife or his children. Above all there is no fire, no
"hearth and home." Going home in fact means
going to bed. An Italian doctor or an Italian lawyer
knows nothing of the cosy evenings of the North, of
the bright fire, the brighter chat round it, or the
quiet book till sleep comes. Somebody has said

truly enough that if a man wanted to see human life at its best he would spend his winters in England and his summers in Italy. We have so much winter that we have faced it, made a study of it, and beaten it. Our houses are a great nuisance in warm weather, but their thick walls and close-fitting windows and broad fireplaces are admirably adapted for cold. Italians, on the other hand, have so little winter that when the cold does come it is completely their master. The large, dark, cool rooms that are so grateful in July are simply ice-houses in December. The large windows are full of crevices and draughts. An ordinary Italian positively dreads a fire from his knowledge of the perils it entails in rooms so draughty as Italian rooms commonly are. He infinitely prefers to rub his blue little hands and wait till this inscrutable mystery of bad weather be overpast. But it is only the thought of what he suffers during the winter, short as it is in comparison with our own, that enables us to understand the ecstasy of his joy at the reappearance of the spring. Everybody meets everybody with greetings on the warmth and the sunshine. The mother comes down again to bask herself at every doorstep, and the little street is once more alive with chat and laughter. The very beggars exchange their whine for a more cheerful tone of insidious persuasion. The women sing as they jog down the hill-paths with the big baskets of olives on their heads. The old dispossessed friar slumbers happily by the roadside. The little tables come out on to the pavement, and the society of the place forms itself afresh into buzzing groups of energetic conversers. The dormouse-life of winter is over, and the spring and the Carnival has come.

Carnival in a little Italian town, as we have said, is no very grand thing, and as a mere question of fun it is no doubt amusing only to people who are ready to be amused. And yet there is a quaint fascination in it as a whole, in the rows of old women with demure little children in their laps ranged on the stone seats along the bridge, the girls on the pavement, the grotesque figures dancing along the road, the harlequins, the mimic Capuchins, the dominoes with big noses, the carriages rolling along amidst a fire of sugarplums, the boys darting in and out and smothering one with their handfuls of flour, the sham cook with his pots and pans wreathed with vine-branches, the sham cavalier in theatrical cloak and trunk hose who dashes about on a pony, the solemn group tossing a doll to a church-like chant in a blanket, the chaff and violet bunches flung from the windows, the fun and life and buzz and colour of it all. It is something very different, one feels, from the common country fair of home. In the first place it is eminently picturesque. As one looks down from the balcony through a storm of sugarplums the eye revels in a perfect feast of colour. Even the russet-brown of every old woman's dress glows in the sunshine into a strange beauty. Every little touch of red or blue in the girls' head-dresses shines out in the intense light. As the oddly attired maskers dart in and out or whirl past in the dance the little street seems like a gay ribbon of shifting hues winding between its grey old houses with touches of fresh tints at every window and balcony. The crimson caps of the peasants stand out in bold relief against the dark green of the lemon-garden behind them. Overhead the wind is just stirring in the big pendent leaves of the two palm-trees in the centre of the street, and the eye once caught by them ranges on to the white mass of the town as it stands glowing on its hill-side, and thence to the brown hill-tops and the intense blue of the sky.

The whole setting of the scene is un-English, and the scene itself is as un-English as its setting. The fun, the enjoyment, is universal. There is nothing of the complicated apparatus which an English fair requires, none of the contrivances to make people laugh — the clowns, the cheap-jacks, the movable theatres, the vans with fat women and two-headed calves, the learned pigs, the peepshows, the peripatetic photographers, the weighing-machines, the swings, the merry-go-rounds. And so there are none of the groups of vacant faces, the joyless chawbacons lounging gloomily from stall to stall, the settled inanity and dreariness of the crowd that drifts through an English fair. An English peasant goes to be amused, and the clown finds it wonderfully hard work to amuse him. The peasant of Italy goes to Carnival to amuse himself and to amuse everybody else. He is full of joyousness and fun, and he wishes everybody to be as funny and as joyous as himself. He has no notion of doing his merriment by deputy. He claps his mask on his face or takes his bag of flour in his hand, and is himself the fun of the fair. His neighbour does precisely the same. The two farmers who were yesterday chaffering over the price of maize meet each other in Carnival as Punch and Harlequin. Every boy has his false nose or his squeaking whistle. The quiet little maiden whom you saw yesterday washing her clothes in the torrent comes tripping up the street with a mask on her face. The very mothers with their little ones in their laps throw in their contribution of smart speeches and merry taunts to the fun of the affair. It is wonderful how simple the elements of their amusement are and how perfectly they are amused. A little masquerading, a little dancing, a little pelting with flour and sugarplums, and everybody is as happy as possible.

And it is a happiness that is free from any coarse intermixture. The badinage is childish enough, but it has none of the foul slang in which an English crowd delights to express its notions of humour. The girls bandy "chaff" with their disguised lovers, but the "chaff" is what their mothers might hear. There is none of the brutal horseplay of home. Harlequin goes by with his little bladder suspended from a string, but the dexterous little touch is a touch and no more. The tiny sugarplums rain like hail on one's face, but there is the fun of catching them and seeing the children hunt after them in the dust. The flour-pelting is the hardest to bear, but the annoyance is redeemed by the burst of laughter from the culprit and the bystanders. It is a rare thing to see anybody lose his temper. It is a yet rarer thing to see anybody drunk. The sulky altercations, the tipsy squabbles, of Northern amusements are unknown. The characteristic "prudence" of the Italian is never better displayed than in his merriment. He knows how far to carry his badinage. He knows when to have done with his fun. The tedious length of an English merrymaking would be unintelligible to him; he doesn't care to spoil the day's enjoyment by making a night of it. A few hours of laughter satisfy him, and when evening falls and the sunshine goes, he goes with the sunshine.

It is in the Carnival that one sees most conspicuously displayed that habit of social equality which is one of the special features of Italian life. Nothing is more unlike the social jealousy of the Frenchman, or the surly incivility with which a Lancashire operative thinks proper to show the world that he is as good a man as his master. In either case one feels the taint of a mere spirit of envious levelling, and a latent confession that the levelling process has still in reality to be accomplished. But the ordinary Italian has nothing

of the leveller about him. The little town is proud
of its Marchese and of the great palazzo that has
entertained a King. It is a matter of public con-
cern when the Count gambles away his patrimony.
An Italian noble is no object of jealousy to his
fellow-citizens, but then no one gives himself less of
the airs of a privileged or exclusive caste. Cavour
was a popular man because, noble as he was, he
would smoke a cigar or stop for a chat with anybody.
The Carnival brings out this characteristic of Italian
manners amusingly enough. The mask, the disguise,
levels all distinctions. The Count's whiskers are
white with the flour just flung at him by the town-
crier. The young nephews of the Baron are the two
harlequins who are exchanging badinage with the
group of country girls at the corner. A general
pelting of sugarplums salutes the appearance of the
Marchese's four-in-hand with the Marchese himself
in an odd mufti on the box.

Social equality is possible, because among rich
and poor alike there is the same social ease. Barber
or donkey-driver chats to you with a perfect frank-
ness and unconsciousness of any need of reserve.
In both rich and poor, too, there is the same social
taste and refinement. The coarse dress of the
peasant girl is worn with as native a dignity as the
robe of a queen. An unconscious elegance breathes
through the very disguises of the Carnival, grotesque
as many of them are. The young fellow who has

wreathed himself with flowers and vine-leaves shows a knowledge of colour and effect which an artist might envy him. But there is not one among the roughest of the peasants or of the townsfolk who has not that indescribable thing we call manner, or who would betray our insular awkwardness when we speak to a lord. And, besides this social equality, there is a family equality too. In England old people enjoy fun, but it is held to be indecorous in them to afford amusement to others. A Palmerston may be a jester at eighty, but the jest must never go beyond words. But in an Italian Carnival the old claim just as much a part in the fun as the young. Grandfathers and grandmothers think it the most natural thing in the world to turn out in odd costumes to give a good laugh to the grandchildren. Papa pops on the most comical mask he can find, and walks down the street arm-in-arm with his boy. In no country perhaps is the filial regard stronger than in Italy; nowhere do mothers claim authority so long over their sons. But this seems to be compatible with a domestic liberty and ease which would be impossible in the graver nations of the North. If once we laughed at our mother's absurdities a mother's influence would be gone. But an Italian will laugh and go on reverencing and obeying in a way we should never dream of. Altogether, it is wonderful how many sides of social life and national character find their illustration in a country carnival.

III

TWO PIRATE TOWNS OF THE RIVIERA

THE view of Monaco, as one looks down on it from the mountain road which leads to Turbia, is unquestionably the most picturesque among all the views of the Riviera. The whole coast-line lies before us for a last look as far as the hills above San Remo, headland after headland running out into blue water, white little towns nestling in the depth of sunny bays or clinging to the brown hill-side, villas peeping white from the dark olive masses, sails gleaming white against the purple sea. The brilliancy of light, the purity and intensity of colour, the clear freshness of the mountain air, tempered as it is by the warm sun-glow, make the long rise from Mentone hard to forget. Mentone itself steals out again and again from under its huge red cliffs to look up at us; we pass by Roccabruna, half rock, half village, hanging high on the hill-side; we leave the orange groves beneath us studded with golden fruit; even the silvery wayward olives fail us, even the pines grow thin and stunted. At last the mountain rises bare above us with only a red rock jutting here and there from its ashen-coloured front. We reach the top, and right in our road rises a vast fragment of Roman masonry, the tower of Turbia, while, thousands of feet beneath, Monaco glows "like a gem" in its setting of dark blue sea. We are on the track of "The Daisy," and the verse of Tennyson's gay little poem comes back to us :—

> What Roman strength Turbia showed
> In ruin, by the mountain road ;
> How like a gem, beneath, the city
> Of little Monaco basking glowed.

Monaco stands on a promontory of rock which falls in bold cliffs into the sea; as one climbs to it from the bay one sees the citadel with its huge bastions frowning on the white buildings of the palace, the long line of grey, ivy-crested walls topping the cliffs, and above them the mass of the little town, broken by a single campanile and a few cypresses. Its situation at once marks the character of the place. It is the one town of the Riviera, which, instead of lying screened in the hollow of some bay, as though eager to escape from pirate or Saracen, juts boldly out into the sea as if on the look-out for prey. Its grim walls, the guns still mounted and shot piled on its battlements, mark the pirate town of the past. At its feet, in trim square of hotel and gambling-house, with a smart Parisian look about it as if the whole had been just caught up out of the Boulevards and dropped on this Italian coast, lies the new Monaco, the pirate town of the present.

Even the least among Italian cities yields so much of interest in its past that we turn with disappointment from the history of Monaco. The place has always been a mere pirate haunt, without a break of liberty or civic life; and yet there is a certain fascination in the perfect uniformity of its existence. The town from which Cæsar sailed to Genoa and Rome vanished before the ravages of the Saracens, and the spot remained desert till it passed by Imperial cession to Genoa, and the Genoese Commune erected a fort which became a refuge alternately for its Guelf or Ghibelline exiles, its Spinolas or its Grimaldis. A church of fine twelfth-century work is the only monument which remains of this earlier time; at the opening of the fourteenth century Monaco passed finally to the Grimaldis, and became in their hands a haunt of buccaneers. Only one of their line rises into historic fame, and he is singularly connected with a great event in English history. Charles Grimaldi was one of the foremost leaders in the Italian wars of his day; he passed as a mercenary into the service of France in her combat with Edward III., and his seventy-two galleys set sail from Monaco with the fifteen thousand Genoese bowmen who appear so unexpectedly in the forefront of the battle of Crécy. The massacre of these forces drove him home again to engage in attacks on the Catalans and Venetians and struggles with Genoa, till the wealth which his piracy had accumulated enabled him to add Mentone and Roccabruna to his petty dominions. It is needless to trace the history of his house any further; corsairs, soldiers of fortune, trimming adroitly in the struggles of the sixteenth century between France and Spain, sinking finally into mere vassals of Louis XIV. and hangers-on at the French Court, the family history of the Grimaldis is one of treason and blood — brother murdering brother, nephew murdering uncle, assassination by subjects avenging the honour of daughters outraged by their master's lust.

Of the town itself, as we have said, there is no history at all; it consists indeed only of a few petty streets streaming down the hill from the palace square. The palace, though spoilt by a gaudy modern restoration, is externally a fine specimen of Italian Renascence work, its court painted all over with arabesques of a rough Caravaggio order, while the State-rooms within have a thoroughly French air, as if to embody the double character of their occupants, at once Lords of Monaco and Ducs de Valentinois. The palace is encircled with a charming little garden, a bit of colour and greenery squeezed in, as it were, between cliff and fortress, from which one looks down over precipices of red rock with the prickly pear clinging to their clefts and ledges, or across a rift of sea to the huge bare front of the Testa del Cane with gigantic euphorbias, cactus, and orange-gardens fringing its base. A bribe administered to Talleyrand is said to have saved the political existence of Monaco at the Congress of Vienna: but it is far more wonderful that, after all the annexations of late years, it should still remain an independent, though the smallest, principality in the world. But even the Grimaldis have not managed wholly to escape from the general luck of their fellow-rulers; Mentone and Roccabruna were ceded to France some few years back for a sum of four million francs, and the present lord of Monaco is the ruler of but a few streets and some two thousand subjects. His army reminds one of the famous war establishment of the older German princelings; one year indeed to the amazement of beholders it rose to the gigantic force of four-and-twenty men; but then, as we were gravely told by an official, "it had been doubled in consequence of the war." Idler and absentee as he is, the Prince is faithful to the traditions of his house; the merchant indeed sails without dread beneath the once dreaded rocks of the pirate haunt; but a new pirate town has risen on the shores of its bay. It is the pillage of a host of gamblers that maintains the heroic army of Monaco, that cleanses its streets, and fills the exchequer of its lord.

There is something exquisitely piquant in the contrast between the gloomy sternness of the older robber hold and the gaiety and attractiveness of the new. Nothing can be prettier than the gardens, rich in fountains and statues and tropical plants, which surround the neat Parisian square of buildings. The hotel is splendidly decorated and its *cuisine* claims to be the best in Europe; there is a pleasant café; the doors of the Casino itself stand hospitably open, and strangers may wander without a question from hall to reading-room, or listen in the concert-room to an excellent band which plays twice a day. The salon itself, the terrible "Hell" which one has pictured with all sorts of Dantesque accompaniments, is a pleasant room, gaily painted, with cosies all round it and a huge mass of gorgeous flowers in the centre. Nothing can be more unlike one's preconceived ideas than the gambling itself, or the aspect of the gamblers around the tables. Of the wild excitement, the frenzy of gain, the outbursts of despair which one has come prepared to witness, there is not a sign. The games strike the bystander as singularly dull and uninteresting; one wearies of the perpetual deal and turn-up of the cards at rouge-et-noir, of the rattle of the ball as it dances into its pigeon-hole at roulette, of the monotonous chant of "Make your game, gentlemen," or "The game is made." The croupiers rake in their gains or poke out the winnings with the passive regularity of machines; the gamblers sit round the table with the vacant solemnity of undertakers. The general air of the company is that of a number of well-to-do people bored out of their lives, and varying their boredom with quiet nods to the croupier and assiduous prickings of little cards.

The boredom is apparently greatest at rouge-et-noir, where the circle is more aristocratic and thousands can be lost and won in a night. Everybody looks tired, absent, inattentive; nobody takes much notice of his neighbour or of the spectators looking on; nobody cares to speak; a finger suffices to direct the croupier to push the stake on to the desired spot, a nod or a look to indicate the winner. The game goes on in a dull uniformity; nobody varies his stake; a few napoleons are added to or subtracted from the heaps before each as the minutes go on; sometimes a little sum is done on a paper beside the player; but there is the same impassive countenance, the same bored expression everywhere. Now and then one player gets quietly up and another sits quietly down. But there is nothing startling or dramatic, no frenzies of hope or exclamations of despair, nothing of the gambler of fiction with "his hands clasped to his burning forehead," and the like. To any one who is not fascinated by the mere look of rolls of napoleons pushed from one colour to another, or of gold raked about in little heaps, there is something very difficult to understand in the spell which a gaming-table exercises. Roulette is a little more amusing, as it is more intelligible to the looker-on. The stakes are smaller, the company changes oftener, and is socially more varied. There is not

such a dead, heavy earnestness about these riskers of
five-franc pieces as about the more desperate gamblers
of rouge-et-noir; the outside fringe of lookers-on
bend over with their stakes to back "a run of luck,"
and there is a certain quiet buzz of interest when
the game seems going against the bank. There is
always some one going and coming, over-dressed girls
lean over and drop their stake and disappear, young
clerks bring their quarter's salary, the casual visitor
"doesn't mind risking a few francs" at roulette.

But even the excitement of roulette is of the gravest
and dullest order. The only player who seems to
throw any kind of vivacity into his gambling is a
gaudy little Jew with heavy watch-chain, who vibrates
between one table and another, sees nothing of the
game save the dropping his stake at roulette and
then rushing off to drop another stake at rouge-et-noir,
and finds time in his marches to spare a merry little
word to a friend or two. But he is the only person
who seems to know anybody. Men who sit by one
another year after year never exchange a word.
There is not even the air of reckless adventure to
excite one. The player who dashes down his all on
any part of the table and trusts to fortune is a mere
creature of fiction; the gambler of fact is a calculator,
a man of business, with a contempt for speculation
and a firm belief in long-studied combination. Each
has his little card, and ticks off the succession of
numbers with the accuracy of a ledger. It is in the

careful study of these statistics that each believes he discovers the secret of the game, the arrangement which, however it may be defeated for a time by inscrutable interference of ill-luck, must in the end, if there is any truth in statistics, be successful. One looks in vain for the "reckless gambler" one has read about and talked about, for "reckless" is the very last word by which one would describe the ring of business-like people who come day after day with the hope of making money by an ingenious dodge.

Their talk, if one listens to it over the dinner-table, turns altogether on this business-like aspect of the question. Nobody takes the least interest in its romantic or poetic side, in the wonderful runs of luck or the terrible stories of ruin and despair which form the stock-in-trade of the novelist. The talk might be that of a conference of commercial travellers. Everybody has his infallible nostrum for breaking the bank; but everybody looks upon the prospect of such a fortune in a purely commercial light. The general opinion of the wiser sort goes against heavy stakes, and "wild play" is only talked about with contempt. The qualities held in honour, so far as we can gather from the conversation, are "judgment," which means a careful study of the little cards and a certain knowledge of mathematics, and "constancy" —the playing not from caprice but on a definite plan and principle. Nobody has the least belief in "luck." A winner is congratulated on his "science." The loser explains the causes of his loss. A portly person who announces himself as one of a company of gamblers who have invested an enormous capital on a theory of winning by means of low stakes and a certain combination excites universal interest. Most of the talkers describe themselves frankly as men of business. No doubt at Monaco, as elsewhere, there is the usual aristocratic fringe—the Russian prince who flings away an estate at a sitting, the half-blind countess from the Faubourg St. Germain, the Polish dancer with a score of titles, the English "milord." But the bulk of the players have the look and air of people who have made their money in trade. It is well to look on at such a scene, if only to strip off the romance which has been so profusely showered over it. As a matter of fact nothing is more prosaic, nothing meaner in tone, nothing more utterly devoid of interest, than a gambling-table. But as a question of profit the establishment of M. Blanc throws into the shade the older piracy of Monaco. The Venetian galleons, the carracks of Genoa, the galleys of Marseilles, brought infinitely less gold to its harbour than these two little groups of the fools of half a continent.

IV

THE WINTER RETREAT

It is odd, when one is safely anchored in a winter refuge, to look back at the terrors and reluctance with which one first faced the sentence of exile. Even if sunshine were the only gain of a winter flitting, it would still be hard to estimate the gain. The cold winds, the icy showers, the fogs we leave behind us, give perhaps a zest not wholly its own to Italian sunshine. But the abrupt plunge into a land of warmth and colour sends a strange shock of pleasure through every nerve. The flinging off of wraps and furs, the discarding of greatcoats, is like the beginning of a new life. It is not till we pass in this sharp, abrupt fashion from the November of one side the Alps to the November of the other that we get some notion of the way in which the actual range and freedom of life is cramped by the "chill north-easters" in which Mr. Kingsley revelled. The unchanged vegetation, the background of dark olive woods, the masses of ilex, the golden globes of the orange hanging over the garden wall, are all so many distinct gains to an eye which has associated winter with leafless boughs and a bare landscape. One has almost a boyish delight in plucking roses at Christmas or hunting for violets along the hedges on New Year's Day. There are chill days of course, and chiller nights, but cold is a relative term and loses its English meaning in spots where snow falls once or twice in a year and vanishes before midday. The mere break of habit is delightful; it is like a laughing defiance of established facts to lounge by the seashore in the hot sun-glare of a January morning. And with this new sense of liberty comes little by little a freedom from the overpowering dread of chills and colds and coughs which only invalids can appreciate. It is an indescribable relief not to look for a cold round every corner. The "lounging" which becomes one's life along the Riviera or the Bay of Naples is only another name for the ease and absence of anxiety which the mere presence of constant sunshine gives to life.

Few people, in fact, actually "lounge" less than the English exiles who bask in the sun of Italy. Their real danger lies in the perpetual temptation to over-exertion which arises from the sense of renewed health. Every village on its hill-top, every white shrine glistening high up among the olives, seems to woo one up the stony paths and the long hot climb to the summit. But the relief from home itself, the break away from all the routine of one's life, is hardly less than the relief from greatcoats. It is not till our life is thoroughly disorganized, till the grave mother of a family finds herself perched on a donkey, or the *habitué* of Pall Mall sees himself sauntering along through the olive groves, that one realizes the iron bounds within which our English existence moves. Every holiday of course brings this home to one more or less, but the long holiday of a whole winter brings it home most of all. England and English ways recede and become unreal. Old prepossessions and prejudices lose half their force when sea and mountains part us from their native soil. It is hard to keep up our vivid interest in the politics of Little Pedlington, or to maintain our old excitement over the matrimonial fortunes of Miss Hominy. It becomes possible to breakfast without the last telegram and to go to bed without the news of a fresh butchery. One's real interest lies in the sunshine, in the pleasure of having sunshine to-day, in the hope of having sunshine to-morrow.

But really to enjoy the winter retreat one must keep as much as possible out of the winter retreat itself. Few places are more depressing in their social aspects than these picturesque little Britains. The winter resort is a colony of squires with the rheumatism, elderly maidens with delicate throats, worn-out legislators, a German princess or two with a due train of portly and short-sighted chamberlains, girls with a hectic flush of consumption, bronchitic parsons, barristers hurried off circuit by the warning cough. The life of these patients is little more than the life of a machine. As the London physician says when he bids them "good-bye," "The nearer you can approach to the condition of a vegetable the better for your chances of recovery." All the delicious uncertainties and irregularities that make up the freedom of existence disappear. The day is broken up into a number of little times and seasons. Dinner comes at midday, and is as exact to its moment as the early breakfast or the "heavy tea." And between each meal there are medicines to be taken, inhalations to be gone through, the due hour of rest to be allotted to digestion, the other due hour to exercise.

The air of the sick-room lingers everywhere about the place; one catches, as it were, the far-off hush of the Campo Santo. Life is reduced to its lowest expression; people exist rather than live. Every one remembers that every one else is an invalid. Voices are soft, conversation is subdued, visits are short. There is a languid, sickly sweetness in the very courtesy of society. Gaiety is simply regarded as a danger. Every hill is a temptation to too long and fatiguing a climb. No sunshine makes "the patient" forget his wraps. No coolness of delicious shade moves him to repose. His whole energy and watchfulness is directed to the avoidance of a chill. Life becomes simply barometrical. An east wind is the subject of public lamentation; the vast mountain range to the north is admired less for its wild grandeur than for the shelter it affords against the terrible mistral. Excitement is a word of dread. Distance itself takes something of the sharpness and vividness off from the old cares and interests of home. The very letters that reach the winter resort are doctored, and "incidents which might excite" are excluded by the care of correspondents. Mamma only hears of Johnny's measles when Johnny is running about again. The young scapegrace at Oxford is far too considerate to trouble his father, against the doctor's orders, with the mention of his failure in the schools. News comes with all colour strained and filtered out of it through the columns of 'Galignani.' The neologian heresy, the debate in Convocation which would have stirred the heart of the parson at home, fall flat in the shape of a brown and aged 'Times.' There are no "evenings out." The first sign of eve is the signal for dispersion homewards, and it is only from the safe shelter of his own room that the winter patient ventures to gaze on the perilous glories of the sunset. The evenings are in fact a dawdle indoors as the day has been a dawdle out, a little music, a little reading of the quiet order, a little chat, a little letter-writing, and an early to-bed.

It is this calm monotony of day after day at which the world of the winter resort deliberately aims, a life like that of the deities of Epicurus, untouched by the cares or interests of the world without. The very gaiety is of the same subdued and quiet order—drives, donkey-rides, picnics of the small-and-early type. An air of slow respectability pervades the place; the bulk of the colonists are people well-to-do, who can afford the expense of a winter away from home and of a villa at £150 the season. The bankrupt element of Boulogne, the half-pay element of Dinan or Avranches, is as rare on the Riviera as the loungers who rejoice in the many-changing toilets of Arcachon or Biarritz. The quiet humdrum tone of the parson best harmonises with that of the winter resort, and parsons of all sorts abound there.

But the chaplain is not here, as in other little Britains, the centre of social life; he is superseded by the doctor. The winter resort in fact owes its origin to the doctor. The little village or the country town looks with awe upon the man who has discovered for it a future of prosperity, at whose call hosts of rich strangers come flocking from the ends of the earth, at whose bidding villas rise white among the olives, and parades stretch along the shore. "I found it a fishing hamlet," the doctor may say with Augustus, "and I leave it a city." It is amusing to see the awful submission which the city-builder expects in return. The most refractory of patients trembles at the threat of his case being abandoned. The doctor has his theories about situation. You are lymphatic, and are ordered down to the very edge of the sea; you are excitable, and must hurry from your comfortable lodgings to the highest nook among the hills. He has his theories about diet, and you sink obediently to milk and water. His one object of hostility and contempt is your London physician. He tears up his rival's prescriptions with contempt, he reverses the treatment. He sighs as you bid him farewell to return to advice which is so likely to prove fatal. The London physician, it is true, hints that though the oracle of the winter resort is a clever man he is also a quack. But a quack soars into a greatness beyond criticism when he creates cities and rules hundreds of patients with his nod.

V

SAN REMO

SAN REMO, though youngest in date, bids fair to become the most popular of all the health resorts of the Riviera. At no other point along the coast is the climate so mild and equable. The rural quiet and repose of the place form a refreshing contrast with the Brighton-like gaiety of Nizza or Cannes, even Mentone looks down with an air of fashionable superiority on a rival almost destitute of promenades; and whose municipality sighs in vain for a theatre. To the charms of quiet and sunshine the place adds that of a peculiar beauty. The Apennines rise like a screen behind the amphitheatre of soft hills that enclose it—hills soft with olive woods, and dipping down into gardens of lemon and orange, and vineyards dotted with palms. An isolated spur juts out from the centre of the semicircle, and from summit to base of it tumbles the oddest of Italian towns, a strange mass of arches and churches and steep lanes, rushing down like a stone cataract to the sea. On either side of the town lie deep ravines, with lemon gardens along their bottoms, and olives thick along their sides. The olive is the characteristic tree of San Remo. As late as the sixteenth century the place was renowned for its palms; a palm tree stands on the civic escutcheon, and the privilege of supplying the papal chapel with palm branches in the week before Easter is still possessed by a family of San Remese. But the palm has wandered off to Bordighera, and the high price of oil during the early part of this century has given unquestioned supremacy to the olive. The loss is after all a very little one, for the palm, picturesque as is its natural effect, assumes any but picturesque forms when grown for commercial purposes, while the thick masses of the olive woods form a soft and almost luxurious background to every view of San Remo.

What strikes one most about the place in an artistic sense is its singular completeness. It lies perfectly shut in by the circle of mountains, the two headlands in which they jut into the sea, and the blue curve of the bay. It is only by climbing to the summit of the Capo Nero or the Capo Verde that one sees the broken outline of the coast towards Genoa or the dim forms of the Estrelles beyond Cannes. Nowhere does the outer world seem more strangely far-off and unreal. But between headland and headland it is hardly possible to find a point from which the scene does not group itself into an exquisite picture with the white gleaming mass of San Remo for a centre. Small too as the space is, it is varied and broken by the natural configuration of the ground; everywhere the hills fall steeply to the very edge of the sea and valleys and ravines go sharply up among the olive woods. Each of these has its own peculiar beauty; in the valley of the Romolo for instance, to the west of the town, the grey mass of San Remo perched on a cliff-like steep, the rocky bed of the torrent below, the light and almost fantastic arch that spans it, the hills in the background with the further snow range just peeping over them, leave memories that are hard to forget. It is easy too for a good walker to reach sterner scenes than those immediately around; a walk of two hours brings one among the pines of San Romolo, an hour's drive plunges one into the almost Alpine scenery of Ceriana. But for the ordinary frequenters of a winter resort the chief attractions of the place will naturally lie in the warmth and shelter of San Remo itself. Protected as it is on every side but that of the sea, it is free from the dreaded mistral of Cannes and from the sharp frost winds that sweep down the torrent-bed of Nizza. In the earlier part of the first winter I spent there, the snow, which lay thick in the streets of Genoa and beneath even the palms of Bordighera, only whitened the distant hill-tops at San Remo. Christmas brought at last a real snowfall, but every trace of it vanished before the sun-glare of midday. From sunset to sunrise indeed the air is sometimes bitterly cold, but the days themselves are often pure summer days.

What gives a special charm to San Remo, as to the other health-stations along the Cornice, is the fact that winter and spring are here the season of flowers. Roses nod at one over the garden-walls, violets peep shyly out along the terraces, a run uphill brings one across a bed of narcissus. It is odd to open one's window on a January morning and count four-and-twenty different kinds of plants in bloom in the garden below. But even were flowers absent, the character of the vegetation excludes from northern eyes the sense of winter. The bare branches of the fig-tree alone remind one that "summer is over and gone." Every homestead up the torrent-valleys is embosomed in the lustrous foliage of its lemon gardens. Every rivulet is choked with maiden-hair and delicate ferns. The golden globes of the orange are the ornament of every garden. The dark green masses of the olive, ruffled by strong winds into sheets of frosted silver, are the background of the whole. And right in front from headland to headland lie the bright waters of the Mediterranean, rising and sinking with a summer's swell, and glancing with a thousand colours even in the gloomiest weather.

The story of San Remo begins with Saracenic inroads from Corsica and Sardinia in the ninth century, to which Nizza, Oneglia, and Genoa owed their walls. But before this time the wild Ligurian coast had afforded hermitages to the earlier bishops of Genoa; to Siro who became its apostle, to Romolo who was destined to give his name to the territory of the town. San Romolo is indeed its invariable designation till the fifteenth century, and it has been conjectured that its present name is owing to no fanciful punning on Romulus and Remus but to a popular contraction of its full ecclesiastical title, "Sancti Romuli in eremo." It was in this "waste," left without inhabitants by the Saracenic inroads, that Theodulf, bishop of Genoa, settled a little agricultural colony round the Carolingian fort and lands which, though within the feudal jurisdiction of the Counts of Ventimiglia, were the property of his see. Two centuries passed quietly over the little town ere the sudden rise of the Consulate here, as at Genoa and Milan, gave it municipal liberty. The civil authority of the bishops passed to the communal Parliament, the free assembly of the citizens in the church of San Stefano; all civil administration, even the right of peace and war, or of alliance, was exercised with perfect freedom from episcopal intervention. The rights of the bishop in fact were reduced to the nomination of the judicial magistrates of the town and the reception of certain fees; rights which were subsequently sold to the Dorias, and transferred by the Dorias to the Republic of Genoa.

This great communal revolution, itself a result of the wave of feeling produced by the Crusades, left its characteristic mark in the armorial bearings of the town, the Crusaders' Palm upon its shield. While its neighbours, Ventimiglia and Albenga, sank into haunts of a feudal noblesse, San Remo became a town of busy merchants, linked by treaties of commerce with the trading cities of the French and Italian coasts. The erection of San Siro marked the wealth and devotion of its citizens. Ruined as it is, like all the churches of the Riviera, by the ochre and stucco of a tasteless restoration, San Siro still retains much of the characteristic twelfth-century work of its first foundation. The alliance of the city with Genoa was that of a perfectly free State. The terms of the treaty which was concluded between the two Republics in 1361 in the Genoese basilica of San Lorenzo are curious as illustrating the federal relations of Italian States. It was in effect little more than a judicial and military convention. Internal legislation, taxation, rights of independent warfare, peace, and alliance were left wholly in the power of the free commune. San Remo was bound to contribute ships and men for service in Genoese warfare, but in return its citizens shared the valuable privileges of those of Genoa in all parts of the world. Genoa, as purchaser of the feudal rights of its lords, nominated the podesta and other judicial officers, but these officers were bound to administer the laws passed or adopted by the commune. The red cross of Genoa was placed above the palm tree of San Remo on the shield of the Republic; and on these terms the federal relations of the two States continued without quarrel or change for nearly four hundred years.

The town continued to prosper till the alliance of Francis I. with the Turks brought the scourge of the Moslem again on the Riviera. The "Saracen towers" with which the coast is studded tell to this day the tale of the raids of Barbarossa and Dragut. The blow fell heavily on San Remo. The ruined quarter beneath its wall still witnesses to the heathen fury. San Siro, which lay without the walls, was more than once desecrated and reduced to ruin. A special officer was appointed by the town to receive contributions for the ransom of citizens carried off by the corsairs of Algiers or Tunis. These terrible razzias, which went on to the very close of the last century, have left their mark on the popular traditions of the coast. But the ruin which they began was consummated by the purposeless bombardment of San Remo by an English fleet during the war of the Austrian Succession, and by the perfidy with which Genoa crushed at a single blow the freedom she had respected for so many centuries. The square Genoese fort near the harbour commemorates the extinction of the liberty of San Remo in 1729. The French revolution found the city ruined and enslaved, and the gratitude of the citizens for their deliverance by Buonaparte was shown by a sacrifice which it is hard to forgive them. A row of magnificent ilexes, which stretched along the ridge from the town to San Romolo, is said to have been felled for the construction of vessels for the French navy.

Some of the criticism which has been lavished on San Remo is fair and natural enough. To any one who has been accustomed to the exquisite scenery around Cannes its background of olives seems tame and monotonous. People who are fond of the bustle and gaiety of Nizza or Mentone in their better days can hardly find much to amuse them in San Remo. It is certainly quiet, and its quiet verges upon dulness. A more serious drawback lies in the scarcity of promenades or level walks for weaker invalids. For people with good legs, or who are at home on a donkey, there are plenty of charming walks and rides up into the hills. But it is not everybody who is strong enough to walk uphill or who cares to mount a donkey. Visitors with sensitive noses may perhaps find reason for growls at the mode of cultivation which is characteristic of the olive groves. The town itself and the country around is, like the bulk of the Riviera, entirely without architectural or archæological interest. There is a fine castle within a long drive at Dolceacqua, and a picturesque church still untouched within a short one at Ceriana, but this is all. Beneficial as the reforms of Carlo Borromeo may have been to the religious life of the Cornice, they have been fatal to its architecture. On the other hand, any one with an artistic eye and a sketch-book may pass his time pleasantly enough at San Remo. The botanist may revel day after day in new "finds" among its valleys and hill-sides. The rural quiet of the place delivers one from the fashionable bustle of livelier watering-places, from the throng of gorgeous equipages that pour along the streets of Nice, or from picnics with a host of flunkeys uncorking the champagne.

The sunshine, the colour, the beauty of the little town, secure its future. The time must soon come when the whole coast of the Riviera will be lined with winter resorts; but we can hardly hope that any will surpass the happy blending of warmth and interest and repose which makes the charm of San Remo.

THE POETRY OF WEALTH

THE POETRY OF WEALTH

THERE is one marvellous tale which is hardly likely to be forgotten so long as men can look down from Notre Dame de la Garde on the sunny beauty of Marseilles. Even if the rest of Dumas's works sink into oblivion, the sight of Château d'If as it rises glowing from the blue waters of the Mediterranean will serve to recall the wonders of 'Monte Christo.' But the true claim of the book to remembrance lies not in its mere command over the wonderful but in the peculiar sense of wonder which it excites. It was the first literary attempt to raise the mere dead fact of money into the sphere of the imagination, and to reveal the dormant poetry of wealth. There has as yet been only a single age in the world's history when wealth has told with any force upon the imagination of men. Unpoetic as the Roman mind essentially was, the sudden burst upon it of the accumulated riches of the older world kindled in senators and proconsuls a sense of romance, which, wild and extravagant as it seems, has in some of its qualities found no parallel since. The feast of Lucullus, the gluttony of Heliogabalus, the sudden upgrowth of vast amphitheatres, the waste of millions on the sport of a day, the encounters of navies in the mimic warfare of the Coliseum, are the freaks of gigantic children tossing about wildly the slowly-hoarded treasures of past generations; but they are freaks which for the first time revealed the strange possibilities which lay in the future of wealth.

It is hard to say whether such a time will ever return. No doubt the world is infinitely richer now than it was in the time of the Romans, and no doubt too there are at least a dozen people in London alone whose actual income far exceeds that of the wealthiest of proconsuls. But the wealth of the modern capitalist is a wealth which has grown by slow accumulations, a wealth which has risen almost insensibly into its enormous mass, and the vastness of which its owner has never had brought home to him with the same sort of shock as that which Lucullus must have felt when he fronted the treasures of Mithridates, or Clive when he threaded his way among the sacks of jewels in the royal vaults of Moorshedabad. So far indeed is wealth from stimulating the imagination nowadays that a banker is the very type of the unimaginative man, and the faintest suspicion of genius is enough to render a financier an object of suspicion to the money market. But it is conceivable in the odd freaks of things that we may yet see the advent of the Poet-Capitalist. It is almost impossible to say what new opportunities the possession of fabulous resources might not add to the fancy of a dreamer or to the speculations of a philanthropist. It is not till after a little thought that we realize how materially the course of human progress is obstructed by sheer want of money at critical moments, or how easily the sum of human happiness might be increased by the sudden descent of a golden shower on the right people at the right time.

There are dreams which men have been dreaming for generation after generation which require nothing for their realization but the appearance of such a capitalist as we have imagined. To take what may seem perhaps an odd instance, just because it is an odd instance, let us remember what a wonderful amount of hope and anticipation has been thrown by a great religious party into the restoration of the Jews. Rightly or wrongly, it is the one theme which sends a throb of excitement through the life of quiet parsonages and kindles a new fire even in the dreariest May meetings at Exeter Hall. But in point of actual fact there is not the slightest necessity to await any great spiritual revolution for the accomplishment of such a dream if its accomplishment were really desirable. A league of Evangelical bankers who fully believed in the prophecies they are so fond of quoting could turn the wildest fancies of Dr. Cumming into sober earnest with very little trouble indeed. Any emigration agent would undertake the transport of Houndsditch bodily to Joppa; the bare limestone uplands of Judæa could be covered again with terraces of olive and vine at precisely the same cost of money and industry as is still required to keep up the cultivation of the Riviera; and Mr. Fergusson would furnish for a due consideration plans and estimates for a restoration of the Temple on Zion. We are not suggesting such a scheme as an opportunity for investing money to any great profit, but it is odd to live in a world of wealthy people who believe firmly that its realization would make this world into a little heaven below and yet never seem to feel that they have the means of bringing it about in their cheque-books. Or to take a hardly less odd instance, but one which has actually been brought a little nearer to practical realization. Some time ago a body of Welsh patriots determined to save the tongue and literature of the Cymry from extinction by founding a new Welsh nation on the shores of Patagonia. Nothing but Welsh was to be spoken, none but Welsh books were to be read, and the laws of the colony were to be an amalgam of the codes of Moses and of Howel the Good. The plan failed simply because its originators were poor and unable to tide over the first difficulties of the project. But conceive an ardent capitalist with a passion for nationalities embracing such a cause, and at the cost of a few hundreds of thousands creating perhaps a type of national life which might directly or indirectly affect the future of the world. Such a man might secure himself a niche in history at less cost and with less trouble than he could obtain a large estate and a share in the commission of the peace for a midland county.

But there is no need to restrict ourselves simply to oddities, although oddities of this sort acquire a grandeur of their own at the touch of wealth. The whole field of social experiment lies open to a great capitalist. The one thing required, for instance, to render the squalor and misery of our larger towns practically impossible would be the actual sight of a large town without squalor or misery; and yet if Liverpool were simply handed over to a great philanthropist with the income of half-a-dozen Dukes of Westminster such a sight might easily be seen. Schemes of this sort require nothing but what we may term the poetic employment of capital for their realization. It is strange that no financial hero makes his appearance to use his great money-club to fell direr monsters than those which Hercules encountered, and by the creation of a city at once great, beautiful, and healthy to realize the conception of the Utopia and the dream of Sir Thomas More. Or take a parallel instance from the country. Those who have watched the issues of the co-operative system as applied to agriculture believe they see in it the future solution of two of our greatest social difficulties—those, we mean, which spring from the increasing hardships of the farmer's position, and those which arise from the terrible serfage of the rural labourer. But the experiments which have been as yet carried on are on too small a scale either to produce any influence on the labour market as a whole, or to make that impression on the public imagination which could alone raise the matter into a "question of the day." What is wanted is simply that two or three dukes should try the experiment of peasant co-operation on a whole county, and try it with a command of capital which would give the experiment fair play. Whether it succeeded or not, such an attempt would have a poetic and heroic aspect of a different order from the usual expenditure of a British peer.

Or we may turn to a wholly different field, the field of art. We are always ready to cry out against "pot boilers" as we wander through the galleries of the Academy, and to grumble at the butchers' bills and bonnet bills which stand between great artists and the production of great works. But the butchers' bills and bonnet bills of all the forty Academicians might be paid by a great capitalist without any deep dip into his money bags, and a whole future opened to English art by the sheer poetry of wealth. There are hundreds of men with special faculties for scientific inquiry who are at the present moment pinned down to the daily drudgery of the lawyer's desk or the doctor's consulting-room by the necessities of daily bread. A Rothschild who would take a score of natural philosophers and enable them to apply their whole energies to investigation would help forward science as really as Newton himself, if less directly. But there are even direct ways in which wealth on a gigantic scale might put out a poetic force which would affect the very fortunes of the world. There are living people who are the masters of twenty millions; and twenty millions would drive a tunnel under the Straits of Dover. If increased intercourse means, as is constantly contended, an increase of friendship and of mutual understanding among nations, the man who devoted a vast wealth to linking two peoples together would rise at once to the level of the great benefactors of mankind. An opportunity for a yet more direct employment of the influence of wealth will some day or other be found in the field of international politics. Already those who come in contact with the big-wigs of the financial world hear whispers of a future when the destinies of peoples are to be decided in bank parlours, and questions of peace and war settled, not by the diplomatist and statesman, but by the capitalist. But as yet these are mere whispers, and no European Gould has risen up to "finance" Downing Street into submission, or to meet the boldest move of Prince Bismarck by a fall of the Stock Exchange. Of all the schemes however which we have suggested, this is probably the nearest to practical realization. If not we ourselves, our children at any rate may see International Congresses made possible by a few people quietly buttoning their breeches-pockets, and the march of "armed nations" arrested by "a run for gold."

Taking however men as they are, it is far more wonderful that no one has hit on the enormous field which wealth opens for the development of sheer downright mischief. The sense of mischief is a sense which goes quietly to sleep as soon as childhood is over from mere want of opportunity. The boy who wants to trip up his tutor can easily find a string to tie across the garden walk; but when one has got beyond the simpler joys of childhood strings are not so easy to find. To carry out a practical joke of the Christopher Sly sort we require, as Shakespere saw, the resources of a prince. But once grant possession of unlimited wealth, and the possibilities of mischief rise to a grandeur such as the world has never realized. The Erie Ring taught us a little of what capital might do in this way, but in the Erie Ring capital was fettered by considerations of profit and loss. Throw these considerations overboard and treat a great question in the spirit of sheer mischief, and the results may be simply amazing. Conceive, for instance, a capitalist getting the railways round London into his power, and then in sheer freak stopping the traffic for a single day. No doubt the day would be a short one, but even twelve hours of such a practical joke would bring about a "Black Monday" such as England has never seen. But there would be no need of such an enormous operation to enable us to realize the power of latent mischief which the owner of great wealth really possesses. An adroit operator might secure every omnibus and every cab in the metropolis and compel us to paddle about for a week in the mud of November before the loss was replaced.

It is quite possible indeed that gigantic mischief of this sort may find its sphere in practical politics. Already Continental Governments watch with anxiety the power which employers possess of bringing about a revolution by simply closing their doors and throwing thousands of unemployed labourers on the street; but it is a power which in some degree or other capital will always possess, and any one who remembers the assistance which Reform derived from the Hyde Park rows will see at once that mischief on the large scale might be made in this way an important factor in political questions.

Ambition has yet a wider sphere of action than even mischief in this poetic use of wealth. A London preacher recently drew pointed attention to the merely selfish use of their riches by great English nobles, and contrasted it with the days when Elizabeth's Lords of the Council clubbed together to provide an English fleet against the Armada, or the nobles of Venice placed their wealth on every great emergency at the service of the State. But from any constitutional point of view there is perhaps nothing on which we may more heartily congratulate ourselves than on the blindness which hides from the great capitalists of England the political power which such a national employment of their wealth would give them—a blindness which is all the more wonderful in what is at once the wealthiest and the most political aristocracy which the world has ever seen. What fame the mere devotion of a quarter of a million to public uses may give to a quiet merchant the recent example of Mr. Peabody abundantly showed. But the case of the Baroness Burdett Coutts is yet more strictly to the point. The mere fact that she has been for years credited with a wide and unselfish benevolence has given her a power over the imagination of vast masses of the London poor which no one who is not really conversant with their daily life and modes of thinking could for an instant imagine. Her bounty is enlarged in the misty air of the slums of Wapping or Rotherhithe to colossal dimensions, and the very quietness and unobtrusiveness of her work gives it an air of mystery which tells like romance on the fancy of the poor.

It was characteristic of the power which such a use of wealth may give that the mobs who smashed the Hyde Park railings stopped to cheer before the house of Lady Burdett Coutts. Luckily none of our political nobles has ever bethought himself of the means by which the great Roman leaders rose habitually to influence or won over the labouring masses by "panem et Circenses." But a nobler ambition might find its field in a large employment of wealth for public ends of a higher sort. Something of the old patrician pride might have spurred the five or six great Houses who own half London to construct the Thames Embankment at their own cost, and to hand it over free from the higglings of Mr. Gore to the people at large. Even now we may hear of some earl whose rent-roll is growing with fabulous rapidity as coming forward to relieve the Treasury by the offer of a National Gallery of Art, or checkmating the jobbers of South Kensington by the erection of a National Museum. It seems to be easy enough for peer after peer to fling away a hundred thousand at Newmarket or Tattersall's, and yet a hundred thousand would establish in the crowded haunts of working London great "Conservatoires" where the finest music might be brought to bear without cost on the coarseness and vulgarity of the life of the poor. The higher drama may be perishing in default of a State subvention, but it never seems to enter any one's head that there are dozens of people among those who grumbled at the artistic taste of Mr. Ayrton who could furnish such a subvention at the present cost of their stable. As yet however we must be content, we suppose, with such a use of wealth as 'Lothair' brings to the front—the purely selfish use of it carried to the highest pitch which selfishness has ever reached. Great parks and great houses, costly studs and costly conservatories, existence relieved of every hitch and discomfort—these are the outlets which wealth has as yet succeeded in finding. For nobler outlets we must wait for the advent of the Poet-Capitalist.

LAMBETH AND THE ARCHBISHOPS

LAMBETH AND THE ARCHBISHOPS

A LITTLE higher up the river, but almost opposite to the huge mass of the Houses of Parliament, lies a broken, irregular pile of buildings, at whose angle, looking out over the Thames, is one grey weather-beaten tower. The broken pile is the archiepiscopal Palace of Lambeth; the grey weatherbeaten building is its Lollards' Tower. From this tower the mansion itself stretches in a varied line, chapel and guard-room and gallery and the stately buildings of the new house looking out on the terrace and garden; while the Great Hall, in which the library has now found a home, is the low picturesque building which reaches southward along the river to the gate.

The story of each of these spots will interweave itself with the thread of our narrative as we proceed; but I would warn my readers at the outset that I do not purpose to trace the history of Lambeth in itself, or to attempt any architectural or picturesque description of the place. What I attempt is simply to mark in incident after incident which has occurred within its walls the relation of the House to the Primates whom it has sheltered for seven hundred years, and through them to the literary, the ecclesiastical, the political history of the realm.

Nothing illustrates the last of these relations better than the site of the house itself. It is doubtful whether we can date the residence of the Archbishops of Canterbury at Lambeth, which was then a manor house of the see of Rochester, earlier than the reign of Eadward the Confessor. But there was a significance in the choice of the spot as there was a significance in the date at which the choice was made. So long as the political head of the English people ruled, like Ælfred or Æthelstan or Eadgar, from Winchester, the spiritual head of the English people was content to rule from Canterbury. It was when the piety of the Confessor and the political prescience of his successors brought the Kings finally to Westminster that the Archbishops were permanently drawn to their suffragan's manor house at Lambeth. The Norman rule gave a fresh meaning to their position. In the new course of national history which opened with the Conquest the Church was called to play a part greater than she had ever known before. Hitherto the Archbishop had been simply the head of the ecclesiastical order—a representative of the moral and spiritual forces on which government was based. The Conquest, the cessation of the great Witenagemots in which the nation, however imperfectly, had till then found a voice, turned him into a Tribune of the People.

Foreigner though he might be, it was the Primate's part to speak for the conquered race the words it could no longer utter. He was in fact the permanent leader (to borrow a modern phrase) of a Constitutional Opposition; and in addition to the older religious forces which he wielded he wielded a popular and democratic force which held the new King and the new baronage in check. It was he who received from the sovereign whom he crowned the solemn oath that he would rule not by his own will, but according to the customs, or as we should say now, the traditional constitution of the realm. It was his to call on the people to declare whether they chose him for their king, to receive the thundered "Ay, ay," of the crowd, to place the priestly unction on shoulder and breast, the royal crown on brow. To watch over the observance of the covenant of that solemn day, to raise obedience and order into religious duties, to uphold the custom and law of the realm against personal tyranny, to guard amid the darkness and brutality of the age those interests of religion, of morality, of intellectual life which as yet lay peacefully together beneath the wing of the Church,—this was the political office of the Primate in the new order which the Conquest created, and it was this office which expressed itself in the site of the house that fronted the King's house over Thames.

From the days of Archbishop Anselm therefore to the days of Stephen Langton, Lambeth only fronted Westminster as the Archbishop fronted the King. Synod met over against Council; the clerical court of the one ruler rivalled in splendour, in actual influence, the baronial court of the other. For more than a century of our history the great powers which together were to make up the England of the future lay marshalled over against each other on either side the water.

With the union of the English people and the sudden arising of English freedom which followed the Great Charter this peculiar attitude of the Archbishops passed necessarily away. When the people itself spoke again, its voice was heard not in the hall of Lambeth but in the Chapter-house which gave a home to the House of Commons in its earlier sessions at Westminster. From the day of Stephen Langton the nation has towered higher and higher above its mere ecclesiastical organization, till the one stands dwarfed beside the other as Lambeth now stands dwarfed before the mass of the Houses of Parliament. Nor was the religious change less than the political. In the Church as in the State the Archbishops suddenly fell into the rear. From the days of the first English Parliament to the days of the Reformation they not only cease to be representatives of the moral and religious forces of the nation but stand actually opposed to them. Nowhere is this better brought out than in their house beside the Thames. The political history of Lambeth lies spread over the whole of its site, from the gateway of Morton to the garden where we shall see Cranmer musing on the fate of Anne Boleyn. Its ecclesiastical interest on the other hand is concentrated in a single spot. We must ask our readers therefore to follow us beneath the groining of the Gate-House into the quiet little court that lies on the river-side of the hall. Passing over its trim grass-plot to a doorway at the angle of Lollards' Tower, and mounting a few steps, they will find themselves in a square antechamber, paved roughly with tiles, and with a single small window looking out towards the Thames. The chamber is at the base of Lollards' Tower; in the centre stands a huge oaken pillar, to which the room owes its name of the "Post-room," and to which somewhat mythical tradition asserts Lollards to have been tied when they were "examined" by the whip. On its western side a doorway of the purest Early English work leads us directly into the palace Chapel.

It is strange to stand at a single step in the very heart of the ecclesiastical life of so many ages, within walls beneath which the men in whose hands the fortunes of English religion have been placed from the age of the Great Charter till to-day have come and gone; to see the light falling through the tall windows with their marble shafts on the spot where Wyclif fronted Sudbury, on the lowly tomb of Parker, on the stately screen-work of Laud, on the altar where the last sad communion of Sancroft originated the Nonjurors. It is strange to note the very characteristics of the building itself, marred as it is by modern restoration, and to feel how simply its stern, unadorned beauty, the beauty of Salisbury and of Lincoln, expressed the very tone of the Church that finds its centre there.

And hardly less strange is it to recall the odd, roystering figure of the Primate to whom, if tradition be true, it owes this beauty. Boniface of Savoy was the youngest of three brothers out of whom their niece Eleanor, the queen of Henry the Third, was striving to build up a foreign party in the realm. Her uncle Amadeus was richly enfeoffed with English lands; the Savoy Palace in the Strand still recalls the settlement and the magnificence of her uncle Peter. For this third and younger uncle she grasped at the highest post in the State save the Crown itself. "The handsome Archbishop," as his knights loved to call him, was not merely a foreigner as Lanfranc and Anselm had been foreigners—strange in manner or in speech to the flock whom they ruled—he was foreign in the worst sense: strange to their freedom, their sense of law, their reverence for piety. His first visit set everything on fire. He retreated to Lyons to hold a commission in the Pope's bodyguard, but even Innocent was soon weary of his tyranny. When the threat of sequestration recalled him after four years of absence to his see, his hatred of England, his purpose soon to withdraw again to his own sunny South, were seen in his refusal to furnish Lambeth. Certainly he went the wrong way to stay here. The young Primate brought with him Savoyard fashions, strange enough to English folk. His armed retainers, foreigners to a man, plundered the City markets. His own archiepiscopal fist felled to the ground a prior who opposed his visitation. It was the Prior of St. Bartholomew's by Smithfield; and London, on the King's refusal to grant redress, took the matter into her own hands. The City bells swung out, and a noisy crowd of citizens were soon swarming beneath the walls of the palace, shouting threats of vengeance.

For shouts Boniface cared little. In the midst of the tumult he caused the sentences of excommunication which he had fulminated to be legally executed in the chapel of his house. But bravado like this soon died before the universal resentment, and "the handsome Archbishop" fled again to Lyons. How helpless the successor of Augustine really was was shown by a daring outrage perpetrated in his absence. Master Eustace, his official, had thrown into prison the Prior of St. Thomas's Hospital for some contempt of court; and the Prior's diocesan, the Bishop of Winchester, a prelate as foreign and lawless as Boniface himself, took up the injury as his own. A party of his knights appeared before the house at Lambeth, tore the gates from their hinges, set Master

Eustace on horseback, and carried him off to the episcopal prison at Farnham. At last Boniface bowed to submission, surrendered the points at issue, recalled his excommunications, and was suffered to return. He had learnt his lesson well enough to remain from that time a quiet, inactive man, with a dash of continental frugality and wit about him. Whether he built the chapel or no, he would probably have said of it as he said of the Great Hall of Canterbury, "My predecessors built, and I discharge the debt for their building. It seems to me that the true builder is the man that pays the bill."

But Boniface never learnt to be an Englishman. When under the guidance of Earl Simon of Montfort the barons wrested the observance of their Charter from the King the Primate of England found shelter in a fresh exile. The Church had in fact ceased to be national. The figure of the first Reformer, as he stands on the chapel floor, is in itself the fittest comment on the age in which the chapel was built, an age when the interests of popular liberty and of intellectual freedom had sheered off from the church which had so long been their protector. With them the moral and spiritual life of the people sheered off too. The vast ecclesiastical fabric rested in the days of Archbishop Sudbury solely on its wealth and its tradition. Suddenly a single man summed up in himself the national, the mental, the moral power it had lost, and struck at the double base on which it rested. Wyclif, the keenest intellect of his day, national and English to the very core, declared its tradition corrupt and its wealth antichrist. The two forces that above all had built up the system of mediæval Christianity, the subtlety of the schoolman, the enthusiasm of the penniless preacher, united to strike it down.

It is curious to mark how timidly the Primate of the day dealt with such a danger as this. Sudbury was acting in virtue of a Papal injunction, but he acted as though the shadow of the terrible doom that was awaiting him had already fallen over him. He summoned the popular Bishop of London to his aid ere he cited the Reformer to his judgment-seat. It was not as a prisoner that Wyclif appeared in the chapel: from the first his tone was that of a man who knew that he was secure. He claimed to have the most favourable construction put upon his words; then, availing himself of his peculiar subtlety of interpretation, he demanded that where they might bear two meanings his judges should take them in an orthodox sense. It was not a noble scene—there was little in it of Luther's "Here stand I—I can none other;" but both sides were in fact acting a part. On the one hand the dead pressure of ecclesiastical fanaticism was driving the Primate into a position from which he sought only to escape; on the other Wyclif was merely gaining time—"beating step," as men say—with his scholastic formulæ. What he looked for soon came. There was a rumour in the City that Papal delegates were sitting in judgment on the Reformer, and London was at once astir. Crowds of angry citizens flocked round the archiepiscopal house, and already there was talk of attacking it when a message from the Council of Regency commanded a suspension of all proceedings in the case. Sudbury dismissed his prisoner with a formal injunction, and the day was for ever lost to the Church.

But if in Sudbury the Church had retreated peaceably before Wyclif, it was not from any doubt of the deadly earnestness of the struggle that lay before her. Archbishop Chichele's accession to the primacy was the signal for the building of Lollards' Tower. Dr. Maitland has shown that the common name rests on a mere error, and that the Lollards' Tower which meets us so grimly in the pages of Foxe was really a western tower of St. Paul's. But, as in so many other instances, the popular voice showed a singular historical tact in its mistake; the tower which Chichele raised marked more than any other in the very date of its erection the new age of persecution on which England was to enter. From a gateway in the northern side of the Post-room worn stone steps lead up to a dungeon in which many a prisoner for the faith must have lain. The massive oaken door, the iron rings bolted into the wall, the one narrow window looking out over the river, tell their tale as well as the broken sentences scratched or carved around. Some are mere names; here and there some light-pated youngster paying for his night's uproar has carved his dice or his "Jesus kep me out of all il compane, Amen." But "Jesus est amor meus" is sacred, whether Lollard or Jesuit graved it in the lonely prison hours, and not less sacred the "Deo sit gratiarum actio" that marks perhaps the leap of a martyr's heart at the news of the near advent of his fiery deliverance. It is strange to think, as one winds once more down the stairs that such feet have trodden, how soon England answered to the challenge that Lollards' Tower flung out over the Thames. The white masonry had hardly grown grey under the buffetings of a hundred years ere Lollard was no longer a word of shame, and the reformation that Wyclif had begun sat enthroned within the walls of the chapel where he had battled for his life.

The attitude of the primates indeed showed that sooner or later such a reformation was inevitable. From the moment when Wyclif stood in Lambeth Chapel the Church sank ecclesiastically as well as politically into non-existence. It survived merely as a vast landowner, whilst its primates, after a short effort to resume their older position as real heads of their order, dwindled into ministers and tools of the Crown. The Gate-tower of the house, · the grand mass of brickwork, whose dark red tones are (or, alas! were till a year or two since) so exquisitely brought out by the grey stone of its angles and the mullions of its broad arch-window, recalls an age—that of its builder, Archbishop Morton—when Lambeth, though the residence of the first minister of the crown, had really lost all hold on the nobler elements of political life. It was raised from this degradation by the efforts of a primate to whose merits justice has hardly as yet been done. First in date among the genuine portraits of the Archbishops of Canterbury which hang round the walls of the Guard-room at Lambeth is the portrait of Archbishop Warham. The plain, homely old man's face still looks down on us line for line as the "seeing eye" of Holbein gazed on it three centuries ago. "I instance this picture," says Mr. Wornum, in his life of the painter, "as an illustration that Holbein had the power of seeing what he looked on, and of perfectly transferring to his picture what he saw." Memorable in the annals of art as the first of that historic series which brings home to us as no age has ever been brought home to eyes of aftertime the age of the English Reformation, it is even more memorable as marking the close of the great intellectual movement which the Reformation swept away.

It was with a letter from Erasmus in his hands that Hans Holbein stood before the aged Archbishop, still young as when he sketched himself at Basel with the fair, frank, manly face, the sweet gentle mouth, the heavy red cap flinging its shade over the mobile, melancholy brow. But it was more than the "seventy years" that he has so carefully noted above it that the artist saw in the Primate's face; it was the still, impassive calm of a life's disappointment. Only ten years before, at the very moment when the painter first made his entry into Basel, Erasmus had been forwarding to England the great work in which he had recalled theologians to the path of sound biblical criticism. "Every lover of letters," the great scholar wrote sadly, after the old man had gone to his rest,— "Every lover of letters owes to Warham that he is the possessor of my 'Jerome';" and with an acknowledgment of the Primate's bounty such as he alone in Christendom could give the edition bore in its forefront his memorable dedication to the Archbishop. That Erasmus could find protection for such a work in Warham's name, that he could address him with a conviction of his approval in words so bold and outspoken as those of his preface, tell us how completely the old man sympathised with the highest tendencies of the New Learning.

Of the Renascence, that "new birth" of the world—for I cling to a word so eminently expressive of a truth that historians of our day seem inclined to forget or to deny—of that regeneration of mankind through the sudden upgrowth of intellectual liberty, Lambeth was in England the shrine. With the Reformation which followed it Lambeth, as we shall see, had little to do. But the home of Warham was the home of the revival of letters. With a singular fitness, the venerable library which still preserves their tradition, ousted from its older dwelling-place by the demolition of the cloister, has in modern days found refuge in the Great Hall, the successor and copy of that hall where the men of the New Learning, where Colet and More and Grocyn and Linacre gathered round the table of Warham.

It was with Grocyn that Erasmus rowed up the river to the Primate's board. Warham addressed a few kindly words to the poor scholar before and after dinner, and then drawing him aside into a corner of the hall (his usual way when he made a present to any one) slipped into his hand an acknowledgment for the book and dedication he had brought with him. "How much did the Archbishop give you?" asked his companion as they rowed home again. "An immense amount!" replied Erasmus, but his friend saw the discontent on his face, and drew from him how small the sum really was. Then the disappointed scholar burst into a string of indignant questions: was Warham miserly, or was he poor, or did he really think such a present expressed the value of the book? Grocyn frankly blurted out the true reason for Warham's economy in his shrewd suspicion that this was not the first dedication that had been prefixed to the "Hecuba," and it is likely enough that the Primate's suspicion was right. At any rate, Erasmus owns that Grocyn's sardonic comment, "It is the way with you scholars," stuck in his mind even when he returned to Paris, and made him forward to the Archbishop a perfectly new translation of the "Iphigenia."

Few men seem to have realised more thoroughly than Warham the new conception of an intellectual and moral equality before which the old social distinctions were to vanish away. In his intercourse with this group of friends he seems utterly unconscious of the exalted station which he occupied in the eyes of men. Take such a story as Erasmus tells of a visit of Dean Colet to Lambeth. The Dean took Erasmus in the boat with him, and read as they rowed along a section called 'The Remedy for Anger' in his friend's popular 'Handbook of the Christian Soldier.' When they reached the hall however Colet plumped gloomily down by Warham's side, neither eating nor drinking nor speaking in spite of the Archbishop's good-humoured attempt to draw him into conversation. It was only by starting the new topic of a comparison of ages that the Archbishop was at last successful; and when dinner was over Colet's ill-temper had utterly fled. Erasmus saw him draw aside an old man who had shared their board, and engage in the friendliest greeting. "What a fortunate fellow you are!" began the impetuous Dean, as the two friends stepped again into their boat; "what a tide of good-luck you bring with you!" Erasmus, of course, protested (one can almost see the half-earnest, half-humorous smile on his lip) that he was the most unfortunate fellow on earth. He was at any rate a bringer of good fortune to his friends, the Dean retorted; one friend at least he had saved from an unseemly outbreak of passion. At the Archbishop's table, in fact, Colet had found himself placed opposite to an uncle with whom he had long waged a bitter family feud, and it was only the singular chance which had brought him thither fresh from the wholesome lessons of the 'Handbook' that had enabled the Dean to refrain at the moment from open quarrel, and at last to get such a full mastery over his temper as to bring about a reconciliation with his kinsman. Colet was certainly very lucky in his friend's lessons, but he was perhaps quite as fortunate in finding a host so patient and good-tempered as Archbishop Warham.

Primate and scholar were finally separated at last by the settlement of Erasmus at Basel, but the severance brought no interruption to their friendship. "England is my last anchor," Erasmus wrote bitterly to a rich German prelate; "if that goes, I must beg." The anchor held as long as Warham lived. Years go by, but the Primate is never tired of new gifts and remembrances to the brave, sensitive scholar at whose heels all the ignorance and bigotry of Europe was yelping. Sometimes indeed he was luckless in his presents; once he sent a horse to his friend, and, in spite of the well-known proverb about looking such a gift in the mouth, got a witty little snub for his pains. "He is no doubt a good steed at bottom," Erasmus gravely confesses, "but it must be owned he is not over-handsome; however he is at any rate free from all mortal sins, with the trifling exception of gluttony and laziness! If he were only a father confessor now! he has all the qualities to fit him for one—indeed, he is only *too* prudent, modest, humble, chaste, and peaceable!" Still, admirable as these characteristics are, he is not quite the nag one expected. "I fancy that through some knavery or blundering on your servant's part, I must have got a different steed from the one you intended for me. In fact, now I come to remember, I had bidden my servant not to accept a horse except it were a good one; but I am infinitely obliged to you all the same." Even Warham's temper must have been tried as he laughed over such a letter as this; but the precious work of art which Lambeth contains proves that years only intensified their friendship. It was, as we have seen, with a letter of Erasmus in his hands, that on his first visit to England Holbein presented himself before Warham; and Erasmus responded to his friend's present of a copy of this portrait by forwarding a copy of his own.

With the Reformation in its nobler and purer aspects Lambeth—as we have said—had little to do. Bucer, Peter Martyr, and Alasco, gathered there for a moment round Cranmer, but it was simply as a resting-place on their way to Cambridge, to Oxford, and to Austin Friars. Only one of the symbols of the new Protestantism has any connection with it; the Prayer-Book was drawn up in the peaceful seclusion of Otford. The party conferences, the rival martyrdoms of the jarring creeds, took place elsewhere. The memories of Cranmer which linger around Lambeth are simply memories of degradation, and that the deepest degradation of all, the degradation of those solemn influences which the Primacy embodies to the sanction of political infamy. It is fair indeed to remember the bitterness of Cranmer's suffering. Impassive as he seemed, with a face that never changed and sleep seldom known to be broken, men saw little of the inner anguish with which the tool of Henry's injustice bent before that overmastering will. But seldom as it was that the silent lips broke into complaint the pitiless pillage of his see wrung fruitless protests even from Cranmer. The pillage had begun on the very eve of his consecration, and from that moment till the king's death Henry played the part of sturdy beggar for the archiepiscopal manors. Concession followed concession, and yet none sufficed to purchase security. The Archbishop lived in the very shadow of death. At one time he heard the music of the royal barge as it passed Lambeth, and hurried to the water-side to greet the King. "I have news for you, my chaplain!" Henry broke out with his rough laugh as he drew

Cranmer on board : " I know now who is the greatest heretic in Kent!" and pulling a paper from his sleeve he showed him his denunciation by the prebendaries of his own cathedral. At another time he was summoned from his bed, and crossed the river to find Henry pacing the gallery at Whitehall and to hear that on the petition of the Council the King had consented to his committal to the Tower. The law of the Six Articles parted him from wife and child. "Happy man that you are," Cranmer groaned to Alexander Ales, whom with his wonted consideration for others he had summoned to Lambeth to warn him of his danger as a married priest; "happy man that you are that you can escape! I would that I could do the same. Truly my see would be no hindrance to me."

The bitter words must have recalled to Ales words of hardly less bitterness which he had listened to on a visit to Lambeth years before. If there was one person upon earth whom Cranmer loved it was Anne Boleyn. When the royal summons had called him to Lambeth to wait till the time arrived when his part was to be played in the murder of the Queen his affection found vent in words of a strange pathos. "I loved her not a little," he wrote to Henry in fruitless intercession, "for the love which I judged her to bear towards God and His Gospel. I was most bound to her of all creatures living." So he wrote, knowing there was wrong to be done towards the woman he loved, wrong which he alone could do, and knowing too that he would stoop to do it. The large garden stretched away northward from his house then as now, but then thick, no doubt, with the elm rows that vanished some thirty years back as the great city's smoke drifted over them, and here in the early morning (it was but four o'clock) Ales, who had found sleep impossible and had crossed the river in a boat to seek calm in the fresh air and stillness of the place, met Cranmer walking. On the preceding day Anne had gone through the mockery of her trial, but to the world outside the little circle of the court nothing was known, and it was in utter unconsciousness of this that Ales told the Archbishop he had been roused by a dream of her beheading. Cranmer was startled out of his usual calm. "Don't you know then," he asked after a moment's silence, "what is to happen to-day?" Then raising his eyes to heaven he added with a wild burst of tears, "She who has been Queen of England on earth will this day become a queen in heaven!" Some hours afterwards the Queen stood before him as her judge, and passed back to the Tower and the block.

Cranmer was freed by his master's death from this helplessness of terror only to lend himself to the injustice of the meaner masters who followed Henry. Their enemies were at least his own, and, kindly as from many instances we know his nature to have been, its very weakness made him spring eagerly in such an hour of deliverance at the opportunity of showing his power over those who so long held him down. On charges of the most frivolous nature Bishop Gardiner and Bishop Bonner were summoned before the Archbishop at Lambeth, deposed from their sees, and flung into prison. It is only the record of their trials, as it still stands in the pages of Foxe, that can enable us to understand the violence of the reaction under Mary. Gardiner with characteristic dignity confined himself to simply refuting the charges brought against him and protesting against the injustice of the court. But the coarser, bull-dog nature of Bonner turned to bay. By gestures, by scoff, by plain English speech, he declared again and again his sense of the wrong that was being done. A temper naturally fearless was stung to bravado by the sense of oppression. As he entered the hall at Lambeth he passed straight by the Archbishop and his fellow-commissioners, still keeping his cap on his head as though in unconsciousness of his presence. One who stood by plucked his sleeve, and bade him do reverence. Bonner turned laughingly round and addressed the Archbishop, "What, my Lord, are you here? By my troth I saw you not." "It was because you would not see," Cranmer sternly rejoined. "Well," replied Bonner, "you sent for me: have you anything to say to me?" The charge was read. The Bishop had been commanded in a sermon to acknowledge that the acts of the King during his minority were as valid as if he were of full age. The command was flatly in contradiction with existing statutes, and the Bishop had no doubt disobeyed it.

But Bonner was too adroit to make a direct answer to the charge. He gained time by turning suddenly on the question of the Sacrament; he cited the appearance of Hooper as a witness in proof that it was really on this point that he was brought to trial, and he at last succeeded in arousing Cranmer's love of controversy. A reply of almost incredible profanity from the Archbishop, if we may trust Foxe's report, rewarded Bonner's perseverance in demanding a statement of his belief. The Bishop was not slow to accept the advantage he had gained. "I am right sorry to hear your Grace speak these words," he said, with a grave shake of his head, and Cranmer was warned by the silence and earnest looks of his fellow-commissioners to break up the session.

Three days after, the addition of Sir Thomas Smith, the bitterest of Reformers, to the number of his assessors emboldened Cranmer to summon Bonner again. The court met in the chapel, and the Bishop was a second time commanded to reply to the charge. He objected now to the admission of the evidence of either Hooper or Latimer on the ground of their notorious heresy. "If that be the law," Cranmer replied hastily, "it is no godly law." "It is the King's law used in the realm," Bonner bluntly rejoined. Again Cranmer's temper gave his opponent the advantage. "Ye be too full of your law," replied the angry Primate; "I would wish you had less knowledge in that law and more knowledge in God's law and of your duty!" "Well," answered the Bishop with admirable self-command, "seeing your Grace falleth to wishing, I can also wish many things to be in your person." It was in vain that Smith strove to brush away his objections with a contemptuous "You do use us thus to be seen a common lawyer." "Indeed," the veteran canonist coolly retorted; "I knew the law ere you could read it!" There was nothing for it but a second adjournment of the court. At its next session all parties met in hotter mood. The Bishop pulled Hooper's books on the Sacrament from his sleeve and began reading them aloud. Latimer lifted up his head, as he alleged, to still the excitement of the people who crowded the chapel; as Bonner believed, to arouse a tumult. Cries of "Yea, yea," "Nay, nay," interrupted Bonner's reading. The Bishop turned round and faced the throng, crying out in humorous defiance, "Ah! Woodcocks! Woodcocks!" The taunt was met with universal laughter, but the scene had roused Cranmer's temper as well as his own. The Primate addressed himself to the people, protesting that Bonner was called in question for no such matter as he would persuade them. Again Bonner turned to the people with "Well now, hear what the Bishop of London saith for his part," but the commissioners forbade him to speak more. The court was at last recalled to a quieter tone, but contests of this sort still varied the proceedings as they dragged their slow length along in chapel and hall.

At last Cranmer resolved to make an end. Had he been sitting simply as Archbishop, he reminded Bonner sharply, he might have expected more reverence and obedience from his suffragan. As it was, "at every time that we have sitten in commission you have used such unseemly fashions, without all reverence or obedience, giving taunts and checks as well unto us, with divers of the servants and chaplains, as also unto certain of the ancientest that be here, calling them fools and daws, with such like, that you have given to the multitude an intolerable example of disobedience." "You show yourself to be a meet judge!" was Bonner's scornful reply. It was clear he had no purpose to yield. The real matter at issue, he contended, was the doctrine of the Sacrament, and from the very court-room he sent his orders to the Lord Mayor to see that no heretical opinions were preached before him. At the close of the trial he once more addressed Cranmer in solemn protest against his breach of the law. "I am sorry," he said, "that I being a bishop am thus handled at your Grace's hand, but more sorry that you suffer abominable heretics to practise as they do in London and elsewhere—answer it as you can!" Then bandying taunts with the throng, the indomitable bishop followed the officers to the Marshalsea.

From the degradation of scenes like these Lambeth was raised to new dignity and self-respect by the primacy of Parker. His consecration in the same chapel which had witnessed Wyclif's confession was the triumph of Wyclif's principles, the close of that storm of the Reformation, of that Catholic reaction, which ceased alike with the accession of Elizabeth. But it was far more than this. It was in itself a symbol of the Church of England as it stands to-day, of that quiet illogical compromise between past and present which Parker and the Queen were to mould into so lasting a shape. Every circumstance of the service marked the strange contrasts which were to be blended in the future of the English Church. The zeal of Edward the Sixth's day had dashed the stained glass from the casements of Lambeth; the zeal of Elizabeth's day was soon to move, if it had not already moved, the holy table into the midst of the chapel. But a reaction from the mere iconoclasm and bareness of Calvinistic Protestantism showed itself in the tapestries hung for the day along the eastern wall and in the rich carpet which was spread over the floor. The old legal forms, the old Ordination Service reappeared, but in their midst came the new spirit of the Reformation, the oath of submission to the royal supremacy, the solemn gift no longer of the pastoral staff but of the Bible. The very dress of the four consecrating bishops showed the same confusion. Barlow, with the Archbishop's chaplains who assisted him in the office of the Communion, wore the silken copes of the older service; Scory and Hodgskins the fair linen surplice of the new. Yet more noteworthy was the aged figure of Coverdale, "Father Coverdale," as men used affectionately to call him, the well-known translator of the Bible, whose life had been so hardly wrung by royal intercession from Mary. Rejecting the very surplice as popery, in his long Genevan cloak he marks the opening of the Puritan controversy over vestments which was to rage so fiercely from Parker on to Laud.

The library of Parker, though no longer within its walls, is memorable in the literary history of Lambeth as the first of a series of such collections made after his time by each successive Archbishop. Many of these indeed have passed away. The manuscripts of Parker form the glory of Corpus College, Cambridge; the oriental collections of Laud are among the most precious treasures of the Bodleian. In puerile revenge for his fall Sancroft withdrew his books from Lambeth, and bequeathed them to Emmanuel College. The library which the munificence of Tenison bequeathed to his old parish of St. Martin's-in-the-Fields has been dispersed by a shameless act of vandalism within our own memories. An old man's caprice deposited the papers of Archbishop Wake at Christ Church. But the treasures thus dispersed are, with the exception of the Parker MSS., far surpassed by the collections that remain. I cannot attempt here to enter with any detail into the nature of the history of the archiepiscopal library. It owes its origin to Archbishop Bancroft, it was largely supplemented by his successor Abbot, and still more largely after a long interval by the book-loving Primates Tenison and Secker. The library of 30,000 volumes still mainly consists of these collections, though it has been augmented by the smaller bequests of Sheldon and Cornwallis and in a far less degree by those of later Archbishops. One has at any rate the repute of having augmented it during his primacy simply by a treatise on gout and a book about butterflies. Of the 1200 volumes of manuscripts and papers, 500 are due to Bancroft and Abbot, the rest mainly to Tenison, who purchased the Carew Papers, the collections of Wharton, and the Codices that bear his name. If Wake left his papers to Christ Church in dread of the succession of Bishop Gibson the bequest of Gibson's own papers more than made up the loss. The most valuable addition since Gibson's day has been that of the Greek Codices collected in the East at the opening of this century by Dr. Carlyle.

The importance of Parker's primacy however was political and ecclesiastical rather than literary. The first Protestant Archbishop was not the man to stoop to servility like Cranmer, nor was Elizabeth the queen to ask such stooping. But the concordat which the two tacitly arranged, the policy so resolutely clung to in spite of Burleigh and

Walsingham, was perhaps a greater curse both to nation and to Church than the meanness of Cranmer. The steady support given by the Crown to the new ecclesiastical organization which Parker moulded into shape was repaid by the conversion of every clergyman into the advocate of irresponsible government. It was as if publicly to ratify this concordat that the Queen came in person to Lambeth in the spring of 1573. On either side the chapel in that day stood a greater and lesser cloister. The last, which lay on the garden side, was swept away by the demolitions of the eighteenth century, the first still fills the space between chapel and hall but has been converted into domestic offices by the "restoration" of our own. Even Mr. Blore might have spared the cloisters from whose gallery on the side towards the Thames Elizabeth looked down on the gay line of nobles and courtiers who leaned from the barred windows beneath and on the crowd of meaner subjects who filled the court, while she listened to Dr. Pearce as he preached from a pulpit set by the well in the midst. At its close the Queen passed to dinner in the Archbishop's chamber of presence, while the noble throng beneath followed Burleigh and Lord Howard to the hall whose oaken roof told freshly of Parker's hand. At four the short visit was over, and Elizabeth again on her way to Greenwich. But, short as it was, it marked the conclusion of a new alliance between Church and State out of which the Ecclesiastical Commission was to spring.

Such an alliance would have been deadly for English religion as for English liberty had not its strength been broken by the obstinate resistance in wise as well as unwise ways of the Puritan party. There are few more interesting memorials of the struggle which followed than the 'Martin Marprelate' tracts which still remain in the collection at Lambeth, significantly scored in all their more virulent passages by the red pencil of Archbishop Whitgift. But the story of that controversy cannot be told here, though it was at Lambeth, as the seat of the High Commission, that it was really fought out. More and more it parted all who clung to liberty from the Church, and knit the episcopate in a closer alliance with the Crown. When Elizabeth set Parker at the head of the new Ecclesiastical Commission, half the work of the Reformation was in fact undone.

Under Laud this great engine of ecclesiastical tyranny was perverted to the uses of civil tyranny of the vilest kind. Under Laud the clerical invectives of a Martin Marprelate deepened into the national fury of 'Canterburie's Doom.' With this political aspect of his life we have not now to deal; what Lambeth Chapel brings out with singular vividness is the strange audacity with which the Archbishop threw himself across the strongest religious sentiments of his time. Men noted as a fatal omen the accident that marked his first entry into Lambeth; the overladen ferry-boat upset in the crossing, and though horses and servants were saved the Primate's coach remained at the bottom of the Thames. But no omen brought hesitation to that bold, narrow mind. His first action, he tells us himself, was the restoration of the chapel, and, as Laud managed it, restoration was the simple undoing of all that the Reformation had done.

"I found the windows so broken, and the chapel lay so nastily," he wrote long after in his Defence, "that I was ashamed to behold, and could not resort unto it but with some disdain." With characteristic energy the Archbishop aided with his own hands in the repair of the windows, and racked his wits "in making up the history of those old broken pictures by help of the fragments of them, which I compared with the story." In the east window his glazier was scandalized at being forced by the Primate's express directions to "repair and new make the broken crucifix." The holy table was set altar-wise against the wall, and a cloth of arras hung behind it embroidered with the history of the Last Supper. The elaborate woodwork of the screen, the richly-embroidered copes of the chaplains, the silver candlesticks, the credence-table, the organ and the choir, the genuflexions to the altar, recalled the elaborate ceremonial of the Royal Chapel.

High-handed however as the Archbishop's course had been, he felt dimly the approaching wreck. At the close of 1639 he notes in his diary a great storm that broke even the boats of the Lambeth watermen to pieces as they lay before his gate. A curious instance of his gloomy prognostications still exists among the relics in the library—a quarry of greenish glass, once belonging to the west window of the gallery of Croydon, and removed when that palace was rebuilt. On the quarry Laud has written with his signet-ring in his own clear, beautiful hand, "Memorand. Ecclesiæ de Micham, Cheme, et Stone cum aliis fulgure combustæ sunt. Januar. 14, 1638-9. Omen avertat Deus."

The omen was far from averted. The Scottish war, the Bellum Episcopale, the Bishops' War, as men called it, was soon going against the King. Laud had been the chief mover in the war, and it was against Laud that the popular indignation at once directed itself. On the 9th of May he notes in his diary: "A paper posted upon the Royal Exchange, animating 'prentices to sack my house on the Monday following." On that Monday night the mob came surging up to the gates. "At midnight my house was beset with 500 of these rascal routers," notes the indomitable little prelate. He had received notice in time to secure the house, and after two hours of useless shouting the mob rolled away. Laud had his revenge; a drummer who had joined in the attack was racked mercilessly, and then hanged and quartered. But retaliation like this was useless. The gathering of the Long Parliament sounded the knell of the sturdy little minister who had ridden England so hard. At the close of October he is in his upper study—it is one of the pleasant scholarly touches that redeem so much in his life—"to see some manuscripts which I was sending to Oxford. In that study hung my picture taken by the life" (the picture is at Lambeth still), "and coming in I found it fallen down upon the face and lying on the floor, the string being broken by which it was hanged against the wall. I am almost every day threatened with my ruin in parliament. God grant this be no omen." On the 18th of December he was in charge of the gentleman-usher of the Lords on impeachment of high treason. In his company the Archbishop returned for a few hours to see his house for the last time, "for a book or two to read in, and such papers as pertained to my defence against the Scots;" really to burn, says Prynne, most of his privy papers. There is the first little break in the boldness with which till now he has faced the popular ill-will, the first little break too of tenderness, as though the shadow of what was to come were softening him, in the words that tell us his last farewell: "I stayed at Lambeth till the evening, to avoid the gaze of the people. I went to evening prayer in my chapel. The Psalms of the day (Ps. 93 and 94) and cap. 50 of Isaiah gave me great comfort. God make me worthy of it, and fit to receive it. As I went to my barge hundreds of my poor neighbours stood there and prayed for my safety and return to my house. For which I bless God and them."

So Laud vanished into the dark December night never to return. The house seems to have been left unmolested for two years. Then "Captain Browne and his company entered my house at Lambeth to keep it for public service." The troopers burst open the door "and offered violence to the organ," but it was saved for the time by the intervention of their captain. In 1643 the zeal of the soldiers could no longer be restrained. Even in the solitude and terror of his prison in the Tower Laud still feels the bitterness of the last blow at the house he held so dear. "May 1. My chapel windows defaced and the steps torn up." But the crowning bitterness was to come. If there were two men living who had personal wrongs to avenge on the Archbishop, they were Leighton and Prynne. It can only have been as a personal triumph over their humbled persecutor that the Parliament appointed the first custodian of Lambeth and gave Prynne the charge of searching the Archbishop's house and chambers for materials in support of the impeachment. Of the spirit in which Prynne executed his task, the famous 'Canterburie's Doom,' with the Breviat of Laud's life which preceded it, still gives pungent evidence. By one of those curious coincidences that sometimes flash the fact upon us through the dust of old libraries, the copy of this violent invective preserved at Lambeth is inscribed on its fly-leaf with the clear, bold "Dum spiro spero, C. R." of the King himself. It is hard to picture the thoughts that must have passed through Charles's mind as he read the bitter triumphant pages that told how the man he had twice pilloried and then flung into prison for life had come out again, as he puts it brutally, to "unkennel that fox," his foe.

Not even the Archbishop's study with its array of Missals and Breviaries and Books of Hours, not even the gallery with its "superstitious pictures," the three Italian masterpieces that he hurried as evidence to the bar of the House of Lords, so revealed to this terrible detective "the rotten, idolatrous heart" of the Primate as the sight of the chapel. It was soon reduced to simplicity. We have seen how sharply even in prison Laud felt the havoc made by the soldiery. But worse profanation was to follow. In 1648 the house passed by sale to the regicide Colonel Scott; the Great Hall was at once demolished, and the chapel turned into the dining-room of the household. The tomb of Parker was levelled with the ground; and if we are to believe the story of the royalists, the new owner felt so keenly the discomfort of dining over a dead man's bones that the remains of the great Protestant primate were disinterred and buried anew in an adjoining field.

The story of the library is a more certain one. From the days of Bancroft to those of Laud it had remained secure in the rooms over the great cloister where Parker's collection had probably stood before it passed to Cambridge. There in Parker's day Foxe had busied himself in work for the later editions of his 'Acts and Monuments;' even in the present library one book at least bears his autograph and the marginal marks of his use. There the great scholars of the seventeenth century, with Selden among them, had carried on their labours. The time was now come when Selden was to save the library from destruction. At the sale of Lambeth the Parliament ordered the books and manuscripts to be sold with the house. Selden dexterously interposed. The will of its founder, Bancroft, he pleaded, directed that in case room should not be found for it at Lambeth his gift should go to Cambridge; and the Parliament, convinced by its greatest scholar, suffered the books to be sent to the University.

When the Restoration brought the Stuart home again, it flung Scott into the Tower and set Juxon in the ruined, desecrated walls. Of the deeper thoughts that such a scene might have suggested few probably found their way into the simple, limited mind of the new primate. The whole pathos of Juxon's position lay in fact in his perfect absorption in the past. The books were reclaimed from their Cambridge Adullam. The chapel was rescued from desecration, and the fine woodwork of screen and stalls replaced as Laud had left them. The demolition of the hall left him a more serious labour, and the way in which he entered on it brought strikingly out Juxon's temper. He knew that he had but a few years to live, and he set himself but one work to do before he died, the replacing everything in the state in which the storm of the rebellion had found it. He resolved therefore not only to rebuild the hall but to rebuild it precisely as it had stood before it was destroyed. It was in vain that he was besieged by the remonstrances of "classical" architects, that he was sneered at even by Pepys as "old-fashioned"; times had changed and fashions had changed, but Juxon would recognize no change at all. He died ere the building was finished, but even in death his inflexible will provided that his plans should be adhered to. The result has been a singularly happy one. It was not merely that the Archbishop has left us one of the noblest examples of that strange yet successful revival of Gothic feeling of which the staircase of Christ Church Hall, erected at much about the same time, furnishes so exquisite a specimen. It is that in his tenacity to the past he has preserved the historic interest of his hall. Beneath the picturesque woodwork of the roof, in the quiet light that breaks through the quaint mullions of its windows, the student may still recall without a jar the figures which make Lambeth memorable, figures such as those of Warham and Erasmus, of Grocyn and Colet and More. Unhappily there was a darker side to this conservatism. The Archbishops had returned like the Bourbons, forgetting nothing and having learned hardly anything. If any man could have learned the lesson of history it was Juxon's successor, the hard sceptical Sheldon, and one of the jottings in Pepys's Diary shows us what sort of lesson he had learned. Pepys had gone down the river at noon to dine with the Archbishop in company with Sir Christopher Wren, "the first time," as he notes, "that I ever was there, and I have long longed for it." Only a few days before he had had a terrible disappointment, for "Mr. Wren and I took boat, thinking to dine with my Lord of Canterbury, but when we came to Lambeth the gate was shut, which is strictly done at twelve o'clock, and nobody comes in afterwards, so we lost our labour." On this occasion Pepys was more fortunate. He found "a noble house and well furnished with good pictures and furniture, and noble attendance in good order, and a great deal of company, though an ordinary day, and exceeding good cheer, nowhere better or so much that ever I think I saw." Sheldon with his usual courtesy gave his visitors kindly welcome, and Pepys was preparing to withdraw at the close of dinner when he heard news which induced him to remain. The almost incredible scene that followed must be told in his own words:—"Most of the company gone, and I going, I heard by a gentleman of a sermon that was to be there; and so I stayed to hear it, thinking it to be serious, till by-and-by the gentleman told me it was a mockery by one Cornet Bolton, a very gentlemanlike man, that behind a chair did pray and preach like a Presbyter Scot, with all the possible imitation in grimaces and voice. And his text about the hanging up their harps upon the willows; and a serious, good sermon too, exclaiming against bishops and crying up of my good Lord Eglington till it made us all burst. But I did wonder to hear the Bishop at this time to make himself sport with things of this kind; but I perceive it was shown to him as a rarity, and he took care to have the room door shut; but there were about twenty gentlemen there, infinitely pleased with the 'novelty.'"

It was "novelties" like these that led the last of the Stuarts to his fatal belief that he could safely defy a Church that had so severed itself from the English religion in doing the work of the Crown. The pen of a great historian has told for all time the Trial of the Seven Bishops, and though their protest was drawn up at Lambeth I may not venture to tell it here. Of all the seven in fact Sancroft was probably the least inclined to resistance, the one prelate to whom the cheers of the great multitude at their acquittal brought least sense of triumph.

No sooner indeed was James driven from the throne than the Primate fell back into the servile king-worship of an England that was passing away. Within the closed gates of Lambeth he debated endlessly with himself and with his fellow-bishops the questions of "de jure" and "de facto" right to the crown. Every day he sheered further and further from the actual world around him. Newton, who was with him at Lambeth when it was announced that the Convention had declared the throne vacant, found that Sancroft's thoughts were not with England or English freedom—they were concentrated on the question whether James's child were a supposititious one or no. "He wished," he said, "they had gone on a more regular method and examined into the birth of the young child. There was reason," he added, "to believe he was not the same as the first, which might easily be known, for he had a mole on his neck." The new Government bore long with the old man, and Sancroft for a time seems really to have wavered. He suffered his chaplains to take the oaths and then scolded them bitterly for praying for William and Mary. He declined to take his seat at the Council board, and yet issued his commission for the consecration of Burnet. At last his mind was made up and the Government on his final refusal to take the oath of allegiance had no alternative but to declare the see vacant.

For six months Sancroft was still suffered to remain in his house, though Tillotson was nominated as his successor. With a perfect courtesy, worthy of the saintly temper which was his characteristic, Tillotson waited long at the deprived Archbishop's door desiring a conference. But Sancroft refused to see him. Evelyn found the old man in a dismantled house, bitter at his fall. "Say 'nolo,' and say it from the heart," he had replied passionately to Beveridge when he sought his counsel on the offer of a bishopric. Others asked whether after refusing the oaths they might attend worship where the new sovereigns were prayed for. "If they do," answered Sancroft, "they will need the Absolution at the end as well as at the beginning of the service." In the answer lay the schism of the Nonjurors, and to this schism Sancroft soon gave definite form. On Whitsunday the new Church was started in the archiepiscopal Chapel. The throng of visitors was kept standing at the palace gate. No one was admitted to the Chapel but some fifty who had refused the oaths. The Archbishop himself consecrated: one Nonjuror reading the prayers, another preaching. A formal action of ejectment was the answer to this open defiance, and on the evening of its decision in favour of the Crown Sancroft withdrew quietly by boat over Thames to the Temple. He was soon followed by many who, amidst the pettiness of his public views, could still realise the grandeur of his self-devotion. To one, the Earl of Aylesbury, the Archbishop himself opened the door. His visitor, struck with the change of all he saw from the pomp of Lambeth, burst into tears and owned how deeply the sight affected him. "O my good lord," replied Sancroft, "rather rejoice with me, for now I live again."

With Sancroft's departure opens a new age of Lambeth's ecclesiastical history. The revolution which flung him aside had completed the work of the great Rebellion in sweeping away for ever the old pretensions of the primates to an autocracy within the Church of England. But it seemed to have opened a nobler prospect in placing them at the head of the Protestant Churches of the world. In their common peril before the great Catholic aggression, which found equal support at Paris and Vienna, the Reformed communities of the Continent looked for aid and sympathy to the one Reformed Church whose position was now unassailable. The congregations of the Palatinate appealed to Lambeth when they were trodden under foot beneath the horse-hoofs of Turenne. The same appeal came from the Vaudois refugees in Germany, the Silesian Protestants, the Huguenot churches that still fought for existence in France, the Calvinists of Geneva, the French refugees who had forsaken their sunny homes in the south for the Gospel and God. In the dry letter-books on the Lambeth shelves, in the records of bounty dispensed through the Archbishop to the persecuted and the stranger, in the warm and cordial correspondence with Lutheran and Calvinist, survives a faint memory of the golden visions which filled Protestant hearts after the accession of the great Deliverer. "The eyes of the world are upon us," was Tenison's plea for union with Protestants at home. " All the Reformed Churches are in expectation of something to be done which may make for union and peace." When a temper so cold as Tenison's could kindle in this fashion it is no wonder that more enthusiastic minds launched into loftier expectations—that Leibnitz hoped to see the union of Calvinist and Lutheran accomplished by a common adoption of the English Liturgy, that a High Churchman like Nicholls revived the plan, which Cranmer had proposed and Calvin had supported, of a general council of Protestants to be held in England. One by one such visions faded before the virulence of party spirit, the narrowness and timidity of Churchmen, the base and selfish politics of the time. Few men had higher or more spiritual conceptions of Christian unity than Tenison; yet the German translation of our Liturgy, stamped with the royal monogram of King Frederick, which still exists in the library, reminds us how in mere jealousy of a Tory triumph Tenison flung away the offer of a union with the Church of Prussia. The creeping ambition of Dubois foiled whatever dreams Archbishop Wake may have entertained of a union with the Church of France.

From the larger field of political and ecclesiastical history we may turn again ere we close to the narrower limits of the Lambeth Library. The storm which drove Sancroft from his house left his librarian, Henry Wharton, still bound to the books he loved so well. Wharton is one of those instances of precocious development which are rarer in the sober walks of historical investigation than in art. It is a strange young face that we see in the frontispiece to his sermons, the impression of its broad, high brow and prominent nose so oddly in contrast with the delicate, feminine curves of the mouth, and yet repeated in the hard, concentrated gaze of the large, full eyes which look out from under the enormous wig. Wharton was the most accomplished of Cambridge students when he quitted the University at twenty-two to aid Cave in his 'Historia Litteraria.' But the time proved too exciting for a purely literary career. At Tenison's instigation the young scholar plunged into the thick of the controversy which had been provoked by the aggression of King James, and his vigour soon attracted the notice of Sancroft. He became one of the Archbishop's chaplains, and was presented in a single year to two of the best livings in his gift. With these however save in his very natural zeal for pluralities he seems to have concerned himself little. It was with the library which now passed into his charge that his name was destined to be associated. Under him its treasures were thrown liberally open to the ecclesiastical antiquaries of his day—to Hody, to Stillingfleet, to Collier, to Atterbury, and to Strype, who was just beginning his voluminous collections towards the illustration of the history of the sixteenth century. But no one made so much use of the documents in his charge as Wharton himself. In them, no doubt, lay the secret of his consent to take the oath, to separate from his earlier patron, to accept the patronage of Tenison. But there was no permanent breach with Sancroft; on his deathbed the Archbishop committed to him the charge of editing Laud's papers, a charge redeemed by his publication of the 'Troubles and Trials' of the Archbishop in 1694.

But this with other labours was mere by-play. The design upon which his energies were mainly concentrated was "to exhibit a complete ecclesiastical history of England to the Reformation," and the two volumes of the 'Anglia Sacra,' which appeared during his life, were intended as a partial fulfilment of this design. Of these, as they now stand, the second is by far the more valuable. The four archiepiscopal biographies by Osbern, the three by Eadmer, Malmesbury's lives of Aldhelm and Wulstan, the larger collection of works by Giraldus Cambrensis, Chaundler's biographies of Wykeham and Bekington, and the collection of smaller documents which accompanied these, formed a more valuable contribution to our ecclesiastical history than had up to Wharton's time ever been made. The first volume contained the chief monastic annals which illustrated the history of the sees whose cathedrals were possessed by monks; those served by canons regular or secular were reserved for a third volume, while a fourth was to have contained the episcopal annals of the Church from the Reformation to the Revolution.

The last however was never destined to appear, and its predecessor was interrupted after the completion of the histories of London and St. Asaph by the premature death of the great scholar. In 1694 Battely writes a touching account to Strype of his interview with Wharton at Canterbury :—" One day he opened his trunk and drawers, and showed me his great collections concerning the state of our Church, and with a great sigh told me his labours were at an end, and that his strength would not permit him to finish any more of that subject." Vigorous and healthy as his natural constitution was, he had worn it out with the severity of his toil. He denied himself refreshment in his eagerness for study, and sat over his books in the bitterest days of winter till hands and feet were powerless with the cold. At last nature abruptly gave way, his last hopes of recovery were foiled by an immoderate return to his old pursuits, and at the age of thirty-one Henry Wharton died a quiet scholar's death. Archbishop Tenison stood with Bishop Lloyd by the grave in Westminster, where the body was laid " with solemn and devout anthems composed by that most ingenious artist, Mr. Harry Purcell ; " and over it were graven words that tell the broken story of so many a student life :—" Multa ad augendam et illustrandam rem literariam conscripsit ; plura moliebatur."

The library no longer rests in those quiet rooms over the great cloister in which a succession of librarians, such as Gibson and Wilkins and Ducarel, preserved the tradition of Henry Wharton. The 'Codex' of the first, the 'Concilia' of the second, and the elaborate analysis of the Canterbury Registers which we owe to the third are, like Wharton's own works, of primary importance to the study of English ecclesiastical history. It was reserved for our own day to see these memories swept away by the degradation of the cloister into a kitchen yard and a scullery; but the Great Hall of Archbishop Juxon, to which by a happy fortune the books were transferred, has seen in Dr. Maitland and Professor Stubbs keepers whose learning more than rivals the learning of Wharton himself. It is not without significance that this great library still lies open to the public as a part and a notable part of the palace of the chief prelate of the English Church. Even if Philistines abound in it the spirit and drift of the English Church have never been wholly Philistine. It has managed somehow to reflect and represent the varying phases of English life and English thought; it has developed more and more a certain original largeness and good-tempered breadth of view; amidst the hundred jarring theories of itself and its position which it has embraced at one time or another it has never stooped to the mere "pay over the counter" theory of Little Bethel. Above all it has as yet managed to find room for almost every shade of religious opinion;

and it has answered at once to every national revival of taste, of beauty, and of art.

Great as are the faults of the Church of England, these are merits which make men who care more for the diffusion of culture than for the propagation of this shade or that shade of religious opinion shrink from any immediate wish for her fall. And they are merits which spring from this, that she is still a learned Church, not learned in the sense of purely theological or ecclesiastical learning, but a Church which is able to show among its clergy men of renown in every branch of literature, critical, poetical, historical, or scientific. How long this distinction is to continue her own it is hard to say; there are signs indeed in the theological temper which is creeping over the clergy that it is soon to cease. But the spirit of intelligence, of largeness of view, of judicious moderation, which is so alien from the theological spirit, can still look for support from the memories of Lambeth. Whatever its influence may have been, it has not grown out of the noisy activity of theological "movement." Its strength has been to sit still and let such "movements" pass by. It is by a spirit the very opposite of theirs—a spirit of conciliation, of largeness of heart, that it has won its power over the Church. None of the great theological impulses of this age or the last, it is sometimes urged, came out of Lambeth. Little of the theological bitterness, of the controversial narrowness of this age or the last, it may fairly be answered, has ever entered its gates. Of Lambeth we may say what Matthew Arnold says of Oxford, that many as are its faults it has never surrendered itself to ecclesiastical Philistines. In the calm, genial silence of its courts, its library, its galleries, in the presence of its venerable past, the virulence, the petty strife, the tumult of religious fanaticism finds itself hushed. Amongst the storm of the Wesleyan revival, of the Evangelical revival, of the Puseyite revival, the voice of Lambeth has ever pleaded for a truth simpler, larger, more human than theirs. Amid the deafening clamour of Tractarian and anti-Tractarian disputants both sides united in condemning the silence of Lambeth. Yet the one word that came from Lambeth will still speak to men's hearts when all their noisy disputations are forgotten. "How," a prelate, whose nearest relative had joined the Church of Rome, asked Archbishop Howley, "how shall I treat my brother?" "As a brother," was the Archbishop's reply.

CHILDREN BY THE SEA

CHILDREN BY THE SEA

AUTUMN brings its congresses — scientific, ecclesiastical, archæological—but the prettiest of autumnal congresses is the children's congress by the sea. It is like a leap from prose into poetry when we step away from Associations and Institutes, from stuffy lecture-rooms and dismal sections, to the strip of sand which the children have chosen for their annual gathering. Behind us are the great white cliffs, before us the reach of grey waters with steamers and their smoke-trail in the offing and waves washing lazily in upon the shore. And between sea and cliff are a world of little creatures, digging, dabbling, delighted. What strikes us at first sight is the number of them. In ordinary life we meet the great host of children in detail, as it were; we kiss our little ones in the morning, we tumble over a perambulator, we dodge a hoop, we pat back a ball. Child after child meets us, but we never realise the world of children till we see it massed upon the sands. Children of every age, from the baby to the schoolboy; big children and tiny children, weak little urchins with pale cheeks and plump little urchins with sturdy legs; children of all tempers, from the screeching child in arms to the quiet child sitting placid and gazing out of large grey eyes; gay little madcaps paddling at the water's edge; busy children, idle children, children careful of their dress, hoydens covered with sand and seaweed, wild children, demure children—all are mustered in the great many-coloured camp between the cliffs and the sea.

It is their holiday as it is ours, but what is a mere refreshment to us is life to them. What a rapture of freedom looks up at us out of the little faces that watch us as we thread our way from group to group! The mere change of dress is a revolution in the child's existence. These brown-holland frocks, rough sunshades, and sandboots, these clothes that they may wet and dirty and tear as they like, mean deliverance from endless dressings—dressings for breakfast and dressings for lunch, dressings to go out with mamma and dressings to come down to dessert—an escape from fashionable little shoes and tight little hats and stiff little flounces that it is treason to rumple. There is an inexpressible triumph in their return at eventide from the congress by the sea, dishevelled, bedraggled, but with no fear of a scolding from nurse. Then too there is the freedom from "lessons." There are no more of those dreadful maps along the wall, no French exercises, no terrible arithmetic. The elder girls make a faint show of keeping up their practising, but the goody books which the governess packed carefully at the bottom of their boxes remain at the bottom unopened. There is no time for books, the grave little faces protest to you; there is only time for the sea. That is why they hurry over breakfast to get early to the sands, and are moody and restless at the length of luncheon. It is a hopeless business to keep them at home; they yawn over picture-books, they quarrel over croquet, they fall asleep over draughts. Home is just now only an interlude of sleeping or dining in the serious business of the day.

The one interest of existence is in the sea. Its novelty, its vastness, its life, dwarf everything else in the little minds beside it. There is the endless watching for the ships, the first peep at the little dot on the horizon, the controversies as it rises about its masts or its flag, the questions as to where it is coming from and where it is going to. There is the endless speculation on the tide, the doubt every morning whether it is coming in or going out, the wonder of its perpetual advance or retreat, the whispered tales of children hemmed in between it and the cliffs, the sense of a mysterious life, the sense of a mysterious danger. Above all there is the sense of a mysterious power. The children wake as the wind howls in the night, or the rain dashes against the window panes, to tell each other how the waves are leaping high over the pier and ships tearing to pieces on reefs far away. So charming and yet so terrible, the most playful of playfellows, the most awful of possible destroyers, the child's first consciousness of the greatness and mystery of the world around him is embodied in the sea.

It is amusing to see the precision with which the children's congress breaks up into its various sections. The most popular and important is that of the engineers. The little members come toddling down from the cliffs with a load of implements, shouldering rake and spade, and dangling tiny buckets from their arms. One little group makes straight for its sand-hole of yesterday, and is soon busy with huge heaps and mounds which are to take the form of a castle. A crowing little urchin beside is already waving the Union Jack which is ready to crown the edifice, if the Fates ever suffer it to be crowned. Engineers of less military taste are busy near the water's edge with an elaborate system of reservoirs and canals, and greeting with shouts of triumph the admission of the water to miniature little harbours. A corps of absolutely unscientific labourers are simply engaged in digging the deepest hole they can, and the blue nets over their sunshades are alone visible above the edge of the excavation. It is delightful to watch the industry, the energy, the absolute seriousness and conviction of the engineers. Sentries warn you off from the limits of the fortress; you are politely asked to "please take care," as your clumsy foot strays along the delicate brink of the canal. Suggestions that have a mechanical turn about them, hints on the best way of reaching the water or the possibility of a steeper slope for the sand-walls, are listened to with attention and respect. You are rewarded by an invitation which allows you to witness the very moment when the dyke is broken and the sea admitted into basin and canal, or the yet more ecstatic moment when the Union Jack waves over the completed castle.

Indolence and adventure charm the dabblers, as industry absorbs the engineers. The sands are of all earthly spots the most delightful; but a greater delight than any earthly spot can afford awaits the dabbler in the sea. It is mostly the girls who dabble; the gaiety and frolic suit them better than the serious industry of castles and canals. Deliverance from shoes and stockings, the first thrill of pleasure and surprise at the cool touch of the water, the wild rush along the brim, the dainty advance till the sea covers the little ankles, the tremulous waiting with an air of defiance as the wave deepens round till it touches the knee, the firm line with which the dabblers grasp hand in hand and face the advancing tide, the sudden panic, the break, the disorderly flight, the tears and laughter, the run after the wave as it retreats again, the fresh advance and defiance—this is the paradise of the dabbler. Hour after hour, with clothes tucked round their waist and a lavish display of stout little legs, the urchins wage their mimic warfare with the sea. Meanwhile the scientific section is encamped upon the rocks. With torn vestments and bruised feet the votaries of knowledge are peeping into every little pool, detecting mussel-shells, picking up seaweed, hunting for anemones. A shout of triumph from the tiny adventurer who has climbed over the rough rock-shelf announces that he has secured a prize for the glass jar at home, where the lumps of formless jelly burst into rosy flowers with delicate tendrils waving gently round them for food. A cry of woe tells of some infantile Whymper who has lost his hold on an Alpine rock-edge some six inches high. Knowledge has its difficulties as well as its dangers, and the difficulty of forming a rock-section in the face of the stern opposition of mothers and nurses is undoubtedly great. Still, formed it is, and science furnishes a goodly company of votaries and martyrs to the congress by the sea.

But of course the naval section bears away the palm. It is for the most part composed of the elder boys and of a few girls who would be boys if they could. Its members all possess a hopeless passion for the sea, and besiege their mothers for promises that their future life shall be that of middies. They wear straw hats and loose blue shirts, and affect as much of the sailor in their costume as they can. Each has a boat, or as they call it a "vessel," and the build and rig of these vessels is a subject of constant discussion and rivalry in the section. Much critical inquiry is directed to the propriety of Arthur's jib, or the necessity of "ballasting" or pouring a little molten lead into Edward's keel. The launch of a new vessel is the event of the week. The coast-guardsman is brought in to settle knotty questions of naval architecture and equipment, and the little seamen listen to his verdicts, his yarns, the records of his voyages, with a wondering reverence. They ask knowingly about the wind and the prospects of the weather; they submit to his higher knowledge their theories as to the nature and destination of each vessel that passes; they come home with a store of naval phrases which are poured recklessly out over the tea-table. The pier is a favourite haunt of the naval section. They delight in sitting on rough coils of old rope. Nothing that is of the sea comes amiss to them. "I like the smell of tar," shouts a little enthusiast. They tell tales among themselves of the life of a middie and the fun of the "fo-castle," and watch the waves leaping up over the pier-head with a wild longing to sing 'Rule Britannia.' Every ship in the offing is a living thing to them, and the appearance of a man-of-war sends them sleepless to bed.

There is but one general meeting of the children's congress, and that is in front of the bathing-machines. Rows of little faces wait for their turn, watching the dash of the waves beneath the wheels, peeping at the black-robed figures who are bobbing up and down in the sea, half longing for their dip, half shrinking as the inevitable moment comes nearer and nearer, dashing forward joyously at last as the door opens and the bathing woman's "Now, my dear," summons them to the quaint little box. One lingers over the sight as one lingers over a bed of flowers. There is all the fragrance, the colour, the sweet caprice, the wilfulness, the delight of childhood in the tiny figures that meet us on the return from their bath, with dancing eyes and flushed cheeks and hair streaming over their shoulders. What a hero the group finds in the urchin who never cries! With what envy they regard the big sister who never wants to come out of the water! It is pleasant to listen to their prattle as they stroll over the sands with a fresh life running through every vein, to hear their confession of fright at the first dip, their dislike of putting their head under water, their chaff of the delicate little sister who "will only bathe with mamma." Mammas are always good-humoured by the sea; papas come out of their eternal newspaper and toss the wee brats on their shoulders, uncles drop down on the merry little group with fresh presents every day. The restraint, the distance of home vanishes with the practical abolition of the nursery and the schoolroom. Home, schoolroom, nursery, all are crammed together in the little cockleshell of a boat where the little ones are packed round father and mother and tossing gaily over the waves. What endless fun in the rising and falling, the creaking of the sail, the gruff voice of the boatman, the sight of the distant cliffs, the flock of sea-gulls nestling in the wave-hollows! The little ones trail their hands in the cool water and fancy they see mermaids in the cool green depths. The big boy watches the boatman and studies navigation. The little brother dips a hook now and then in a fond hope of whiting. The tide has come in ere they return, and the little voyagers are lifted out, tired and sleepy, in the boatman's arms, to dream that night of endless sailings over endless seas.

It is a terrible morning that brings the children news of their recall to the smoke and din of town. They wander for a last visit down to the beach, listen for the last time to the young bandit in his Spanish sombrero who charms the nursery-maids with lays of love, club their pence for a last interview with the itinerant photographer. It is all over; the sands are thinner now, group after group is breaking up, autumn is dying into winter, and rougher winds are blowing over the sea. But the sea is never too rough for the little ones. With hair blown wildly about their faces they linger disconsolately along the brink, count the boats they shall never see again, make pilgrimages to the rock caves to tell its separate story of enjoyment in each of them, and fling themselves with a last kiss on the dear, dear sands! Then they shoulder their spade and rake, and with one fond look at the cliffs turn their backs on the sea. But the sea is with them still, even when the crowded train has whirled them far from waves that the white gull skims over.

They have their tales of it to tell to their governess, their memories of it to count over before they fall asleep, their dreams of it as they lie asleep, their hopes of seeing it again when weary winter and spring and summer have at last slipped away. They listen to stories of wrecks, and find a halfpenny for the sham sailor who trolls his ballads in the street. Now and then they look lovingly at the ships and the sand-buckets piled away in the play-cupboard. So with one abiding thought at their little hearts the long days glide away till autumn finds them again children by the sea.

THE FLORENCE OF DANTE

THE FLORENCE OF DANTE

THE one story in the history of the modern world which rivals in concentrated interest the story of Athens is the story of Florence in the years just before and after the opening of the fourteenth century —the few years, that is, of its highest glory in freedom, in letters, in art. Never since the days of Pericles had such a varied outburst of human energy been summed up in so short a space. Architecture reared the noble monuments of the Duomo and Santa Croce. Cimabue revolutionized painting, and then "the cry was Giotto's." Italian poetry, preluded by the canzonets of Guido Cavalcanti and his rivals, rose to its fullest grandeur in the 'Commedia' of Dante. Italian prose was born in the works of Malaspina and Dino. Within, the Florentines worked out patiently and bravely amidst a thousand obstacles the problem of free and popular government. Without, they covered sea and land with their commerce; their agents supplied the Papal treasury, while private firms were already beginning that career of vast foreign loans which at a later time enabled the victor of Creçy to equip his armies with Florentine gold.

We can only realise the attitude of Florence at this moment by its contrast with the rest of Europe. It was a time when Germany was sinking down into feudal chaos under the earlier Hapsburgs. The system of despotic centralization invented by St. Louis and perfected by Philippe le Bel was crushing freedom and vigour out of France. If Parliamentary life was opening in England, literature was dead, and a feudalism which had become embittered by the new forms of law which the legal spirit of the age gave it was pressing harder and harder on the peasantry. Even in Italy Florence stood alone. The South lay crushed beneath the oppression of its French conquerors. In the North the earlier communal freedom had already made way for the rule of tyrants when it was just springing into life in the city by the Arno. For it is noteworthy that of all the cities of Italy Florence is the most modern. Genoa and Pisa had been rivals in commercial activity a hundred years before the merchants of Florence were known out of Tuscany. Sicily had caught the gift of song from the Provençal troubadours half a century before the Florentine singers. Too insignificant to share in the great struggle of the Empire and the Papacy, among the last to be divided into Guelph and Ghibelline, Florence emerged into communal greatness when that of Milan or Bologna was already in decay.

The City of the Lily came late to the front to

inherit and give fresh vigour to the gifts of all. As the effigies of Byzantine art became living men and women beneath the pencil of Giotto, so the mere imitative poetry of the Sicilian Court became Italian literature in Dante and Boccaccio. Freedom, slow as it seemed in awakening, nowhere awakened so grandly, nowhere fought so long and stubbornly for life. Dino Compagni sets us face to face with this awakening, with this patient pitiful struggle. His 'Chronicle' indeed has been roughly attacked of late by the sweeping scepticism of German critics, but the attack has proved an unsuccessful one. The strongest evidence of its genuineness indeed lies in the impression of a distinct personality which is left on us by a simple perusal of the 'Chronicle' itself. Some of its charm no doubt rises from the naive simplicity of Dino's story-telling. With him and with his contemporaries, Malaspina, Dante, and Villani, Italian prose begins; and we can hardly fancy a better training in style for any young Italian than to be brought face to face in Dino with the nervous picturesque accents that marked the birth of his mother-tongue. But the charm is more one of character than one of style. Throughout we feel the man, a man whose temper is so strongly and clearly marked in its contrast with so reflective a temper as Villani's that the German theory which makes his chronicle a mere cento from the later work hardly needs discussion. Dino has the quaint directness, the dramatic force, the tenderness of Froissart, but it is a nobler and more human tenderness; a pity not for the knight only, but for knight and burgher as well. The sham tinsel of chivalry which flutters over the pages of the gay Canon of Liège is exchanged in Dino for a manly patriotism, a love of civic freedom, of justice, of religion. In his quiet way he is a great artist. There is an Herodotean picturesqueness as well as an Herodotean simplicity in such a picture as that of Dante's first battle-field, the Florentine victory of Campaldino :—

"On the appointed day the men of Florence "advanced their standards to go into the enemies' "land, and passed by Casentino along an ill road "where, had the enemy found them, they had re- "ceived no little damage; but such was not the will "of God. And they came near to Bibbiena, at a "place called Campaldino where was the enemy, and "there they halted in array of battle. The captains "of war sent the light-armed foot to the front; and "each man's shield, with a red lily on a white ground, "was stretched out well before him. Then the "Bishop, who was short-sighted, asked, 'Those there: "'what walls be they?' They answered him, 'The "'shields of the enemy.' Messer Barone de' Man- "giadori da San Miniato, a chevalier frank and well "skilled in deeds of arms, gathered his men-at-arms "together and said to them, 'My masters, in Tuscan "'wars men were wont to conquer by making a stout "'onset, and that lasted but a while, and few men

" 'died, for it was not in use to kill. Now is the
" 'fashion changed, and men conquer by holding
" ' their ground stoutly, wherefore I counsel you that
" ' ye stand firm and let them assault you.' And so
" they settled to do. The men of Arezzo made their
" onset with such vigour and so great force that the
" body of the Florentines fell back not a little. The
" fight was hard and keen. Messer Corso Donati
" with a brigade of the men of Pistoja charged the
" enemy in flank; the quarrels from the crossbows
" poured down like rain; the men of Arezzo had
" few of them, and were withal charged in flank
" where they were exposed; the air was covered
" with clouds, and there was a very great dust. Then
" the footmen of Arezzo set themselves to creep
" under the bellies of the horses, knife in hand, and
" disembowelled them, and some of them penetrated
" so far that in the very midst of the battalion were
" many dead of either part. Many that were counted
" of great prowess were shown vile that day, and
" many of whom none spoke word won honour. . . .
" The men of Arezzo were broken, not by cowardice
" or little prowess, but by the greater number of their
" enemies were they put to the rout and slain. The
" soldiers of Florence that were used to fighting slew
" them; the villeins had no pity."

"Pity" is almost the characteristic word of Dino
Compagni—pity alike for foe or friend; for the
warriors of Arezzo or the starved-out patriots of

Pistoja as well as for the heroes of his own Florence; pity for the victims of her feuds, and even for the men who drove them into exile; pity, most of all, for Florence herself. We read his story indeed at first with a strange sense of disappointment and surprise. To the modern reader the story of Florence in the years which Dino covers is above all the story of Dante. As the 'Chronicle' jots patiently down the hopes and fears, the failures and successes of the wiser citizens in that struggle for order and good government which brought Dante to his long exile, we feel ourselves standing in the very midst of events out of which grew the threefold Poem of the After-World and face to face with the men who front us in the 'Inferno' and 'Paradiso.' But this is not the world Dino stands in. Of what seem to us the greater elements of the life around him he sees and tells us nothing. Of art or letters his 'Chronicle' says never a word. The name of Dante is mentioned but once, and then without a syllable of comment. It is not in Dante that Dino interests himself: his one interest, his one passion, is Florence.

And yet as we read page after page a new interest in the story grows on us, the interest that Dino himself felt in the tragedy around him. Our sympathies go with that earnest group of men to which he belonged, men who struggled honestly to reconcile freedom and order in a State torn with antipathies of the past, with jealousies and ambitions and feuds of the present. The terrible sadness of the 'Divina Commedia' becomes more intelligible as we follow step by step the ruin of those hopes for his country which Dante entertained as well as Dino. And beyond this interest there is the social picture of the Florence of the fourteenth century itself, its strange medley of past and present, the old world of feudalism jostling with the new world of commerce, the trader elbowing the noble and the artisan the trader, an enthusiastic mystical devotion jealous of the new classicalism or the scepticism of men like Guido Cavalcanti, the petty rivalries of great houses alternating with large schemes of public policy, the tenderest poetry with brutal outrage and lust, the art of Giotto with the slow, patient bloodthirst of the vendetta.

What was the cause—the question presses on us through every page of Dino or of Dante—what was the cause of that ruin which waited in Florence as in every Italian city on so short a burst of freedom? What was it that foiled alike the counsel of statesmen and the passionate love of liberty in the people at large? What was it which drove Dante into exile and stung the simple-hearted Dino into a burst of eloquent despair? The answer—if we set aside the silly talk about "democracy" and look simply at the facts themselves—is a very simple one. The ruin of Florentine liberty, like the ruin of liberty elsewhere throughout Italy, lay wholly with its *noblesse*. It was equally perilous for an Italian town to leave its nobles without the walls or to force them to reside within. In their own robber-holds or their own country estates they were a scourge to the trader whose wains rolled temptingly past their walls. Florence, like its fellow Italian States, was driven to the demolition of the feudal castles, and to enforcing the residence of their lords within its own civic bounds. But the danger was only brought nearer home. Excluded by civic jealousy, wise or unwise, from all share in municipal government, their huge palazzi rose like fortresses in every quarter of the city. Within them lay the noble, a wild beast all the fiercer for his confinement in so narrow a den, with the old tastes, hatreds, preferences utterly unchanged, at feud as of old with his fellow-nobles, knit to them only by a common scorn of the burghers and the burgher life around them, stung to madness by his exclusion from all rule in the commonwealth, bitter, revengeful, with the wilfulness of a child, shameless, false, unprincipled.

The story which lies at the opening of the great feud between Guelph and Ghibelline in Florence throws a picturesque light on the temper of its nobility. Buondelmonte, the betrothed lover of a daughter of Oderigo Giantrufetti, passes beneath a palace of the Donati at whose window stands Madonna Aldruda with her two fair daughters. Seeing him pass by Aldruda calls aloud to him, pointing with her finger to the damsel by her side. "Whom have you taken to wife?" she says. "This is the wife I kept for you." The damsel pleased the youth, but his troth bound him, and he answered, "I can wed none other, now at any rate!" "Yes," cried Aldruda, "for I will pay the penalty for thee." "Then will I have her," said Buondelmonte. "Cosa fatta capo ha," was the famous comment of the outraged house —"stone dead has no fellow"—and as Dino puts it, in the most ordinary way in the world, "they settled to kill him the day he was to have married the damsel, and so they did." "Kill, kill," echoes everywhere through the story of these Florentine nobles. Assassination is an event of every day. Corso Donati sends murderers to kill an enemy among the Cerchi. Guido Cavalcanti strives to stab Corso in the back as he passes him. Where the dagger fails, they try poison without scruple. The best of them decline a share in a murder much as an Irish peasant may decline a share in an agrarian outrage, with a certain delicacy and readiness to stand by and see it done. When the assassination of the Bishop of Arezzo was decided on, Guglielmo da Pazzi, who was in the counsel, protested "he would have been content had it been done without his knowledge, but were the question put to him he might not be guilty of his blood."

Among such men even Corso Donati towers into a certain grandeur:—

"Knight he was of great valour and renown, gentle of blood and manners, of a most fair body even to old age, comely in figure, with delicate features, and a white skin; a pleasing, prudent, and eloquent speaker; one who ever aimed at great ends; friend and comrade of great lords and nobles; a man too of many friends and great fame throughout all Italy. Foe he was of the people and its leaders; the darling of soldiers, full of evil devices, evil-hearted, cunning."

Such was the man who drove Dante into exile:—

"Who for his pride was called 'Il Barone,' so that when he passed through the land many cried 'Viva Il Barone!' and the land seemed all his own."

He stood not merely at the head of the Florentine nobility, but at the head of the great Guelph organization which extended from city to city throughout Tuscany—a league with its own leaders, its own policy, its own treasure. In the attempt to seize this treasure for the general service of the State the most popular of Florentine leaders, Giano della Bella, had been foiled and driven into exile. An honest attempt to secure the peace of the city by the banishment of Corso and his friends brought about the exile of Dante. It is plain that powerless as they were before the united forces of the whole people the nobles were strong enough by simply biding their time and availing themselves of popular divisions to crush one opponent after another. And yet the struggle against them was one of life and death for the city. No atom of the new civilization, the new spirit of freedom or humanity, seems to have penetrated among them. Behind the gloomy walls of their city fortresses they remained the mere murderous tyrants of a brutal feudalism. "I counsel, lords, that we free ourselves from this slavery," cried Berto Frescobaldi to his brother nobles in the church of San Jacopo; "let us arm ourselves and run on to the Piazza, and there kill friend and foe alike as many as we find, so that neither we nor our children be ever subject to them more." Those who, like Sismondi, censure the sternness of the laws which pressed upon the nobles forget what wild beasts they were intended to hold down. Their outbreaks were the blind outbreaks of mere ruffians. The victory of Corso over Dante and the wiser citizens was followed by a carnival of bloodshed, firing of houses, pillage and lawlessness which wrings from Dino curses as bitter as those of the 'Inferno.'

From the hopeless task of curbing the various elements of disorder by the single force of each isolated city the wiser and more patriotic among the men of that day turned in despair to the Empire. Guelph and Ghibelline, Papalist and Imperialist, were words which as Dante saw had now lost their old meaning. In the twelfth century the Emperor was at once the foe of religion and the one obstacle to the rising freedom of the towns. In the fourteenth that freedom had either perished by its own excesses, or, as at Florence, was strong enough to defy even an Imperial assailant. Religion found its bitterest enemy in such a Pope as Boniface VIII., or the church over which he ruled. Whatever might have been its fortune under happier circumstances, the great experiment of democratic self-government, of free and independent city-states, had failed, whether from the wars of city with city, or from the civil feuds that rent each in sunder. The papacy could furnish no centre of union; its old sanctity was gone, its greed and worldliness weakened it every day. On the other hand, the remembrance of the tyranny of Barbarossa, of the terrible struggle by which the peace of Constance had been won, had grown faint and dim in the course of years. It was long since Italy had seen an Emperor at all.

But the old Ghibellinism had recovered new vigour from an unlooked-for quarter. As the revival of the Roman law had given an artificial prestige to the Empire in the twelfth century, so the revival of classical literature threw a new halo around it in the fourteenth. To Dante, penetrated with the greater Latin authors, Henry of Luxemburg is no stranger from over the Alps, but the descendant of the Augustus whom his own Vergil had loved and sung. The same classical feeling tells on Dino. With him

Florence is "the daughter of Rome." The pages of Sallust and of Livy have stirred him to undertake her annals. "The remembrance of ancient histories has long spurred my mind to write the events, full of danger yet reaching to no prosperous end, that this noble city, daughter of Rome, has encountered." It was the same sense that united with his own practical appreciation of the necessities of the time in his impatient longing for the intervention of the new Emperor. As Prior, Dino had acted the part of a brave and honest man, striving to conciliate party with party, refusing to break the law, chased at last with the rest of the magistracy from the Palace of the Signory by the violence of Corso Donati and the nobles. If he did not share Dante's exile, he had at any rate acted with Dante in the course of policy which brought that penalty on him. Both were Priors together in 1300; both have the same passionate love of Florence, the same haughty disdain of the factions that tore it to pieces. If the appeal of Dino to his fellows in Santa Trinità is less thrilling than the verse of Dante, it has its own pathetic force:—"My masters, why will ye confound and undo so good a city? Against whom do ye will to fight? Against your brethren? What victory will ye gain?—none other than weeping!" The words fell on deaf ears, and the smoke of burning streets, slaughter, and exile forced Dino to look to the stranger. There is something strangely touching in the dry, passionless way in which he tracks Henry of Luxemburg from city to city, the fire of his real longing only breaking out here and there in pettish outbursts at each obstacle the Emperor finds. The weary waiting came to nothing. Dino leaves us still looking for Henry's coming; Dante tells us of the death that dashed all hope to the ground. Even in the hour of his despair the poet could console himself by setting his "divino Arrigo" in the regions of the blest. What comfort the humble chronicler found whose work we have been studying none can know.

BUTTERCUPS

BUTTERCUPS

IT is not the least debt we owe to the holidays that they give us our buttercups back again. Few faces have stirred us with a keener touch of pity through the whole of the season than the face of the pale, awkward girl who slips by us now and then on the stairs, a face mutinous in revolt against its imprisonment in brick and mortar, dull with the boredom of the schoolroom, weary of the formal walk, the monotonous drive, the inevitable practice on that hated piano, the perpetual round of lessons from the odd creatures who leave their odder umbrellas in the hall. It is amazingly pleasant to meet the same little face on the lawn, and to see it blooming with new life at the touch of freedom and fresh air. It blooms with a sense of individuality, a sense of power. In the town the buttercup was nobody, silent, unnoticed, lost in the bustle and splendour of elder sisterdom. Here among the fields and the hedges she is queen. Her very laugh, the reckless shout that calls for mamma's frown and dooms the governess to a headache, rings out like a claim of possession. Here in her own realm she rushes at once to the front, and if we find ourselves enjoying a scamper over the common or a run down the hillside, it is the buttercup that leads the way.

All the silent defiance of her town bondage vanishes in the chatty familiarities of home. She has a story about the elm and the pond, she knows where Harry landed the trout last year, she is intimate with the keeper, and hints to us his mysterious hopes about the pheasants. She is great in short cuts through the woods, and has made herself wondrous lurking-places which she betrays under solemn promises of secrecy. She is a friend of every dog about the place, and if the pony lies nearest to her heart her lesser affections range over a world of favourites. It is hard to remember the pale, silent, school-girl of town in the vivid, chatty little buttercup who hurries one from the parrot to the pigeon, from the stables to the farm, and who knows and describes the merits of every hound in the kennels.

It is natural enough that the dethroned beauties who meet us at luncheon should wonder at our enthusiasm for nymphs of bread-and-butter, and ask with a certain severity. of scorn the secret of our happy mornings. The secret is simply that the buttercup is at home, and that with the close of her bondage come a grace and a naturalness that take her out of the realms of bread-and-butter. However difficult it may be for her maturer rivals to abdicate, it is the buttercup in fact who gives the tone to the holidays. There is a subtle contagion about pleasure, and it is from her that we catch the sense of largeness and liberty and physical enjoyment that gives a new zest to life. She laughs at our moans about sunshine as she laughs at our moans about mud, till we are as indifferent to mud and sunshine as she is herself. The whole atmosphere of our life is in fact changed, and it is amusing to recognize how much of the change we owe to the buttercup.

It is impossible perhaps to be whirled in this fashion out of the whisperings and boredoms of town without longing to know a little more of the pretty magician who works this wonderful transformation scene. But it is no easy matter to know much of the buttercup. Her whole charm lies in her freedom from self-consciousness; she has a reserved force of shyness behind all her familiarity, and of a very defiant sort of shyness. Her character in fact is one of which it is easier to feel the beauty than to analyse or describe it. Like all transitional phases, girlhood is full of picturesque inequalities, strange slumbers of one faculty and stranger developments of another; full of startling effects, of contrasts and surprises, of light and shade, that no other phase of life affords. Unconsciously month after month drifts the buttercup on to womanhood; consciously she lives in the past of the child. She comes to us trailing clouds of glory

—as Wordsworth sings—from her earlier existence, from her home, her schoolroom, her catechism. The girl of twenty summers whose faith has been wrecked by clerical croquet looks with amazement on the implicit faith which the buttercup retains in the clergy. Even on the curate, shy and awkward as he is, she looks as on a being sacred and ineffable. Perhaps his very shyness and awkwardness creates a sympathy between the two, and rouses a keener remorse for her yawns under his sermons and a keener gratitude for the heavenly generosity with which he bestowed on her the confirmation ticket. Free as she is from fancies, her conception of the daily life of her clergyman shows amusingly enough that she can attain a very fair pitch of idealism. We remember the story of a certain parson of our acquaintance who owned to a meek little buttercup his habit of carrying a book in his pocket for reading in leisure hours. "Ah, yes," replied the eager little auditor, with a hush of real awe in her voice—"the Bible, of course!" Unluckily it was the *Physiologie du Goût*.

Still more does the sister of a couple of seasons wonder at the ardour and fidelity of buttercup friendships. In after-life men have friends and women have lovers. The home and the husband and the child absorb the whole tenderness of a woman where they only temper and moderate the old external affections of her spouse. But then girl-friendship is a much more vivid and far more universal thing than friendship among boys. The one means, in nine cases out of ten, an accident of neighbourhood in school that fades with the next remove, or a partnership in some venture, or a common attachment to some particular game. But the school friendship of a girl is a passionate idolatry and devotion of friend for friend. Their desks are full of little gifts to each other. They have pet names that no strange ear may know, and hidden photographs that no strange eye may see. They share all the innocent secrets of their hearts, they are fondly interested in one another's brothers, they plan subtle devices to wear the same ribbons and to dress their hair in the same fashion. No amount of affection ever made a boy like the business of writing his friend a letter in the holidays, but half the charm of holidays to a girl lies in the letters she gets and the letters she sends. Nothing save friendship itself is more sacred to girlhood than a friend's letter; nothing more exquisite than the pleasure of stealing from the breakfast-table to kiss it and read it, and then tie it up with the rest that lie in the nook that nobody knows but the one pet brother. The pet brother is as necessary an element in buttercup life as the friend. He is generally the dullest, the most awkward, the most silent of the family group. He takes all this sisterly devotion as a matter of course, and half resents it as a matter of boredom. He is fond of informing his adorer that he hates girls, that they are always kissing and crying, and that they can't play cricket. The buttercup rushes away to pour out her woes to her little nest in the woods, and hurries back to worship as before. Girlhood indeed is the one stage of feminine existence in which woman has brothers. Her first season out digs a gulf between their sister and "the boys" of the family that nothing can fill up. Henceforth the latter are useful to get tickets for her, to carry her shawls, to drive her to Goodwood or to Lord's. In the mere fetching and carrying business they sink into the general ruck of cousins, grumbling only a little more than cousins usually do at the luck that dooms them to hew wood and draw water for the belle of the season. But in the pure equality of earlier days the buttercup shares half the games and all the secrets of the boys about her, and brotherhood and sisterhood are very real things indeed.

Unluckily the holidays pass away, and the buttercup passes away like the holidays. There is a strange humour about the subtle gradations by which girlhood passes out of all this free, genial, irreflective life into the self-consciousness, the reserve, the artificiality of womanhood. It is the sudden discovery of a new sense of enjoyment that first whirls the buttercup out of her purely family affections. She laughs at the worship of her new adorer. She is as far as Dian herself from any return of it; but the sense of power is awakened, and she has a sort of Puckish pride in bringing her suitor to her feet.

Nobody is so exacting, so capricious, so uncertain, so fascinating as a buttercup, because no one is so perfectly free from love. The first touch of passion renders her more exacting and more charming than ever. She resents the suspicion of a tenderness whose very novelty scares her, and she visits her resentment on her worshipper. If he enjoys a kind farewell overnight, he atones for it by the coldest greeting in the morning. There are days when the buttercup runs amuck among her adorers, days of snubbing and sarcasm and bitterness. The poor little bird beats savagely against the wires that are closing her round. And then there are days of pure abandon and coquetry and fun. The buttercup flirts, but she flirts in such an open and ingenuous fashion that nobody is a bit the worse for it. She tells you the fun she had overnight with that charming young fellow from Oxford, and you know that to-morrow she will be telling that hated Guardsman what fun she has had with you. She is a little dazzled with the wealth and profusion of the new life that is bursting on her, and she wings her way from one charming flower to another with little thought of more than a sip from each. Then there is a return of pure girlhood, days in which the buttercup is simply the buttercup again. Flirtations are forgotten, conquests are abandoned, brothers are worshipped with the old worship; and we start back, and rub our eyes, and wonder whether life is all a delusion, and whether this pure creature of home and bread-and-butter is the volatile, provoking little puss who gave our hand such a significant squeeze yesterday.

But it is just this utterly illogical, unreasonable, inconsequential character that gives the pursuit of the buttercup its charm. There is a pleasure in this irregular warfare, with its razzias and dashes and repulses and successes and skirmishes and flights, which we cannot get out of the regular operations of the sap and the mine. We sympathize with the ingenious gentleman who declined to study astronomy on the ground of his dislike to the sun for the monotonous regularity of its daily rising and setting. There is something delightfully cometary about the affection of the buttercup. Any experienced strategist in the art of getting married will tell us the exact time within which her elder sister may be reduced, and sketch for us a plan of the campaign. But the buttercup lies outside of the rules of war. She gives one the pleasure of adoration in its purest and most ideal form, and she adds to this the pleasure of *rouge et noir*. One feels in the presence of a buttercup the possibility of combining enjoyments which are in no other sphere compatible with each other—the delight, say, of a musing over 'In Memoriam' with the fiercer joys of the gaming-table. And meanwhile the buttercup drifts on, recking little of us and of our thoughts, into a world mysterious and unknown to her. Tones of deeper colour flush the pure white light of her dawn, and announce the fuller day of womanhood.

And with the death of the dawn the buttercup passes insensibly away. The next season steals her from us; it is only the holidays that give her to us, and dispel half our conventionality, our shams, our conceit with the laugh of the buttercup.

ABBOT AND TOWN

ABBOT AND TOWN

THE genius of a great writer of our own days has made Abbot Sampson of St. Edmunds' the most familiar of mediæval names to the bulk of Englishmen. By a rare accident the figure of the silent, industrious Norfolk monk who at the close of Henry the Second's reign suddenly found himself ruler of the wealthiest, if not the greatest, of English abbeys starts out distinct from the dim canvas of the annals of his house. Annals indeed in any strict sense St. Edmunds has none; no national chronicle was ever penned in its *scriptorium* such as that which flings lustre round its rival, St. Albans; nor is even a record of its purely monastic life preserved such as that which gives a local and ecclesiastical interest to its rival of Glastonbury. One book alone the abbey has given us, but that one book is worth a thousand chronicles. In the wandering, gossipy pages of Jocelyn of Brakeland the life of the twelfth century, so far as it could penetrate abbey walls, still glows distinct for us round the figure of the shrewd, practical, kindly, imperious abbot who looks out, a little travestied perhaps, from the pages of Mr. Carlyle.

It is however to an incident in this abbot's life, somewhat later than most of the events told so vividly in 'Past and Present,' that I wish to direct my readers' attention. A good many eventful years had passed by since Sampson stood abbot-elect in the court of King Henry; it was from the German prison where Richard was lying captive that the old abbot was returning, sad at heart, to his stately house. His way lay through the little town that sloped quietly down to the abbey walls, along the narrow little street that led to the stately gate-tower, now grey with the waste of ages, but then fresh and white from the builder's hand. It may have been in the shadow of that gateway that a group of townsmen stood gathered to greet the return of their lord, but with other business on hand besides kindly greeting. There was a rustling of parchment as the alderman unfolded the town-charters, recited the brief grants of Abbots Anselm and Ording and Hugh, and begged from the Lord Abbot a new confirmation of the liberties of the town.

As Sampson paused a moment—he was a prudent, deliberate man in all his ways—he must have read in the faces of all the monks who gathered round him, in the murmured growl that monastic obedience just kept within bounds, very emphatic counsel of refusal. On the other hand there was the alderman pleading for the old privileges of the town—for security of justice in its own town-mote, for freedom of sale in its market, for just provisions to enforce the recovery of debts—the simple, efficient liberty that stood written in the parchment with the heavy seals—the seals of Anselm and Ording and Hugh. "Only the same words as your predecessor used, Lord Abbot, simply the same words"—and then came the silvery jingle of the sixty marks that the townsmen offered for their lord's assent. A moment more and the assent was won, "given pleasantly too," the monks commented bitterly, as "murmuring and grunting," to use their own emphatic phrase, they led Sampson to the chapter-house. But murmurings and gruntings broke idly against the old abbot's imperious will. "Let the brethren murmur," he flashed out when one of his friends told him there was discontent in the cloister at his dealings with the townsmen; "let them blame me, and say among themselves what they will. I am their father and abbot. So long as I live I will not give mine honour to another."

The words were impatient, wilful enough; but it was the impatience of a man who frets at the blindness of others to what is clear and evident to his own finer sense. The shrewd, experienced eye of the old Churchman read with a perfect sagacity the signs of the times. He had just stood face to face in his German prison with one who, mere reckless soldier as he seemed, had read them as clearly, as sagaciously as himself. When History drops her drums and trumpets and learns to tell the story of Englishmen, it will find the significance of Richard, not in his crusade or in his weary wars along the Norman border, but in his lavish recognition of municipal life. When, busy with the preparations for his Eastern journey, the King sold charter after charter to the burgesses of his towns, it seemed a mere outburst of royal greed, a mere carrying out of his own bitter scoff that he would have sold London itself could he have found a purchaser. But the hard cynical words of the Angevins were veils which they flung over political conceptions too large for the comprehension of their day. Richard was in fact only following out the policy which had been timidly pursued by his father, which was to find its fullest realization under John.

The silent growth and elevation of the English people was the real work of their reigns, and in this work the boroughs led the way. Unnoticed and despised, even by the historian of to-day, they had alone preserved the full tradition of Teutonic liberty. The right of self-government, the right of free speech in free parliament, the right of equal justice by one's peers,—it was these that the towns had brought safely across the ages of Norman rule, these that by the mouth of traders and shopkeepers asked recognition from the Angevin kings. No liberty was claimed in the Great Charter for the realm at large which had not in borough after borough been claimed and won beforehand by plain burgesses whom the "mailed barons" who wrested it from their king would have despised. That out of the heap of borough-charters which he flung back to these townsmen that Charter was to be born, Richard could not know; but that a statesman so keen and far-sighted as he really was could have been driven by mere greed of gold, or have been utterly blind to the real nature of the forces to which he gave legal recognition, is impossible. We have no such pithy hints of what was passing in his mind as we shall find Abbot Sampson dropping in the course of our story. But Richard can hardly have failed to note what these hints proved his mitred counsellor to have noted well—the silent revolution which was passing over the land, and which in a century and a half had raised serfs like those of St. Edmunds into freeholders of a town.

It is only in such lowly records as those which we are about to give that we can follow the progress of that revolution. But simple as the tale is there is hardly better historic training for a man than to set him frankly in the streets of a quiet little town like Bury St. Edmunds, and bid him work out the history of the men who lived and died there. In the quiet, quaintly-named streets, in the town-mead and the market-place, in the lord's mill beside the stream, in the ruffed and furred brasses of its burghers in the church, lies the real life of England and Englishmen, the life of their home and their trade, their ceaseless, sober struggle with oppression, their steady, unwearied battle for self-government. It is just in the pettiness of its details, in its commonplace incidents, in the want of marked features and striking events, that the real lesson of the whole story lies. For two centuries this little town of Bury St. Edmunds was winning liberty for itself, and yet we hardly note as we pass from one little step to another little step how surely that liberty was being won. It is hard indeed merely to catch a glimpse of the steps. The monks were too busy with royal endowments and papal grants of mitre and ring, too full of their struggles with arrogant bishops and encroaching barons, to tell us how the line of tiny hovels crept higher and higher from the abbey gate up the westerly sunlit slope. It is only by glimpses that we catch sight of the first steps towards civic life, of market and market-toll, of flax-growing and women with distaffs at their door, of fullers at work along the abbey-stream, of gate-keepers for the rude walls, of town-meetings summoned in old Teutonic fashion by blast of horn.

It is the Great Survey of the Conqueror that gives us our first clear peep at the town. Much that had been plough-land in the time of the Confessor was covered with houses under the Norman rule. No doubt the great abbey-church of stone that Abbot Baldwin was raising amidst all the storm of the Conquest drew its craftsmen and masons to mingle with the ploughers and reapers of the broad domain. The troubles of the time too did their part here as elsewhere; the serf, the fugitive from justice or his lord, the trader, the Jew, would naturally seek shelter under the strong hand of St. Edmund. On the whole the great house looked kindly on a settlement which raised the value of its land and brought fresh pence to the cellarer. Not a settler that held his acre for a year and a day but paid his pence to the treasury and owned the abbot for his lord. Not a serf but was bound to plough a rood of the abbot's land, to reap in the abbot's harvest field, to fold his sheep in the abbey folds, to help bring the annual catch of eels from the abbey-waters. Within the four crosses that bounded the abbot's domain, land and water were his; the cattle of the townsmen paid for their pasture on the common; if the fullers refused the loan of their cloth, the cellarer would withhold the use of the stream, and seize their looms wherever he found them. Landlord's rights passed easily as ever into landlord's wrongs. No toll, for instance, might be levied on a purchaser of produce from the abbey farms, and the house drove better bargains than its country rivals. First-purchase was a privilege even more vexatious, and we can catch the low growl of the customers as they waited with folded hands before shop and stall till the buyers of the Lord Abbot had had their pick of the market. But there was little chance of redress, for if they growled in the town-mote there were the abbot's officers before whom the meeting must be held; and if they growled to their alderman, he was the abbot's nominee and received the symbol of office, the mot-horn, the town-horn, at his hands.

By what process these serfs of a rural hamlet had grown into the busy burgesses whom we saw rustling their parchments and chinking their silver marks in the ears of Abbot Sampson in Richard's time, it is hard to say. Like all the greater revolutions of society, this advance was a silent one. The more galling and oppressive instances of serfdom seem to have slipped unconsciously away. Some, like the eel-fishery, were commuted for an easy rent; others, like the slavery of the fullers and the toll of flax, simply disappeared. No one could tell when the retainers of the abbey came to lose their exemption from local taxation and to pay the town-penny to the alderman like the rest of the burgesses. "In some way, I don't know how,"—as Jocelyn grumbles about just such an unnoted change,—by usage, by omission, by downright forgetfulness, here by a little struggle, there by a little present to a needy abbot, the town won freedom. But progress was not always unconscious, and one incident in the history of Bury St. Edmunds, remarkable if only regarded as marking the advance of law, is yet more remarkable as indicating the part which a new moral sense of human right to equal justice was to play in the general advance of the realm.

The borough, as we have seen, had preserved the

old English right of meeting in full assembly of the townsmen for government and law. In the presence of the burgesses justice was administered in the old English fashion, and the accused acquitted or condemned by the oath of his neighbours, the "compurgators," out of whom our jury was to grow. Rough and inadequate as such a process seems to us, it insured substantial justice; the meanest burgher had his trial by his peers as thoroughly as the belted earl. Without the borough bounds however the system of the Norman judicature prevailed. The rural tenants who did suit and service at the cellarer's court were subject to the "judicial duel" which the Conqueror had introduced. In the twelfth century however the strong tendency to national unity told heavily against judicial inequality, and the barbarous injustice of the foreign system became too apparent even for the baronage or the Church to uphold it. "Kebel's case," as a lawyer would term it, brought the matter to an issue at Bury St. Edmunds. In the opinion of his neighbours Kebel seems to have been guiltless of the robbery with which he had been charged; but he was "of the cellarer's fee," and subject to the feudal jurisdiction of his court. The duel went against him and he was hanged just without the gates. The taunts of the townsmen woke the farmers to a sense of their wrong. "Had Kebel been a dweller within the borough," said the burgesses, "he would have got his acquittal from the oaths of his neighbours, as our liberty is." The scandal at last moved the convent itself to action. The monks were divided in opinion, but the saner part determined that their tenants "should enjoy equal liberty" with the townsmen. The cellarer's court was abolished; the franchise of the town was extended to the rural possessions of the abbey; the farmers "came to the toll-house, and were written in the alderman's roll, and paid the town-penny."

A moral revolution like this is notable at any time, but a change wrought avowedly "that all might enjoy equal liberty" is especially notable in the twelfth century. Cases like Kebel's were everywhere sounding the knell of feudal privilege and of national division, long before freedom fronted John by the sedges of Runnymede. Slowly and fitfully through the reign of his father the new England which had grown out of conquered and conquerors woke to self-consciousness. It was this awakening that Abbot Sampson saw and noted with his clear, shrewd eyes. To him, we can hardly doubt, the revolt of the town-wives, for instance, was more than a mere scream of angry women. The "rep-silver," the commutation for that old service of reaping in the abbot's fields, had ceased to be exacted from the richer burgesses. At last the poorer sort refused to pay. Then the cellarer's men came seizing gate and stool by way of distress till the women turning out, distaff in hand, put them ignominiously to flight. Sampson had his own thoughts about the matter, saw perhaps that the days of inequality were over, that in the England that was coming there would be one law for rich and poor. At any rate he quietly compromised the question for twenty shillings a year.

The convent was indignant. "Abbot Ording, who lies there," muttered an angry monk, as he pointed to the tomb in the choir, "would not have done this for five hundred marks of silver." That their abbot should capitulate to a mob of infuriated town-wives was too much for the patience of the brotherhood. All at once they opened their eyes to the facts which had been going on unobserved for so many long years. There was their own town growing, burgesses encroaching on the market space, settlers squatting on their own acre with no leave asked, aldermen who were once only the abbey servants taking on themselves to give permission for this and that, tradesmen thriving and markets increasing, and the abbey never one penny the richer for it all. It was quite time that Abbot Sampson should be roused to do his duty, and to do it in very sharp fashion indeed. However we will let one of the monks tell his own tale in his own gossiping way:—

"In the tenth year of Abbot Sampson's abbacy we monks, after full deliberation in chapter, laid our formal plaint before the abbot in his court. We said that the rents and revenues of all the good towns and boroughs in England were steadily growing and increasing to the enrichment of their lords, in every case save in that of our town of St. Edmund. The customary rent of £40 which it pays never rises higher. That this is so we imputed solely to the conduct of the townspeople, who are continually building new shops and stalls in the market-place without any leave of the convent" (abbey-land though it was). "The only permission, in fact, which they ask is that of their alderman, an officer who himself was of old times a mere servant of our sacrist, and bound to pay into his hands the yearly rent of the town, and removable at his pleasure."

Never, Jocelyn evidently thinks, was a case plainer; but into the justice or injustice of it the burgesses refused sturdily to enter. When they were summoned to make answer they pleaded simple possession. "They were in the King's justice, and no answer would they make concerning tenements which they and their fathers had held in peace for a year and a day." Such answer would in fact, they added, be utterly contrary to the freedom of the town. No plea could have been legally more complete, as none could have been more provoking. The monks turned in a rage upon the abbot, and simply requested him to eject their opponents. Then they retired angrily into the chapter-house, and waited in a sort of white heat to hear what the abbot would do. This is what Sampson did. He quietly bade the townsmen wait; then he "came into chapter just like one of ourselves, and told us privily that he would right us as far as he could, but that if he were to act it must be by law. Be the case right or wrong, he did not dare eject without trial his free men from land and property which they had held year after year; in fact, if he did so, he would at once fall into the King's justice. At this moment in came the townsfolk into the chapter-house, and offered to compromise the matter for an annual quit rent of a hundred shillings. This offer we refused. We preferred a simple adjournment of our claim in the hope that in some other abbot's time we might get all back again."

Notwithstanding his many very admirable qualities, in fact, this present abbot was on these municipal points simply incorrigible. Was it quite by an oversight, for instance, that in Sampson's old age, "in some way, I don't quite know how, the new alderman of the town got chosen in other places than in chapter, and without leave of the house,"—in simple town-motes, that is, and by sheer downright delegation of power on the part of his fellow-burgesses? At any rate it was by no oversight that Sampson granted his charter on the day he came back from Richard's prison, when "we monks were murmuring and grumbling" in his very ear! And yet was the abbot foolish in his generation? This charter of his ranks lineally among the ancestors of that Great Charter which his successor was first to unroll on the altar-steps of the choir (we can still measure off the site in the rough field by the great piers of the tower arch that remain) before the baronage of the realm. At any rate, half a century after that scene in chapter, the new England that Sampson had foreseen came surging stormily enough against the abbey gates. Later abbots had set themselves sturdily against his policy of concession and conciliation; and riots, lawsuits, royal commissions, mark the troubled relations of Town and Abbey under the first two Edwards. Under the third came the fierce conflict of 1327.

On the 25th of January in that year the townsmen of Bury St. Edmunds, headed by Richard Drayton, burst into the Abbey. Its servants were beaten off, the monks driven into choir, and dragged thence with their prior (for the abbot was away in London) to the town prison. The abbey itself was sacked; chalices, missals, chasubles, tunicles, altar frontals, the books of the library, the very vats and dishes of the kitchen, all disappeared. Chattels valued at £10,000, £500 worth of coin, 3000 "florins,"—this was the abbey's estimate of its loss. But neither florins nor chasubles were what their assailants really aimed at. Their next step shows what were the grievances which had driven the burgesses to this fierce outbreak of revolt. They were as much personal as municipal. The gates of the town indeed were still in the abbot's hands. He had succeeded in enforcing his claim to the wardship of orphans born within his domain. From claims such as these the town could never feel itself safe so long as mysterious charters from Pope and King, interpreted yet more mysteriously by the wit of the new lawyer class, were stored in the abbey archives. But the archives contained other and yet more formidable documents. The religious houses, untroubled by the waste of war, had profited more than any landowners by the general increase of wealth. They had become great proprietors, money-lenders to their tenants, extortionate as the Jew whom they had banished from the land. There were few townsmen of St. Edmund who had not some bond laid up in the abbey registry. Nicholas Fowke and a band of debtors had a covenant lying there for the payment of 500 marks and fifty casks of wine. Philip Clopton's mark bound him to discharge a debt of £22; a whole company of the wealthier burgesses were joint debtors in a bond for no less a sum than £10,000. The new spirit of commercial enterprise, joined with the troubles of the time, seems to have thrown the whole community into the abbot's hands.

It was from the troubles of the time that the burghers looked for escape; and the general disturbance which accompanied the deposition of Edward II. seems to have quickened their longing into action. Their revolt soon disclosed its practical aims. From their prison in the town the trembling prior and his monks were brought back to their own chapter-house.

The spoil of their registry—the papal bulls and the royal charters, the deeds and bonds and mortgages of the townsmen—were laid before them. Amidst the wild threats of the mob, they were forced to execute a grant of perfect freedom and of a guild to the town, and a full release to their debtors. Then they were left masters of the ruined house. But all control over the town was gone. Through spring and summer no rent or fine was paid. The bailiffs and other officers of the abbey did not dare to show their faces in the streets. Then news came that the abbot was in London, appealing for aid to King and Court, and the whole county was at once on fire. A crowd of rustics, maddened at the thought of revived claims of serfage, of interminable suits of law which had become a tyranny, poured into the streets of the town. From thirty-two of the neighbouring villages the priests marched at the head of their flocks to this new crusade. Twenty thousand in number, so men guessed, the wild mass of men, women, and children rushed again on the abbey. For four November days the work of destruction went on unhindered, whilst gate, stables, granaries, kitchen, infirmary, hostelry, went up in flames. From the wreck of the abbey itself the great multitude swept away too the granges and barns of the abbey farms. The monks had become vast agricultural proprietors: 1000 horses, 120 oxen, 200 cows, 300 bullocks, 300 hogs, 10,000 sheep were driven off for spoil, and as a last outrage, the granges and barns were burnt to the ground.

£60,000, the justiciaries afterwards decided, would hardly cover the loss.

Weak as was the government of Mortimer and Isabella, there never was a time in English history when government stood with folded hands before a scene such as this. The appeal of the abbot was no longer neglected; a royal force quelled the riot and exacted vengeance for this breach of the King's peace. Thirty carts full of prisoners were despatched to Norwich; twenty-four of the chief townsmen, thirty-two of the village priests, were convicted as aiders and abettors. Twenty were at once summarily hanged. But with this first vigorous effort at repression the danger seemed again to roll away. Nearly 200 persons remained indeed under sentence of outlawry, and for five weary years their case dragged on in the King's courts. At last matters ended in a lawless, ludicrous outrage. Out of patience and irritated by repeated breaches of promise on the abbot's part, the outlawed burgesses seized him as he lay in his manor of Chevington, robbed, bound, and shaved him, and carried him off to London. There he was hurried from street to street, lest his hiding-place should be detected, till opportunity offered for his shipping off to Brabant. The Archbishop of Canterbury, the Pope himself, levelled their excommunications against the perpetrators of this daring outrage in vain.

The prison of their victim was at last discovered;

he was released and brought home. But the lesson seems to have done good. The year 1332 saw a concordat arranged between the Abbey and Town. The damages assessed by the royal justiciaries, a sum enormous now but incredible then, were remitted, the outlawry was reversed, the prisoners were released. On the other hand, the deeds were again replaced in the archives of the abbey, and the charters which had been extorted from the trembling monks were formally cancelled. In other words, the old process of legal oppression was left to go on. The spirit of the townsmen was, as we shall see, crushed by the failure of their outbreak of despair. It was from a new quarter that help was for a moment to come. No subject is more difficult to treat, as nothing is more difficult to explain, than the communal revolt which shook the throne of Richard II., and the grievances which prompted it. But one thing is clear; it was a revolt against oppression which veiled itself under the form of law. The rural tenants found themselves in a mesh of legal claims—old services revived, old dues enforced, endless suits in the King's courts grinding them again to serfage. Oppression was no longer the rough blow of the rough baron; it was the delicate, ruthless tyranny of the lawyer-clerk.

Prior John of Cambridge, who, in the vacancy of the abbot, was now in charge of the house, was a man skilled in all the arts of his day. In sweetness of voice, in knowledge of sacred song, his eulogists pronounced him the superior of Orpheus, of Nero, of one yet more illustrious but, save in the Bury cloisters, more obscure, the Breton Belgabred. He was a man "industrious and subtle ; " and subtlety and industry found their scope in suit after suit with the farmers and burgesses around. " Faithfully he strove," says his monastic eulogist, "with the villeins of Bury for the rights of his house." The townsmen he owned as his foes, his "adversaries ; " but it was the rustics who were especially to show how memorable a hate he had won. It was a perilous time in which to win men's hate. We have seen the private suffering of the day, but nationally too, England was racked with despair and the sense of wrong; with the collapse of the French war, with the ruinous taxation, with the frightful pestilence that had swept away half the population ; with the iniquitous labour-laws that, in the face of such a reduction, kept down the rate of wages in the interest of the landlords; with the frightful law of settlement that, to enforce this wrong, reduced at a stroke the free labourer again to a serfage from which he has yet fully to emerge. That terrible revolution of social sentiment had begun which was to turn law into the instrument of the basest interests of a class, which was with the Statute of Labourers and the successive labour-regulations that followed to create pauperism, and with pauperism to create that hatred of class to class which hangs like a sick dream over us to-day.

The earliest, the most awful instance of such a hatred was gathering round Prior John, while at his manor-house of Mildenhall he studied his parchments and touched a defter lute than Nero or the Breton Belgabred. In a single hour hosts of armed men arose, as it were, out of the earth. Kent gathered round Wat Tyler; in Norfolk, in Essex, fifty thousand peasants hoisted the standard of Jack Straw. It was no longer a local rising or a local grievance, no longer the old English revolution headed by the baron and priest. Priest and baron were swept away before this sudden storm of national hate. The howl of the great multitude broke roughly in on the delicate chanting of Prior John. He turned to fly, but his own serfs betrayed him, judged him in rude mockery of the law that had wronged them, condemned him, killed him.[1] Five days the corpse lay half-stripped in the open field, none daring to bury it—so ran the sentence of his murderers—while the mob poured unresisted into Bury. The scene was liker some wild orgy of the French Revolution than any after-scenes in England. Bearing the prior's head on a lance before them through the streets, the frenzied throng reached at last the gallows where the head of Cavendish, the chief justice, stood already impaled,

[1] To one who knows what frightful cruelty and oppression may lie in simple legal phrases, the indignant sentence in which Walsingham tells his death is the truest comment on the scene: "Non tam villanorum prædictæ villæ de Bury, suorum adversariorum, sed propriorum servorum et nativorum arbitrio simul et judicio addictus morti."

and pressing the cold lips together, in fierce mockery of the old friendship between the two, set them side by side.

Another head soon joined them. The abbey gates had been burst open, the cloister was full of the dense maddened crowd, howling for a new victim, John Lackenheath. Warden of the barony as he was, few knew him as he stood among the group of trembling monks; there was still amidst this outburst of frenzy the dread of a coming revenge, and the rustic who had denounced him had stolen back silent into the crowd. But if Lackenheath resembled the French nobles in the hatred he had roused, he resembled them also in the cool contemptuous courage with which they fronted death. "I am the man you seek," he said, stepping forward; and in a moment, with a mighty roar of "Devil's son! monk! traitor!" he was swept to the gallows and his head hacked from his shoulders. Then the crowd rolled back again to the abbey-gate and summoned the monks before them. They told them that now for a long time they had oppressed their fellows, the burgesses of Bury; wherefore they willed that in the sight of the Commons they should forthwith surrender their bonds and their charters. The monks brought the parchments to the market-place; many which might have served the purposes of the townsmen they swore they could not find. The Commons disbelieved them, and bade the burgesses inspect the documents.

But the iron had entered too deeply into these men's souls. Not even in their hour of triumph could they shake off their awe of the trembling black-robed masters who stood before them. A compromise was patched up. The charters should be surrendered till the popular claimant of the abbacy should confirm them. Then, unable to do more, the great crowd ebbed away.

Common history tells the upshot of the revolt; the despair when in the presence of the boy-king Wat Tyler was struck down by a foul treason; the ruin when the young martial Bishop of Norwich came trampling in upon the panic-stricken multitude at Barton. Nationally the movement had wrought good; from this time the law was modified in practice, and the tendency to reduce a whole class to serfage was effectually checked. But to Bury it brought little but harm. A hundred years later the town again sought freedom in the law-courts, and again sought it in vain. The abbey charters told fatally against mere oral customs. The royal council of Edward IV. decided that "the abbot is lord of the whole town of Bury, the sole head and captain within the town." All municipal appointments were at his pleasure, all justice in his hands. The townsmen had no communal union, no corporate existence. Their leaders paid for riot and insult by imprisonment and fine.

The dim, dull lawsuit was almost the last incident

in the long struggle, the last and darkest for the town. But it was the darkness that goes before the day. Fifty years more and abbot and abbey were swept away together, and the burghers were building their houses afresh with the carved ashlar and the stately pillars of their lord's house. Whatever other aspects the Reformation may present, it gave at any rate emancipation to the one class of English to whom freedom had been denied, the towns that lay in the dead hand of the Church. None more heartily echoed the Protector's jest, "We must pull down the rooks' nests lest the rooks may come back again," than the burghers of St. Edmunds. The completeness of the Bury demolitions hangs perhaps on the long serfdom of the town, and the shapeless masses of rubble that alone recall the graceful cloister and the long-drawn aisle may find their explanation in the story of the town's struggles. But the story has a pleasanter ending. The charter of James—for the town had passed into the King's hands as the abbot's successor—gave all that it had ever contended for, and crowned the gift by the creation of a mayor. Modern reform has long since swept away the municipal oligarchy which owed its origin to the Stuart king. But the essence of his work remains; and in its mayor, with his fourfold glory of maces borne before him, Bury sees the strange close of the battle waged through so many centuries for simple self-government.

HOTELS IN THE CLOUDS

HOTELS IN THE CLOUDS

WHEN the snow has driven everybody home again from the Oberland and the Rigi and all the Swiss hotelkeepers have resumed their original dignity as Landammans of their various cantons, it is a little amusing to reflect how much of the pleasure of one's holiday has been due to one's own countrymen. It is not that the Englishman abroad is particularly entertaining, for the Frenchman is infinitely more vivacious; nor that he is peculiarly stolid, for he yields in that to most of the German students who journey on the faith of a nightcap and a pipe ; or that he is especially boring, for every American whom one meets whips him easily in boredom. It is that he is so nakedly and undisguisedly English. We never see Englishmen in England. They are too busy, too afraid of Mrs. Grundy, too oppressed with duties and responsibilities and insular respectabilities and home decencies to be really themselves. They are forced to dress decently, to restrain their temper, to affect a little modesty ; there is the pulpit to scold them, and the 'Times' to give them something to talk about, and an infinite number of grooves and lines and sidings along which they can be driven in a slow and decent fashion, or into which as a last resort they can be respectably shunted. But grooves and lines end with the British Channel. The true Englishman has no awe for 'Galignani'; he has a slight contempt for the Continental chaplain. He can wear what hat he likes, show what temper he likes, and be himself. It is he whose boots tramp along the Boulevards, whose snore thunders loudest of all in the night train, who begins his endless growl after "a decent dinner" at Basle, and his endless contempt for "Swiss stupidity" at Lucerne. We track him from hotel to hotel, we meet him at station after station, we revel in the chase as coat after coat of the outer man peels away and the inner Englishman stands more plainly revealed. But it is in the hotels of the higher mountains that we first catch the man himself.

There is a sort of snow-line of nations, and nothing amazes one more in a run through the Alps than to see how true the various peoples among their visitors are to their own specific level. As a rule the Frenchman clings to the road through the passes, the American pauses at the end of the mule-track, the German stops at the chalet in the pine-forest. It is only at the Alpine *table d'hôte*, with a proud consciousness of being seven thousand feet above the sea-level, that one gets the Englishman pure. It is a very odd sensation, in face of the huge mountain-chains, and with the glacier only an hour's walk overhead, to find one's self again in a little England, with the very hotelkeeper greeting one in one's native tongue, and the guides exchanging English oaths over their trinkgelt. Cooped up within four walls one gets a better notion of the varieties, the lights and shadows, of home-life than one gets in Pall Mall. The steady old Indian couple whose climb is so infinitely slow and sure, the Oxford freshman who comes blooming up the hill-side to declare Titiens beautiful and to gush over the essays of Frederick Robertson, the steady man of business who does his Alps every summer, the jaded London curate who lingers with a look of misery round the stove, the British mother, silken, severe, implacable as below, the British maiden sitting alone in the rock-clefts and reviewing the losses and gains of the last season—all these are thrown together in an odd jumble of rank and taste by the rain, fog, and snowdrift which form some two-thirds of the pleasures of the Alps. But, odd as the jumble is, it illustrates in a way that nothing else does some of the characteristics of the British nation, and impresses on one in a way that one never forgets the real native peculiarities of Englishmen.

In the first place, no scene so perfectly brings out the absolute vacuity of the British mind when one can get it free from the replenishing influences of the daily paper. Alpine talk is the lowest variety of conversation, as the common run of Alpine writing is the lowest form of literature. It is in fact simply drawing-room talk as drawing-room talk would be if all news, all scandal, all family details were suddenly cut off. In its way it throws a pleasant light on English education and on the amount of information about other countries which it is considered essential to an English gentleman to possess. The guardsman swears that the Swiss are an uneducated nation, with a charming unconsciousness that their school system is without a rival in Europe; the young lady to one's right wonders why such nice people should be republicans; the Cambridge man across the table exposes the eccentricity of a friend who wished to know in what canton he was travelling; the squire with the pink and white daughters is amazed at the absence of police. In the very heart of the noblest home of liberty which Europe has seen our astonishing nation lives and moves with as contented and self-satisfied an ignorance of the laws, the history, the character of the country or its people, as if Switzerland were Timbuctoo. Still, even sublime ignorance such as this is better than to listen to the young thing of thirty-five summers, with her drivel about William Tell; and one has always the resource of conceiving a Swiss party tramping about England with no other notion of Englishmen than that they are extortionate hotelkeepers, or of the English Constitution than that it is democratic and absurd, or of English history than that Queen Eleanor sucked the poison from her husband's arm.

The real foe of life over an Alpine table is that

weather-talk, raised to its highest power, which forms nine-tenths of the conversation. The beautiful weather one had on the Rigi, the execrable weather one had at the Furca, the unsettled weather one had on the Lake of Thun; the endless questions whether you have been here and whether you have been there; the long catechism as to the insect-life and the tariff of the various hotels; the statements as to the route by which they have come, the equally gratuitous information as to the route by which they shall go; the "oh, so beautiful" of the gusher in ringlets, the lawyer's "decidedly sublime," the monotonous "grand, grand" of the man of business; the constant asseveration of all as to every prospect which they have visited that they never have seen such a beautiful view in their life—form a cataract of boredom which pours down from morn to dewy eve. It is in vain that one makes desperate efforts to procure relief, that the inventive mind entraps the spinster into discussion over ferns, tries the graduate on poetry, beguiles the squire towards politics, lures the Indian officer into a dissertation on coolies, leads the British mother through flowery paths of piety towards the new vacancies in the episcopal bench. The British mother remembers a bishop whom she met at Lucerne, the Indian officer gets back by the Ghauts to the Schreckhorn, the graduate finds his way again through 'Manfred' to the precipices. In an instant the drone recommences, the cataract pours down again, and there is nothing for it but to wander out on the terrace of six feet by four, and wonder what the view would be if there were no fog.

But even a life like this must have its poetry and its hero, and at seven thousand feet above the sea-level it is very natural to find one's poetry in what would be dull enough below. The hero of the Bell Alp or the Œggischorn is naturally enough the Alpine Clubbist. He has hurried silent and solitary through the lower country, he only blooms into real life at the sight of "high work." It is wonderful how lively the little place becomes as he enters it, what a run there is on the landlord for information as to his projects, what endless consultations of the barometer, what pottering over the pages of 'Peaks, Passes, and Glaciers.' How many guides will he take, has he a dog, will he use the rope, what places has he done before?—a thousand questions of this sort are buzzing about the room as the hero sits quietly down to his dinner. The elderly spinster remembers the fatal accident of last season, and ventures to ask him what preparations he has made for the ascent. The hero stops his dinner politely, and shows her the new little box of lip-salve with which he intends to defy the terrors of the Alps. To say the truth, the Alpine climber is not an imaginative man. With him the climb which fills every bystander with awe is "a good bit of work, but nothing out of the way you know." He has never done this particular peak, and so he has to do it; but it has been too often done before to fill him with any particular interest in the matter. As to the ascent itself, he sets about planning it as practically as if he were planning a run from London to Lucerne. We see him sitting with his guides, marking down the time-table of his route, ascertaining the amount of meat and wine which will be required, distributing among his followers their fair weights of blankets and ropes. Then he tells us the hour at which he shall be back to-morrow, and the file of porters set off with him quietly and steadily up the hill-side. We turn out and give him a cheer as he follows, but the thought of the provisions takes a little of the edge off our romance. Still, there is a great run that evening on 'Peaks, Passes, and Glaciers,' and a constant little buzz round the fortunate person who has found the one record of an ascent of this particular peak.

What is it which makes men in Alpine travel-books write as men never write elsewhere? What is the origin of a style unique in literature, which misses both the sublime and the ridiculous, and constantly hops from tall-talk to a mirth feeble and inane? Why is it that the senior tutor, who is so hard on a bit of bad Latin, plunges at the sight of an Alp into English inconceivable, hideous? Why does page after page look as if it had been dredged with French words through a pepper-castor? Why is the sunrise or the scenery always "indescribable," while the appetite of the guides lends itself to such reiterated description?

These are questions which suggest themselves to quiet critics, but hardly to the group in the hotel. They have found the hole where the hero is to snatch a few hours of sleep before commencing the ascent. They have followed him in imagination round the edge of the crevasses. All the old awe and terror that disappeared in his presence revive at the eloquent description of the *arête*. There is a gloom over us as we retire to bed and think of the little company huddled in their blankets, waiting for the dawn. There is a gloom over us at breakfast as the spinster recalls one "dreadful place where you look down five thousand feet clear." The whole party breaks up into little groups, who set out for high points from which the first view of the returning hero will be caught. Everybody comes back certain they have seen him, till the landlord pronounces that everybody has mistaken the direction in which he must come. At last there is a distant *jodel*, and in an hour or so the hero arrives. He is impassive and good-humoured as before. When we crowd around him for the tidings of peril and adventure, he tells us, as he told us before he started, that it is "a good bit of work, but nothing out of the way." Pressed by the spinster, he replies, in the very words of 'Peaks and Passes,' that the sunrise was "indescribable," and then, like the same inspired volume, enlarges freely on the appetite of his guides. Then he dines, and then he tells us that what he has really gained from his climb is entire faith in the efficacy of his little box for preventing all injury from sun or from snow. He is a little proud, too, to have done the peak in twenty minutes less time than Jones, and at ten shillings less cost. Altogether, it must be confessed, the Alpine Clubbist is not an imaginative man. His one grief in life seems to be the failure of his new portable cooking apparatus, and he pronounces "Liebig's Extract" to be the great discovery of the age. But such as he is, solid, practical, slightly stupid, he is the hero of the Alpine hotel.

At such an elevation the religious development of the British mind becomes strangely jerky and irregular. The arrival of Sunday is suddenly revealed to the group round the breakfast-table by the severity with which the spinster's eye is fixed on an announcement over the stove that the English service in the hotel is at ten o'clock. But the announcement is purely speculative. The landlord "hopes" there will be service, and plunges again into the kitchen. Profane sounds of fiddling and dancing reach the ear from an outbuilding where the guides and the maids are celebrating the day by a dance. The spinster is in earnest, but the insuperable difficulty lies in the non-existence of a parson. The Indian civilian suggests that we should adopt the naval usage, and that the senior layman read prayers. But the attorney is the senior layman, and he objects to such a muddling of the professions. The young Oxford undergraduate tells his little tale of a service on board ship where the major, unversed in such matters, began with the churching service, and ended with the office for the burial of the dead. Then he withers beneath the stony stare of the British mother, who is reading her "lessons" in the corner. At last there is a little buzz of excitement, and every eye is fixed upon the quiet-looking traveller in a brown shooting-coat and a purple tie, who is chipping his egg and imbibing his coffee in silence and unconsciousness. The spinster is sure that the stranger is Mr. Smith. The attorney doubts whether such a remarkable preacher would go about in such a costume. The British mother solves the whole difficulty by walking straight up to him, and with an eye on the announcement in question, asking point-blank whether she has the pleasure of addressing that eminent divine. Smith hesitates, and is lost. His egg and coffee disappear. The table is cleared, and the chairs arranged with as little regard to comfort as may be. The divine retires for the sermon which—prescient of his doom—he has slipped into his valise. The landlord produces two hymn-books of perfectly different origins, and some time is spent in finding a hymn which is common to both. When the time comes for singing it, the landlord joins in with a fine but wandering bass, catching an English word here and there as he goes along. The sermon is as usual on the Prodigal Son, and the Indian civilian nods at every mention of "going into a far country," as a topic specially appropriate for the occasion. But the divine is seen no more. His cold becomes rapidly serious, and he takes to his bed at the very hour of afternoon service. The British maiden wanders out to read Tennyson in the rock-clefts, and is wonder-struck to come upon the unhappy sufferer reading Tennyson in the rock-clefts too. After all, bed is not good for a cold, and the British Sunday is insufferable, and poetry is the expression of the deepest and most sacred emotions. This is the development which religion takes with a British maiden and a British parson in regions above the clouds.

ÆNEAS: A VERGILIAN STUDY

ÆNEAS: A VERGILIAN STUDY

In the revival side by side of Homeric and Vergilian study it is easy to see the reflection of two currents of contrasted sentiment which are telling on the world around us. A cry for simpler living and simpler thinking, a revolt against the social and intellectual perplexities in which modern life loses its direct and intensest joys, a craving for a world untroubled by the problems that weigh on us, express themselves as vividly in poems like the "Earthly Paradise" as in the return to the Iliad. The charm of Vergil on the other hand lies in the strange fidelity with which across so many ages he echoes those complex thoughts which make the life of our own. Vergil is the Tennyson of the older world; his power, like that of the Laureate, lies in the sympathy with which he reflects the strength and weakness of his time, its humanity, its new sense of human brotherhood, its pitifulness, its moral earnestness, its high conception of the purpose of life and the dignity of man, its attitude of curious but condescending interest towards the past, its vast dreams of a future, embodied by the one poet in the vague dreamland of

'Locksley Hall,' by the other in the enduring greatness of Rome.

From beginning to end the Æneid is a song of Rome. Throughout it we feel ourselves drawing nearer and nearer to that sense of the Roman greatness which filled the soul of Vergil; with him in verse after verse "tendimus in Latium." Nowhere does the song rise to a higher grandeur than when the singer sings the majesty of that all-embracing empire, the wide peace of the world beneath its sway. But the Æneid is no mere outburst of Roman pride. To Vergil the time in which he lived was at once an end and a beginning, a close of the long struggles which had fitted Rome to be the mistress of the world, an opening of her new and mightier career as a reconciler and leader of the nations. His song is broken by divine prophecies, not merely of Roman greatness, but of the work Rome had to do in warring down the rebels against her universal sway, in showing clemency to the conquered, in binding hostile peoples together, in welding the nations into a new human race. The Æneid is a song of the future rather than of the present or past, a song not of pride but of duty. The work that Rome has done points throughout to the nobler work which Rome has yet to do. And in the very forefront of this dream of the future Vergil sets the ideal of the new Roman by whom this mighty task shall be wrought, the picture of one who by loyalty to a higher purpose had fitted himself to demand loyalty from those whom he ruled, one who by self-mastery had learned to be master of men.

It is this thought of self-mastery which is the key to the Æneid. Filled as he is with a sense of the greatness of Rome, the mood of Vergil seems constantly to be fluctuating between a pathetic consciousness of the toils and self-devotion, the suffering and woe, that run through his national history and the final greatness which they bought. His poem draws both these impressions together in the figure of Æneas. Æneas is the representative of that "piety," that faith in his race and in his destiny, which had drawn the Roman from his little settlement on the hills beside Tiber to a vast empire "beyond the Garamantians and the Indians." All the endurance, the suffering, the patriotism, the self-devotion of generation after generation is incarnate in him. It is by his mouth that in the darkest hours of national trial Roman seems to say to Roman, "O passi graviora, dabit Deus his quoque finem." It is to this "end" that the wanderings of Æneas, like the labours of consul and dictator, inevitably tend, and it is the firm faith in such a close that gives its peculiar character to the pathos of the Æneid.

Rome is before us throughout, "per tot discrimina rerum tendimus in Latium." It is not as a mere tale of romance that we follow the wanderings of "the man who first came from Trojan shores to Italy." They are the sacrifice by which the father of the Roman race wrought out the greatness of his people, the toils he endured "dum conderet urbem." "Italiam quæro patriam" is the key-note of the Æneid, but the Quest of Æneas is no self-sought quest of his own. "Italiam non sponte sequor," he pleads as Dido turns from him in the Elysian Fields with eyes of speechless reproach. He is the chosen instrument of a Divine purpose working out its ends alike across his own buffetings from shore to shore or the love-tortures of the Phœnician Queen. The memorable words that Æneas addresses to Dares, "Cede Deo," "bend before a will higher as well as stronger than thine own," are in fact the faith of his own career.

But it is in this very submission to the Divine order that he himself soars into greatness. The figure of the warrior who is so insignificant in the Homeric story of the fight around Troy becomes that of a hero in the horror of its capture. Æneas comes before us the survivor of an immense fall, sad with the sadness of lost home and slaughtered friends, not even suffered to fall amidst the wreck, but driven forth by voices of the Fates to new toils and a distant glory. He may not die; his "moriamur" is answered by the reiterated "Depart" of the gods, the "Heu, fuge!" of the shade of Hector. The vision of the great circle of the gods fighting against Troy drives him forth in despair to a life of exile, and the carelessness of despair is over him as he drifts from land to land. "Sail where you will," he cries to his pilot; "one land is as good as another now Troy is gone." More and more indeed as he wanders he recognizes himself as the agent of a Divine purpose, but all personal joy in life has fled. Like Dante he feels the bitterness of exile, how hard it is to climb another's stairs, how bitter to eat is another's bread. Here and there he meets waifs and strays of the great wreck, fugitives like himself, but who have found a refuge and a new Troy on foreign shores. He greets them, but he may not stay. At last the very gods themselves seem to give him the passionate love of Dido, but again the fatal "Depart" tears him from her arms. The chivalrous love of Pallas casts for a moment its light and glory round his life, but the light and glory sink into gloom again beneath the spear of Turnus. Æneas is left alone with his destiny to the very end, but it is a destiny that has grown into a passion that absorbs the very life of the man.

"Italiam magnam Grynæus Apollo,
Italiam Lyciæ jussere capessere sortes.
Hic amor, hæc patria est!"

It is in the hero of the Idylls and not in the hero of the Iliad that we find the key to such a character as this. So far is Vergil from being the mere imitator of Homer, that in spite of his close and loving study of the older poem its temper seems to have roused him only to poetic protest. He recoils from the vast personality of Achilleus, from that incarnate "wrath," heedless of divine purposes, measuring itself boldly with the gods, careless as a god of the fate and fortunes of men. In the face of this destroyer the Roman poet sets a founder of cities and peoples, self-forgetful, patient, loyal to a divine aim, calm with a Roman calmness, yet touched as no Roman had hitherto been touched with pity and tenderness for the sorrows of men. The one poem is a song of passion, a mighty triumph of the individual man, a poem of human energy in defiant isolation. The other is an epic of social order, of a divine law manifesting itself in the fortunes of the world, of the bonds which link man to his fellow-men, a song of duty, of self-sacrifice, of reverence, of "piety."

It is in realizing the temper of the poem that we realize the temper of its hero. Æneas is the Arthur of the Vergilian epic, with the same absorption of all individuality in the nobleness of his purpose, the same undertone of melancholy, the same unearthly vagueness of outline and remoteness from the meaner interests and passions of men. As the poet of our own day has embodied his ideal of manhood in the king, so Vergil has embodied it in the hero-founder of his race. The temper of Æneas is the highest conception of human character to which the old world ever attained. The virtues of the Homeric combatants are there: courage, endurance, wisdom in council, eloquence, chivalrous friendship, family affection, faith to plighted word; but with these mingle virtues unknown to Hector or Achilleus, temperance, self-control, nobleness and unselfishness of aim, loyalty to an inner sense of right, the piety of self-devotion and self-sacrifice, refinement of feeling, a pure and delicate sense of the sweetness of woman's love, pity for the fallen and the weak.

In the Homeric picture Achilleus sits solitary in his tent, bound as it were to the affections of earth by the one tie of his friendship for Patroclos. No figure has ever been painted by a poet's pen more terrible in the loneliness of its wrath, its sorrow, its revenge. But from one end of his song to the other Vergil has surrounded Æneas with the ties and affections of home. In the awful night with which his story opens, the loss of Creusa, the mocking embrace in which the dead wife flies from his arms, form his farewell to Troy. "Thrice strove I there to clasp my arms about her neck,"—everyone knows the famous lines :—

"Thrice I essayed her neck to clasp,
Thrice the vain semblance mocked my grasp,
As wind or slumber light."

Amid all the terror of the flight from the burning city the figure of his child starts out bright against the darkness, touched with a tenderness which Vergil seems to reserve for his child-pictures.[1] But the

[1] "Dextræ se parvus Iulus
Implicuit, sequiturque patrem non passibus æquis."
"His steps scarce matching with my stride."
Mr. Conington's translation hardly renders the fond little touch of the Vergilian phrase, a phrase only possible to a lover of children.

whole escape is the escape of a family. Not merely child and wife, but father and household accompany Æneas. Life, he tells them when they bid him leave them to their fate, is worthless without them; and the "commune periclum, una salus" runs throughout all his wanderings. The common love of his boy is one of the bonds that link Dido with Æneas, and a yet more exquisite touch of poetic tenderness makes his affection for Ascanius the one final motive for his severance from the Queen. Not merely the will of the gods drives him from Carthage, but the sense of the wrong done to his boy.[1] His friendship is as warm and constant as his love for father or child. At the two great crises of his life the thought of Hector stirs a new outpouring of passionate regret. It is the vision of Hector which rouses him from the slumber of the terrible night when Troy is taken; the vision of the hero not as glorified by death, but as the memory of that last pitiful sight of the corpse dragged at the chariot wheels of Achilleus had stamped it for ever on the mind of his friend. It is as though all recollection of his greatness had been blotted out by the shame and terror of his fall ("quantum mutatus ab illo Hectore!"), but the gory hair and the mangled form only quicken the passionate longing of Æneas.[2]

[1] "Me puer Ascanius, capitisque injuria cari,
    Quem regno Hesperiæ fraudo et fatalibus arvis."
[2] "Quibus Hector ab oris
    Expectate venis?"

The tears, the "mighty groan," burst forth again as in the tapestry of the Sidonian temple he sees pictured anew the story of Hector's fall. In the hour of his last combat the thought of his brother-in-arms returns to him, and the memory of Hector is the spur to nobleness and valour which he bequeaths to his boy.

But throughout it is this refinement of feeling, this tenderness and sensitiveness to affection, that Vergil has loved to paint in the character of Æneas. To him Dido's charm lies in her being the one pitying face that has as yet met his own. Divine as he is, the child, like Achilleus, of a goddess, he broods with a tender melancholy over the sorrows of his fellow-men. "Sunt lacrymæ rerum et mentem mortalia tangunt," are words in which Sainte-Beuve has found the secret of the Æneid; they are at any rate the key to the character of Æneas. Like the poet of our own days, he longs for "the touch of a vanished hand, and the sound of a voice that is still."[1] He stands utterly apart from those epical heroes "that delight in war." The joy in sheer downright fighting which rings through Homer is wholly absent from the Æneid. Stirring and picturesque as is "The gathering of the Latin Clans," brilliant as is the painting of the last combat with Turnus, we feel everywhere the touch of a poet of

[1] "Cur dextræ jungere dextram
Non datur, ac veras audire et reddere voces?"

peace. Nothing is more noteworthy than the careful exclusion of the Roman cruelty, the Roman ambition, from the portrait of Æneas. Vergil seems to protest in his very hero against the poetic compulsion that drags him to the battle-field. On the eve of his final triumph, Æneas

> "incusat voce Latinum;
> Testaturque deos iterum se ad prœlia cogi."

Even when host is marshalled against host the thought of reconciliation is always kept steadily to the front, and the bitter cry of the hero asks in the very hour of the combat why bloodshed should divide peoples who are destined to be one.

It is the conflict of these two sides of the character of Æneas, the struggle between this sensitiveness to affection and his entire absorption in the mysterious destiny to which he is called, between his clinging to human ties and his readiness to forsake all and follow the divine voice which summons him, the strife in a word between love and duty, which gives its meaning and pathos to the story of Æneas and Dido. Attractive as it undoubtedly is, the story of Dido is in the minds of nine modern readers out of ten fatal to the effect of the Æneid as a whole. The very beauty of the tale is partly the cause of this. To the schoolboy and to thousands who are schoolboys no longer the poem is nothing more than the love story of the Trojan leader and the Tyrian queen. Its human interest ends with the funeral fires of Dido, and the books which follow are read merely as ingenious displays of the philosophic learning, the antiquarian research, and the patriotism of Vergil. But the story is yet more directly fatal in the way in which it cuts off the hero himself from modern sympathies. His desertion of Dido makes, it has been said, "an irredeemable poltroon of him in all honest English eyes." Dryden can only save his character by a jest, and Rousseau damns it with an epigram. Mr. Keble supposes that in the interview among the Shades the poet himself intended the abasement of his hero, and Mr. Gladstone has capped this by a theory that Vergil meant to draw his readers' admiration, not to Æneas but to Turnus.

It is wiser perhaps to turn from the impressions of Vergil's critics to the impression which the story must have left in the mind of Vergil himself. It is surely needless to assume that the first of poetic artists has forgotten the very rudiments of his art in placing at the opening of his song a figure which strips all interest from his hero. Nor is it needful to believe that such a blunder has been unconscious, and that Vergil has had to learn the true effect of his episode on the general texture of his poem from the reader of to-day. The poet who paints for us the character of Dido must have felt, ere he could have painted it, that charm which has ever since bewitched the world. Every nerve in Vergil must have thrilled at the consummate beauty of this woman of his own creation, her self-abandonment, her love, her suffering, her despair. If he deliberately uses her simply as a foil to the character of Æneas it is with a perception of this charm infinitely deeper and tenderer than ours. But he does use her as a foil. Impulse, passion, the mighty energies of unbridled will are wrought up into a figure of unequalled beauty, and then set against the true manhood of the founder and type of Rome, the manhood of duty, of self-sacrifice, of self-control.

To the stoicism of Vergil, steadied by a high sense of man's worth and work in the world, braced to patience and endurance for noble ends, passion—the revolt of the individual self against the world's order—seemed a light and trivial thing. He could feel and paint with exquisite delicacy and fire the charm of woman's utter love; but woman with all her loveliness wanted to him the grandeur of man's higher constancy to an unselfish purpose, "varium et mutabile semper foemina." Passion on the other hand is the mainspring of modern poetry, and it is difficult for us to realize the superior beauty of the calmer and vaster ideal of the poets of old. The figure of Dido, whirled hither and thither by the storms of warring emotions, reft even of her queenly dignity by the despair of her love, degraded by jealousy and disappointment to a very scold, is to the calm, serene figure of Æneas as modern sculpture, the sculpture of emotion, is to the sculpture of classic art. Each, no doubt, has its own peculiar beauty, and the work of a true criticism is to view either from its own standpoint and not from the standpoint of its rival. But if we would enter into the mind of Vergil we must view Dido with the eyes of Æneas and not Æneas with the eyes of Dido.

When Vergil first sets the two figures before us, it is not on the contrast but on the unity of their temper and history that he dwells. Touch after touch brings out this oneness of mood and aim as they drift towards one another. The same weariness, the same unconscious longing for rest and love, fills either heart. It is as a queen, as a Dian overtopping her nymphs by the head, that Dido appears on the scene, distributing their task to her labourers as a Roman Cornelia distributed wool to her house-slaves, questioning the Trojan strangers who sought her hospitality and protection. It is with the brief, haughty tone of a ruler of men that she bids them lay by their fears and assures them of shelter. Around her is the hum and stir of the city-building, a scene in which the sharp, precise touches of Vergil betray the hand of the town-poet. But within is the lonely heart of a woman. Dido, like Æneas, is a fugitive, an exile of bitter, vain regrets. Her husband, "loved with a mighty love," has fallen by a brother's hand; and his ghost, like that of Creusa, has driven her in flight from her Tyrian fatherland.

Like Æneas too she is no solitary wanderer; she guides a new colony to the site of the future Carthage as he to the site of the future Rome. When Æneas stands before her, it is as a wanderer like herself. His heart is bleeding at the loss of Creusa, of Helen, of Troy. He is solitary in his despair. He is longing for the touch of a human hand, the sound of a voice of love. He is weary of being baffled by the ghostly embraces of his wife, by the cloud that wraps his mother from his view. He is weary of wandering, longing with all the old-world intensity of longing for a settled home. "O fortunati quorum jam mœnia surgunt," he cries as he looks on the rising walls of Carthage. His gloom has been lightened indeed by the assurance of his fame which he gathers from the pictures of the great Defence graven on the walls of the Tyrian temple. But the loneliness and longing still press heavily on him when the cloud which has wrapt him from sight parts suddenly asunder, and Dido and Æneas stand face to face.

Few situations in poetry are more artistic than this meeting of Æneas and the Queen in its suddenness and picturesqueness. A love born of pity speaks in the first words of the hero,[1] and the reply of Dido strikes the same sympathetic note.[2] But the fervour of passion is soon to supersede this compassionate

---

[1] "O sola infandos Trojæ miserata labores."
[2] "Non ignara mali, miseris succurrere disco."

regard. Love himself in the most exquisite episode of the Æneid takes the place of Ascanius; while the Trojan boy lies sleeping on Ida, lapped on Earth's bosom beneath the cool mountain shade, his divine "double" lies clasped to Dido's breast, and pours his fiery longings into her heart. Slowly, unconsciously, the lovers draw together. The gratitude of Æneas is still at first subordinate to his quest. "Thy name and praise shall live," he says to Dido, "whatever lands call me." In the same way, though the Queen's generosity has shown itself in her first offer to the sailors ("urbem quam statuo vestra est"), it is still generosity and not passion. Passion is born in the long night through which, with Eros still folded in her arms, Dido listens to the "Tale of Troy."

The very verse quickens with the new pulse of love. The preface of the Æneid, the stately introduction that foretells the destinies of Rome and the divine end to which the fates were guiding Æneas, closes in fact with the appearance of Dido. The poem takes a gayer and lighter tone. The disguise and recognition of Venus as she appears to her son, the busy scene of city-building, the sudden revelation of Æneas to the Queen, have the note of exquisite romance. The honey-sweet of the lover's tale, to use the poet's own simile,[1] steals subtly on the graver epic. Step by step Vergil leads us on through every stage of pity, of fancy, of reverie, of restlessness, of

[1] "Fervet opus, redolentque thymo fragrantia mella."

passion, to the fatal close. None before him had painted the thousand delicate shades of love's advance; none has painted them more tenderly, more exquisitely since. As the Queen listens to the tale of her lover's escape she showers her questions as one that could never know enough.

"Multa super Priamo rogitans, super Hectore multa."

Her passion feeds through sleepless nights on the recollection of his look, on the memory of his lightest words. Even the old love of Sychæus seems to revive in and blend with this new affection.[1] Her very queenliness delights to idealize her lover, to recognize in the hero before whom she falls "one of the race of the gods." For a while the figure of Dido is that of happy, insatiate passion. The rumours of war from the jealous chieftains about her fall idly on her ear. She hovers round her hero with sweet observances of love, she hangs at his side the jewelled sword and the robe of Tyrian purple woven by her queenly hands.

But even in the happiest moments of his story the consummate art of the poet has prepared for the final catastrophe. Little words, like "misera," "infelix," "fati nescia," sound the first undertones of a woe to come, even amidst the joy of the first meeting or the glad tumult of the hunting-scene. The restlessness, the quick alternations of feeling in the hour

[1] "Agnosco veteris vestigia flammæ."

of Dido's triumph, prepare us for the wild swaying of the soul from bitterest hate to pitiful affection in the hour of her agony. She is the first in the sensitiveness of her passion to catch the change in Æneas, and the storm of her indignation sweeps away the excuses of her lover, as the storm of her love had swept away his earlier resolve. All dignity, all queenliness breaks before the "fury of a woman scorned." She dashes herself against the rooted purpose of Æneas as the storm-winds, to use Vergil's image, dash themselves from this quarter and that against the rooted oak. The madness of her failure drives her through the streets like a Mænad in the nightly orgies of Cithæron; she flies at last to her chamber like a beast at bay, and gazes out distracted at the Trojan shipmen putting off busily from the shores. Yet ever and again the wild frenzy-bursts are broken by notes of the old pathetic tenderness. In the midst of her taunts and menaces she turns with a woman's delicacy to protest against her own violence, "heu, furiis incensa feror!" She humbles herself even to pray for a little respite, if but for a few hours.[1] She pleads her very loneliness; she catches as it were from Æneas the thought of the boy whose future he had pleaded as one cause of his departure and finds in it a plea for pity.

Sometimes her agony is too terrible for speech;

[1] "Tempus inane peto, requiem spatiumque furori,
Dum mea me victam doceat fortuna dolere."

she can only answer with those "speechless eyes" with which her shade was once more to meet Æneas in the Elysian fields. But her wonderful energy forbids her to lie, like weaker women, crushed in her despair. She hurries her sister to the feet of her lover that nothing may be left untried. From the first she stakes her life on the issue; it is as one "about to die" that she prays Æneas not to leave her. When all has failed and hope itself deserts her the weariness of life gathers round and she "tires of the sight of day."

Never have the mighty energies of unbridled human will been wrought up into a form of more surpassing beauty; never have they been set more boldly and sharply against the manhood of duty, of self-sacrifice, of self-control. If the tide of Dido's passion sweeps away for the moment the consciousness of a divine mission which has borne Æneas to the Tyrian shore, the consciousness lies still in the very heart of the man and revives at the new call of the gods. The call bids him depart at once; and without a struggle he "burns to depart." He stamps down and hides within the deep recesses of his heart the "care" that the wild entreaties of the woman he loved arouse within him; the life that had swung for an hour out of its course returns to its old bearings; once more Italy and his destiny become aim and fatherland, "hic amor, hæc patria est." Æneas bows to the higher will, and from that moment all that has turned him from his course is of the past. Dido becomes a part of his memory as of the things that were.[1]

Æneas is as "resolute to depart" as Dido is "resolute to die." And in both the resolve lifts the soul out of its lower passion-life into a nobler air. The queen rises into her old queenliness as she passes "majestic to the grave;" and her last curse as the Tyrian ships quit her shore is no longer the wild imprecation of a frenzied woman; it is the mighty curse of the founder of a people calling down on the Roman race ages of inextinguishable hate. "Fight shore with shore: fight sea with sea!" is the prophecy of that struggle with Carthage which all but wrecked for a moment the destinies of Rome. But Vergil saw in the character of Dido herself a danger to Rome's future far greater than the sword of Hannibal. His very sense of the grandeur of Rome's destinies frees him from the vulgar self-confidence of meaner men. Throughout his poem he is haunted by the memories of civil war, by the sense of instability which clings to men who have grown up in the midst of revolutions. The grandest picture in the Æneid reflects the terror of that hour of suspense when the galleys of Augustus jostled against the galleys of Antony. From that moment, as Vergil's prescience foresaw, the dangers of Rome were to spring from a single source. Passion, greed,

[1] "Nec me meminisse pigebit Elissæ."

lawless self-seeking, personal ambition, the decay of the older Roman sense of unselfish duty, of that "pietas" which subordinated the interest of the individual man to the common interest of the state, this was henceforth to be the real enemy of Rome. More and more, as the Roman peace drew the world together, the temper of the East, the temper which Vergil has embodied in his sketch of Dido, would tell and tell fatally on the temper of the West. Orontes —to borrow Juvenal's phrase—was already flowing into Tiber, and the sterner virtues of the conquerors were growing hourly more distasteful beside the variety, the geniality, the passionate flush and impulse of the conquered.

It was their common sense of this danger which drew together Vergil and the Emperor. It is easy to see throughout his poem what critics are accustomed to style a compliment to Augustus. But the loving admiration and reverence of Vergil had no need to stoop to the flattery of compliment. To him Augustus was in a deep and true sense the realization of that ideal Roman whom his song was meant to set in the forefront of Rome. When Antony in the madness of his enchantment forgot the high mission to which Rome was called, the spell had only been broken by the colder "piety" of Cæsar. To Vergil Augustus was the founder of a new Rome, the Æneas who after long wanderings across the strife of civil war had brought her into quiet waters and bound warring factions into a peaceful people. Vergil felt, as even we can feel so many ages later, the sense of a high mission, the calm silent recognition of a vast work to be done, which lifted the cold, passionless Imperator into greatness. It was the bidding of Augustus that had called him from his "rustic measure" to this song of Rome, and the thought of Augustus blended, whether he would or not, with that Rome of the future which seemed growing up under his hands. Unlike too as Vergil was to the Emperor, there was a common undertone of melancholy that drew the two men together. The wreck of the older faiths, the lingering doubt whether good was after all the strongest thing in the world, whether "the gods" were always on the side of justice and right, throws its gloom over the noblest passages of the Æneid. It is the same doubt, hardened by the temper of the man into a colder and more mocking scepticism, that sounds in the "plaudite et valete" of the deathbed of Augustus. The Emperor had played his part well, but it was a part that he could hardly persuade himself was real. All that wisdom and power could do had been done, but Augustus had no faith in the great fabric he had reared. Vergil drew faith in the fortunes of Rome from his own enthusiasm, but to him too the moral order of the world brought only the melancholy doubt of Hamlet. Everywhere we feel "the pity on't." The religious theory of the universe, the order of the world around him, jars at every step with his moral faith. Æneas is the reflection of a time out of joint. Everywhere among good men there was the same moral earnestness, the same stern resolve after nobleness and grandeur of life, and everywhere there was the same inability to harmonize his moral life with the experience of the world.

A noble stoicism breathes in the character of Æneas, the virtue of the virtuous man, refined and softened by a poet's pitifulness, heightened above all by the lingering doubt whether there were any necessary connection between virtue and the divine order of things around it.

> "Di tibi, si qua pios respectant numina, si quid
> Usquam Justitia est et mens sibi conscia recti,
> Præmia digna ferant!"

The words glow, so to speak, with moral earnestness, but through them we feel the doubt whether, after all, uprightness and a good conscience were really the object of a divine care. Heaven had flown further off from earth than in the days of the Iliad. The laws of the universe, as time had revealed them, the current of human affairs, the very might of the colossal Empire in which the world of civilization found itself prisoned, all seemed to be dwarfing man. Man remained, the sad stern manhood of the Stoic, the spirit that breathes through the character of Æneas, enduring, baffled, yet full of a faith that the very storms that drove him from sea to sea were working out some mysterious and divine order. Man was greater than his fate:—

> "Quo fata trahunt retrahuntque sequamur,
> Quicquid erit, superanda omnis fortuna ferendo est."

There is the same sad Cato-like stoicism in the words with which Æneas addresses himself to his final combat:—

> "Disce, puer, virtutem ex me verumque laborem,
> Fortunam ex aliis."

But the "dîs aliter visum" meets us at every step. Ripheus is the most just and upright among the warriors of Troy, but he is the first to fall. An inscrutable mystery hangs around the order of the world. Men of harder, colder temper shrug their shoulders, and like Augustus repeat their "vanitas vanitatum" with a smile of contempt at the fools who take life in earnest. Nobler and more sensitive souls like that of Vergil carry about with them "the pity of it." It is this melancholy that flings its sad grace over the verse of the Æneid. We close it as we close the Idylls with the King's mournful cry in our ears. But the Roman stoicism is of harder and manlier stuff than the chivalrous spiritualism of Arthur. The ideal of the old world is of nobler, sterner tone than the ideal of the new. Even with death and ruin around him, and the mystery of the world darkening his soul, man remains man and master of his fate. The suffering and woe of the individual find amends in the greatness and welfare of the race. We pity the wandering of Æneas, but his wanderings found the city. The dream of Arthur vanishes as the dark boat dies into a dot upon the mere; the dream of Æneas becomes Rome.

TWO VENETIAN STUDIES

VENICE AND ROME

IT is the strangeness and completeness of the contrast which makes one's first row from Venice to Torcello so hard to forget. Behind us the great city sinks slowly into a low line of domes and towers; around us, dotted here and there over the gleaming surface, are the orange sails of trailing market-boats; we skirt the great hay-barges of Mazorbo, whose boatmen bandy *lazzi* and badinage with our gondolier; we glide by a lonely cypress into a broader reach, and in front, across a waste of brown sedge and brushwood, the tower of Torcello rises sharply against the sky. There is something weird and unearthly in the suddenness with which one passes from the bright, luminous waters of the lagoon, barred with soft lines of violet light and broken with reflections of wall and bell-tower, into this presence of desolation and death. A whole world seems to part those dreary flats broken with lifeless inlets, those patches of sodden fields flung shapelessly among sheets of sullen water, from the life and joy of the Grand Canal. And yet really to understand the origin of Venice, those ages of terror and flight and exile in which the Republic took its birth, we must study them at Torcello. It was from the vast Alpine chain which hangs in the haze of midday like a long dim cloud-line to the north that the hordes of Hun and Goth burst on the Roman world. Their path lay along the coast trending round to the west, where lost among little villages that stand out white in the distant shadow lie the sites of Heraclea and Altinum. Across these grey shallows cut by the blue serpentine windings of deeper channels the Romans of the older province of Venetia on the mainland fled before Attila or Theodoric or Alboin to found the new Venetia of the lagoon. Eastward over Lido the glimmer of the Adriatic recalls the long centuries of the Pirate war, that struggle for life which shaped into their after-form the government and destinies of the infant state. Venice itself, the crown and end of struggle and of flight, lies over shining miles of water to the south. But it is here that one can best study the story of its birth; it is easier to realize those centuries of exile and buffeting for life amid the dreary flats, the solitude, the poverty of Torcello, than beneath the gleaming front of the Ducal Palace or the mosaics of St. Mark.

Here in fact lies the secret of Venetian history, the one key by which it is possible to understand the strange riddle of the Republic. For thirteen centuries Venice lay moored as it were off the coast of Western Europe, without political analogue or social parallel. Its patriciate, its people, its government were not what government or people or patriciate were in other countries of Western Christendom. The difference lay not in any peculiar institutions which it had developed, or in any novel form of social or administrative order which it had invented, but in the very origin of the State itself. We see this the better if we turn from Venice to our own homeland. The same age saw the birth of the two great maritime Powers of modern Europe, for the settlements of the English in Britain cover the same century with those of the Roman exiles in the Venetian Lagoon. But the English colonization was the establishment of a purely Teutonic State on the wreck of Rome, while the Venetian was the establishment of a purely Roman State in the face of the Teuton. Venice in its origin was simply the Imperial province of Venetia floated across to the islands of the shore. Before the successive waves of the northern inroad the citizens of the coast fled to the sandbanks which had long served them as gardens or merchant-ports. The "Chair of Attila," the rough stone seat beside the church of San Fosco, preserves the memory of one destroyer before whom a third part of the people of Altinum fled to Torcello and the islands around. Their city—even materially— passed with them. The new houses were built from the ruins of the old. The very stones of Altinum served for the "New Altinum" which arose on the desolate isle, and inscriptions, pillars, capitals came in the track of the exiles across the lagoon to be worked into the fabric of its cathedral.

Neither citizens nor city were changed even in name. They had put out for security a few miles to sea, but the sandbanks on which they landed were still Venetia. The fugitive patricians were neither more nor less citizens of the imperial province because they had fled from Padua or Altinum to Malamocco or Torcello. Their political allegiance was still due to the Empire. Their social organization remained unaffected by the flight. So far were they from being severed from Rome, so far from entertaining any dreams of starting afresh in the "new democracy" which exists in the imagination of Daru and his followers, that the one boast of their annalists is that they are more Roman than the Romans themselves. Their nobles looked with contempt on the barbaric blood which had tainted that of the Colonnas or the Orsini, nor did any Isaurian peasant ever break the Roman line of Doges as Leo broke the line of Roman Emperors. Venice—as she proudly styled herself in after time—was "the legitimate daughter of Rome." The strip of seaboard from the Brenta to the Isonzo was the one spot in the Empire from the Caspian to the Atlantic where foot of barbarian never trod. And as it rose, so it set. From that older world of which it was a part the history of Venice stretched on to the French Revolution untouched by Teutonic influences. The old Roman life which became strange even to the Capitol lingered unaltered, unimpaired, beside the palace of the duke. The strange ducal cap, the red ducal slippers, the fan of bright feathers borne before the ducal chair, all came unchanged from ages when they were the distinctions of every great officer of the Imperial State. It is startling to think that almost within the memory of living men Venice brought Rome—the Rome of Ambrose and Theodosius—to the very doors of the Western World; that the living and unchanged tradition of the Empire passed away only with the last of the Doges. Only on the tomb of Manin could men write truthfully, "Hic jacet ultimus Romanorum."

It is this simple continuance of the old social organization which the barbarians elsewhere overthrew that explains the peculiar character of the Venetian patriciate. In all other countries of the West the new feudal aristocracy sprang from the Teutonic invaders. In Italy itself the nobles were descendants of Lombard conquerors, or of the barons who followed Emperor after Emperor across the Alps. Even when their names and characters had alike been moulded into Southern form, the "Seven Houses" of Pisa boasted of their descent from the seven barons of Emperor Otto. But the older genealogies of the senators whose names stood written in the Golden

Book of Venice ran, truly or falsely, not to Teutonic but to Roman origins. The Participazii, the Dandoli, the Falieri, the Foscari, told of the flight of their Roman fathers before the barbarian sword from Pavia, Gaeta, Fano, Messina. Every quarter of Italy had given its exiles, but above all the coast round the head of the Gulf from Ravenna to Trieste. It was especially a flight and settlement of nobles. As soon as the barbaric hordes had swept away to the South the farmer or the peasant would creep back to his fields and his cabin and submit to the German master whom the conquest had left behind it. But the patrician had filled too great a place in the old social order to stoop easily to the new. He remained camped as before in his island-refuge, among a crowd of dependants, his fishermen, his dock-labourers. Throughout the long ages which followed, this original form of Venetian society remained unchanged. The populace of dependants never grew into a people. To the last fisherman and gondolier clung to the great houses of which they were the clients, as the fishers of Torcello had clung to the great nobles of Altinum. No difference of tradition or language or blood parted them. Tradition, on the contrary, bound them together. No democratic agitator could appeal from the present to the past, as Rienzi invoked the memories of the Tribunate against the feudal tyranny of the Colonnas. In Venice the past and present were one. The patrician of Venice simply governed the State as his fathers, the curials of Padua or Aquileia, had governed the State ten centuries before him.

It is this unity of Venetian society which makes Venetian history so unlike the history of other Italian towns, and to which Venice owes the peculiar picturesqueness and brightness which charms us still in its decay. Elsewhere the history of mediæval Italy sprang from the difference of race and tradition between conquered and conquerors, between Lombard noble and Italian serf. The communal revolt of the twelfth century, the democratic constitutions of Milan or of Bologna, were in effect a rising of race against race, the awakening of a new people in the effort to throw off the yoke of the stranger. The huge embattled piles which flung their dark shadows over the streets of Florence tell of the ceaseless war between baronage and people. The famous penalty by which some of the democratic communes condemned a recreant cobbler or tinker to "descend" as his worst punishment "into the order of the *noblesse*," tells of the hate and issue of the struggle between them. But no trace of struggle or of hate breaks the annals of Venice. There is no people, no democratic Broletto, no Hall of the Commune. And as there was no "people," so in the mediæval sense of the word there was no "baronage." The nobles of Venice were not Lombard barons but Roman patricians, untouched by feudal traditions or by the strong instinct of personal independence which created feudalism. The shadow of the Empire is always over them, they look for greatness not to independent power or strife, but to joint co-operation in the government of the State. Their instinct is administrative, they shrink from disorder as from a barbaric thing, they are citizens, and nobles only because they are citizens. Of this political attitude of its patricians Venice is itself the type. The palaces of Torcello or Rialto were houses, not of war, but of peace; no dark masses of tower and wall, but bright with marbles and frescoes, and broken with arcades of fretted masonry.

Venice, in a word, to her very close was a city of nobles, the one place in the modern world where the old senatorial houses of the fifth century lived and ruled as of old. But it was a city of Roman nobles. Like the Teutonic passion for war, the Teutonic scorn of commerce was strange and unknown to the curial houses of the Italian municipalities, as it had been strange and unknown to the greatest houses of Rome. The Senator of Padua or Aquileia, of Concordia, Altinum, or Ravenna, had always been a merchant, and in his new refuge he remained a merchant still. Venice was no "crowd of poor fishermen," as it has been sometimes described, who were gradually drawn to wider ventures and a larger commerce. The port of Aquileia had long been the emporium of a trade which reached northwards to the Danube and eastward to Byzantium. What the Roman merchants of

Venetia had been at Aquileia they remained at Grado. The commerce of Altinum simply transferred itself to Torcello. The Paduan merchants passed to their old port of Rialto. Vague and rhetorical as is the letter of Cassiodorus, it shows how keen was the mercantile activity of the State from its beginning. Nothing could be more natural, more continuous in its historical development; nothing was more startling, more incomprehensible to the new world which had grown up in German moulds. The nobles of Henry VIII.'s Court could not restrain their sneer at "the fishermen of Venice," the stately patricians who could look back from merchant-noble to merchant-noble through ages when the mushroom houses of England were unheard of. Only the genius of Shakspere seized the grandeur of a social organization which was still one with that of Rome and Athens and Tyre. The merchant of Venice is with him "a royal merchant." His "argosies o'ertop the petty traffickers." At the moment when feudalism was about to vanish away, the poet comprehended the grandeur of that commerce which it scorned and the grandeur of the one State which had carried the nobler classic tradition across ages of brutality and ignorance. The great commercial State, whose merchants are nobles, whose nobles are Romans, rises in all its majesty before us in the 'Merchant of Venice.'

II

VENICE AND TINTORETTO

The fall of Venice dates from the League of Cambray, but her victory over the crowd of her assailants was followed by half a century of peace and glory such as she had never known. Her losses on the mainland were in reality a gain, enforcing as they did the cessation of that policy of Italian aggression which had eaten like a canker into the resources of the State and drawn her from her natural career of commerce and aggrandizement on the sea. If the political power of Venice became less, her political influence grew greater than ever. The statesmen of France, of England, and of Germany studied in the cool, grave school of her Senate. We need only turn to 'Othello' to find reflected the universal reverence for the wisdom of her policy and the order of her streets. No policy, however wise, could indeed avert her fall. The Turkish occupation of Egypt and the Portuguese discovery of a sea route round the Cape of Good Hope were destined to rob the Republic of that trade with the East which was the life-blood of its commerce. But, though the blow was already dealt, its effects were for a time hardly discernible. On the contrary, the accumulated wealth of centuries poured itself out in an almost riotous prodigality. A new Venice, a Venice of loftier palaces, of statelier colonnades, rose under Palladio and Sansovino along the line of its canals. In the deep peace of the sixteenth century, a peace unbroken even by religious struggles (for Venice was the one State exempt from the struggle of the Reformation), literature and art won their highest triumphs. The press of the Aldi gave for the first time the masterpieces of Greek poetry to Europe. The novels of Venice furnished plots for our own drama, and became the origin of modern fiction. Painting reached its loftiest height in Giorgione, Titian, Tintoret, and Paul Veronese.

The greatest of colourists sprang from a world of colour. Faded, ruined as the city is now, the frescoes of Giorgione swept from its palace fronts by the sea-wind, its very gondoliers bare and ragged, the glory of its sunsets alone remains vivid as of old. But it is not difficult to restore the many-hued Venice out of which its painters sprang. There are two pictures by Carpaccio in the Accademia which bring back vividly its physical aspect. The scene of the first, the 'Miracle of the Patriarch of Grado' as it is called, lies on the Grand Canal immediately in front of the Rialto. It is the hour of sunset, and darker-edged clouds are beginning to fleck the golden haze of the west which still arches over the broken sky-line, roof and turret and bell-tower and chimneys of strange fashion with quaint conical tops. The canal lies dusk in the eventide, but the dark surface throws into relief a crowd of gondolas, and the lithe, glowing figures of their gondoliers. The boats themselves are long and narrow as now, but without the indented prora which has become universal; the sumptuary law of the Republic has not yet robbed them of colour, and instead of the present "coffin" we see canopies of gaily-hued stuffs supported on four light pillars. The gondolier himself is commonly tricked out in almost fantastic finery; red cap with long golden curls flowing down over the silken doublet, slashed hose, the light dress displaying those graceful attitudes into which the rower naturally falls. On the left side of the canal its white marble steps are crowded with figures of the nobler Venetian life; a black robe here or there breaking the gay variety of golden and purple and red and blue, while in the balcony above a white group of clergy, with golden candlesticks towering overhead, are gathered round the dæmoniac whose cure forms the subject of the picture.

But the most noteworthy point in it is the light it throws on the architectural aspect of Venice at the close of the fifteenth century. On the right the houses are wholly of mediæval type, the flat marble-sheeted fronts pierced with trefoil-headed lights; one of them splendid with painted arabesques dipping at its base into the very waters of the canal and mounting up to enwreathe in intricate patterns the very chimney of the roof. The left is filled by a palace of the early Renascence, but the change of architectural style, though it has modified the tone and extent of colour, is far from dismissing it altogether. The flat pilasters which support the round arches of its base are sheeted with a delicately-tinged marble; the flower-work of their capitals and the mask enclosed within it are gilded like the continuous billet moulding which runs round in the hollow of each arch, while the spandrils are filled in with richer and darker marbles, each broken with a central medallion of gold. The use of gold indeed seems a "note" of the colouring of the early Renascence; a broad band of gold wreathes the two rolls beneath and above the cornice, and lozenges of gold light up the bases of the light pillars in the colonnade above. In another picture of Carpaccio, the 'Dismissal of the Ambassadors,' one sees the same principles of colouring extended to the treatment of interiors. The effect is obtained partly by the contrast of the lighter marbles with those of deeper colour or with porphyry, partly by the contrast of both with gold. Everywhere, whether in the earlier buildings of mediæval art or in the later efforts of the Renascence, Venice seemed to clothe itself in robes of Oriental splendour, and to pour over Western art before its fall the wealth and gorgeousness of the East.

Of the four artist-figures who—in the tradition of Tintoret's picture—support this "Golden Calf" of Venice, Tintoret himself is the one specially Venetian. Giorgione was of Castel Franco; Titian came from the mountains of Cadore; Paolo from Verona. But Jacopo Robusti, the "little dyer," the Tintoretto, was born, lived, and died in Venice. His works, rare elsewhere, crowd its churches, its palaces, its galleries. Its greatest art-building is the shrine of his faith. The school of San Rocco has rightly been styled by Mr. Ruskin "one of the three most precious buildings in the world"; it is the one spot where all is Tintoret. Few contrasts are at first sight more striking than the contrast between the building of the Renascence which contains his forty masterpieces and the great mediæval church of the Frari which stands beside it. But a certain oneness after all links the two buildings together. The Friars had burst on the caste spirit of the middle age, its mere classification of brute force, with the bold recognition of human equality which ended in the socialism of Wyclif and the Lollards. Tintoret found himself facing a new caste-spirit in the Renascence, a classification of mankind founded on æsthetic refinement and intellectual power; and it is hard not to see in the greatest of his works a protest as energetic as theirs for the common rights of men. Into the grandeur of the Venice about him, her fame, her wealth, her splendour, none could enter more vividly. He rises to his best painting, as Mr. Ruskin has observed, when his subjects are noble—doges, saints, priests, senators clad in purple and jewels and gold. But Tintoret is never quite Veronese. He cannot be untrue to beauty, and the pomps and glories of earth are beautiful to him; but there is a beauty too in earth, in man himself. The brown half-naked gondolier lies stretched on the marble steps which the Doge in one of his finest pictures has ascended. It is as if he had stripped off the stately robe and the ducal cap, and shown the soul of Venice in the bare child of the lagoons. The "want of dignity" which some have censured in his scenes from the Gospels is in them just as it is in the Gospels themselves. Here, as there, the poetry lies in the strange, unearthly mingling of the commonest human life with the sublimest divine. In his 'Last Supper,' in San Giorgio Maggiore, the apostles are peasants; the low, mean life of the people is there, but hushed and transfigured by the tall standing figure of the Master who bends to give bread to the disciple by His side. And above and around crowd in the legions of heaven, cherubim and seraphim mingling their radiance with the purer radiance from the halo of their Lord; while amid all this conflict of celestial light the twinkling candles upon the board burn on, and the damsel who enters bearing food, bathed as she is in the very glory of heaven, is busy, unconscious—a serving-maid, and nothing more.

The older painters had seen something undivine

in man; the colossal mosaic, the tall unwomanly Madonna, expressed the sense of the Byzantine artist that to be divine was to be unhuman. The Renascence, with little faith in God, had faith in man, but only in the might and beauty and knowledge of man. With Tintoret the common life of man is ever one with heaven. This was the faith which he flung on "acres of canvas" as ungrudgingly as apostle ever did, toiling and living as apostles lived and toiled. This was the faith he found in Old Testament and New, in saintly legend or in national history. In the 'Annunciation' at San Rocco a great bow of angels streaming either way from the ethereal Dove sweeps into a ruined hut, a few mean chairs its only furniture, the mean plaster dropping from the bare brick pilasters; without, Joseph at work unheeding, amid piles of worthless timber flung here and there. So in the 'Adoration of the Magi' the mother wonders with a peasant's wonder at the jewels and gold. Again, the 'Massacre of the Innocents' is one wild, horror-driven rush of pure motherhood, reckless of all in its clutch at its babe. So in the splendour of his 'Circumcision' it is from the naked child that the light streams on the High Priest's brow, on the mighty robe of purple and gold held up by stately forms like a vast banner behind him. The peasant mother to whose poorest hut that first stir of child-life has brought a vision of angels, who has marvelled at the wealth of precious gifts which a babe brings to her breast, who has felt the sword piercing her own bosom also as danger threatened it, on whose mean world her child has flung a glory brighter than glory of earth, is the truest critic of Tintoret.

What Shakspere was to the national history of England in his great series of historic dramas, his contemporary Tintoret was to the history of Venice. It was perhaps from an unconscious sense that her annals were really closed that the Republic began to write her history and her exploits in the series of paintings which covers the walls of the Ducal Palace. Her apotheosis is like that of the Roman Emperors; it is when death has fallen upon her that her artists raise her into a divine form, throned amid heavenly clouds and crowned by angel hands with the laurel wreath of victory. It is no longer St. Mark who watches over Venice, it is Venice herself who bends from heaven to bless boatman and senator. In the divine figure of the Republic with which Tintoret filled the central cartoon of the Great Hall every Venetian felt himself incarnate. His figure of 'Venice' in the Senate Hall is yet nobler; the blue sea-depths are cleft open, and strange ocean-shapes wave their homage and yet more unearthly forms dart up with tribute of coral and pearls to the feet of the Sea Queen as she sits in the silken state of the time with the divine halo around her. But if from this picture in the roof the eye falls suddenly on the fresco which fills the close of the room, we can hardly help reading the deeper comment of Tintoret on the glory of the State. The Sala del Consiglio is the very heart of Venice. In the double row of plain seats running round it sat her nobles; on the raised dais at the end, surrounded by the graver senators, sat her duke. One long fresco occupies the whole wall above the ducal seat; in the background the blue waters of the Lagoon with the towers and domes of Venice rising from them; around a framework of six bending saints; in front two kneeling Doges in full ducal robes with a black curtain of clouds between them. The clouds roll back to reveal a mighty glory, and in the heart of it the livid figure of a dead Christ taken from the Cross. Not one eye of all the nobles gathered in council could have lifted itself from the figure of the Doge without falling on the figure of the dead Christ. Strange as the conception is, it is hard to believe that in a mind so peculiarly symbolical as that of Tintoret the contrast could have been without a definite meaning. And if this be so, it is a meaning that one can hardly fail to read in the history of the time. The brief interval of peace and glory had passed away ere Tintoret's brush had ceased to toil. The victory of Lepanto had only gilded that disgraceful submission to the Turk which preluded the disastrous struggle in which her richest possessions were to be wrested from the Republic. The terrible plague of 1576 had carried off Titian. Twelve years after Titian Paul Veronese passed away. Tintoret, born almost at its opening, lingered till the very close of the century to see

Venice sinking into powerlessness and infamy and decay. May not the figure of the dead Christ be the old man's protest against a pride in which all true nobleness and effort had ceased to live, and which was hurrying to so shameful a fall?

THE DISTRICT VISITOR

THE DISTRICT VISITOR

IT would be hard to define exactly the office and duties of the District Visitor. Historically she is the direct result of the Evangelical movement which marked the beginning of this century; the descendant of the "devout women not a few" who played, like Hannah More, the part of mothers in Israel to the Simeons and Wilberforces of the time. But the mere tract-distributor of fifty years ago has grown into a parochial and ecclesiastical force of far greater magnitude. The District Visitor of to-day is parson and almoner in one; the parochial censor of popular morals, the parochial instructor in domestic economy. She claims the same right as the vicar to knock at every door and obtain admission into every house. But once within it her scope of action is far larger than the parson's. To the spiritual influence of the tract or "the chapter" she adds the more secular and effective power of the bread-ticket. "The way to the heart of the poor," as she pithily puts it, "lies through their stomachs." Her religious exhortations are backed by scoldings and fussiness. She is eloquent upon rags and tatters, and severe upon dirty floors. She flings open the window and lectures her flock on the advantages of fresh air. She hurries little Johnny off to school and gets Sally out to service. She has a keen nose for drains and a passion for clean hands and faces. What worries her most is the fatalism and improvidence of the poor. She is full of exhortations to "lay by" for the rainy day, and seductive in her praises of the Penny Bank. The whole life of the family falls within her supervision. She knows the wages of the husband and the occasional jobs of the wife. She inquires what there is for dinner and gives wise counsels on economical cookery. She has her theory as to the hour when children ought to be in bed, and fetches in Tommy, much weeping, from the last mud-pie of sunset. Only "the master" himself lies outside of her rule. Between the husband and the District Visitor there exists a sort of armed neutrality. Her visits are generally paid when he is at work. If she arrives when he happens to be at home, he calls for "missus," and retires sheepishly to the 'Blue Boar.' The energetic Dorcas who fixes him in a corner gets little for her pains. He "supposes" that "missus" knows where and when the children go to school, and that "missus" may some day or other be induced to go to church. But the theory of the British labourer is that with his home or his family, their religion or their education, he has nothing personally to do. And so he has nothing to do with the District Visitor. His only demand is that she should let him alone, and the wise District Visitor soon learns, as parson and curate have long learnt, to let him alone.

Like theirs, her work lies with wife and children, and as we have seen it is of far wider scope even here than the work of the clergy. But, fussy and dictatorial as she is, the District Visitor is as a rule more popular than the clergyman. In the first place, the parson is only doing a duty he is bound to do while the District Visitor is a volunteer. The parson, as the poor roughly say, is paid for it. Again, however simple-hearted and courteous he may be, he never gets very close home to the poor. Their life is not his life, nor their ways his ways. They do not understand his refinement, his delicacy about interference, his gentlemanly reticence, his abhorrence of gossip and scandal. They are accustomed to be ordered about, to rough words, to gossip over their neighbours. And so the District Visitor is "more in their way," as they tell her. She is profuse of questions, routing out a thousand little details that no parson would ever know. She has little of the sensitive pride that hinders the vicar from listening to scandal, or of the manly objection to "telling tales" which hurries him out of the room when neighbour brings charges against neighbour. She is entirely unaffected by his scruples against interference with the conscience or religion of the poor. "Where do you go to church?" and "Why don't you go to church?" are her first stock questions in her cross-examination of every family. Her exhortations at the sick-bed have a somewhat startling peremptoriness about them. We can hardly wonder at the wish of a poor patient that she were a rich one, because then she could "die in peace, and have nobody to come in and pray over her." What irritates the District Visitor in cases where she has bestowed special religious attention is that people when so effectively prepared for death "won't die." But hard, practical action such as this does not jostle against the feelings of the poor as it would against our own. Women especially forgive all because the District Visitor listens as well as talks. They could no more pour out their little budget of domestic troubles to the parson than to a being from another world. But the District Visitor is the recipient of all. The washerwoman stops her mangle to talk about the hard times and the rise of a halfpenny on the loaf. The matron next door turns up her sleeve to show the bruise her husband bestowed on her on his return from the 'Chequers.' She enters largely and minutely into the merits and defects of her partner's character, and protests with a subtle discrimination that "he's a good father when he ain't bothered with the children, and a good husband when he's off the drink." The old widow down the lane is waiting for "the lady" to write a letter for her to her son in Australia, and to see the "pictur," the cheap photograph of the grandchildren she has never seen or will see, that John has sent home. A girl home from her "place" wants the District Visitor to intercede with her mistress, and listens in all humility to a lecture on her giddiness and love of finery.

The society in fact of the little alley is very much held together by the District Visitor. In her love of goody gossip she fulfils the office which in an Italian town is filled by the barber. She retails tittle-tattle for the highest ends. She relates Mrs. A.'s misdemeanour for the edification and correction of Mrs. B. She has the true version of the quarrel between Smith and his employer. She is the one person to whom the lane looks for accurate information as to the domestic relations of the two Browns, whose quarrels are the scandal of the neighbourhood. Her influence in fact over the poor is a strange mixture of good and evil, of real benevolence with an interference that saps all sense of self-respect, of real sympathy and womanly feeling with a good deal of womanly meddling, curiosity, and babble.

But her influence on the parish at large is a far more delicate question. To the outer world a parish seems a sheer despotism. The parson prays, preaches, changes the order of service, distributes the parochial charities at his simple discretion. One of the great cries of the Church reformer is generally for the substitution of some constitutional system, some congregational council, some lay co-operation, for this clerical tyranny. But no one in fact feels the narrow limits of his power more keenly than the parson himself. As the old French monarchy was a despotism tempered by epigrams, so the rule of a parish is a despotism tempered by parochial traditions, by the observation of neighbouring clergymen, by the suggestions of the squire, by the opposition of churchwardens, by the hints and regrets of "Constant Attendants," by the state of the pew-letting or the ups and downs of the offertory, by the influences of local opinion, by the censorship of the District Visitor. What the assembly of his "elders" is to a Scotch minister, the District Visitors' meeting is to the English clergyman. He has to prove in the face of a standing jealousy that his alms have been equally distributed between district and district. His selection of tracts is freely criticised. Mrs. A. regrets that her poor people have seen so little of their vicar lately. Mrs. B. is sorry to report the failure of her attempts to get her sheep to church, in face of the new Ritualistic development, the processions, and the surplices. Mrs. C., whose forte is education, declines any longer to induce mothers to send their children to "such" a master. The curates shudder as Mrs. D. laments their frequent absence from the Penny Bank, not that they can do any good there, but "we are always glad of the presence and sympathy of our clergy." The curates promise amendment of life. The vicar engages to look out for another schoolmaster, and be more diligent in his attentions to Muck Lane. A surreptitious supply of extra tickets to the ultra-Protestant appeases for the moment her wrath against the choir surplices. But the occasional screw of the monthly meeting is as nothing to the daily pressure applied by the individual District Visitor. At the bottom of every alley the vicar runs up against a parochial censor. The "five minutes' conversation" which the District Visitor expects as the reward of her benevolence becomes a perpetual trickle of advice, remonstrance, and even reproof. A strong-minded parson of course soon makes himself master of his District Visitors, but the ordinary vicar generally feels that his District Visitors are masters of him. The harm that comes of this feminine despotism is the feminine impress it leaves on the whole aspect of the parish. Manly preaching disappears before the disappointed faces the preacher encounters on Monday. A policy of expedients and evasions takes the place of any straightforward attempt to meet or denounce local evils. The vicar's time and energy are frittered away on a thousand little jealousies and envyings, his temper is tried in humouring one person and conciliating another, he learns to be cautious and reserved and diplomatic, to drop hints and suggestions, to become in a word the first District Visitor of his parish. He flies to his wife for protection, and finds in her the most effective buffer against parochial collisions. Greek meets Greek when the vicar's wife meets the District Visitor. But the vicar himself sinks into a parochial nobody, a being as sacred and as powerless as the Lama of Thibet.

It was hardly to be expected that the progress of religion and charitable feeling should fail to raise up formidable rivals to the District Visitor. To the more ecclesiastical mind she is hardly ecclesiastical enough for the prominent part she claims in the parochial system. Her lace and Parisian bonnet are an abomination. She has a trick of being terribly Protestant, and her Protestantism is somewhat dictatorial. On the other hand, to the energetic organizer whose ideal of a parish is a well-oiled machine turning out piety and charity without hitches or friction she is simply a parochial impediment. She has no system. Her visiting days are determined by somewhat eccentric considerations. Her almsgiving is regulated by no principle whatever. She carries silly likes and dislikes into her work among the poor. She rustles into wrath at any attempt to introduce order into her efforts, and regards it as a piece of ungrateful interference. She is always ready with threats of resignation, with petty suspicions of ill-treatment, with jealousies of her fellow-workers. We can hardly wonder that in ecclesiastical quarters she is retreating before the Sister of Mercy, while in the more organized parishes she is being superseded by the Deaconess. The Deaconess has nothing but contempt for the mere "volunteer" movement in charity. She has a strong sense of order and discipline, and a hatred of "francs-tireurs." Above all she is a woman of business. She is without home or child, and her time and labour are arranged with military precision. She has her theory of the poor and of what can be done for the poor, and she rides her hobby from morning to night with an equal contempt for the sentimental almsgiving of the District Visitor and for the warnings of the political economist. No doubt an amazing deal of good is done, but it is done in a methodical fashion that is a little trying to ordinary flesh and blood. The parish is elaborately tabulated. The poor are grouped and ticketed. The charitable agencies of the parish are put in connection with the hospital and the workhouse. This case is referred to the dispensary, that to the overseer. The Deaconess prides herself on not being "taken in." The washerwoman finds that her "outdoor allowance" has been ascertained and set off against her share in the distribution of alms. The pious old woman who has played off the charity of the church against the charity of the chapel is struck off the list. The miserable creature who drags out existence on a bit of bread and a cup of tea is kindly but firmly advised to try "the house." Nothing can be wiser, nothing more really beneficial to the poor, than the work of the Deaconess, but it is a little dry and mechanical. The ill-used wife of the drunkard sighs after the garrulous sympathy of the District Visitor. The old gossip and dawdle have disappeared from the parochial charity, but with them has gone a good deal of the social contact, the sympathy of rich with poor, in which its chief virtue lay. The very vicar sighs after a little human imperfection and irregularity as he reads the list of sick cases "to be visited this morning."

The one lingering touch of feminine weakness in the Deaconess comes out in her relations with the clergy. The Deaconess is not a "Sister"—she is most precise in enforcing the distinction—but she is a woman with a difference. She has not retired from the world, but a faint flavour of the nun hangs about her. She has left behind all thought of coquetry, but she prefers to work with a married clergyman. Her delicacy can just endure a celibate curate, but it shrinks aghast from a bachelor incumbent. We know a case where a bishop, anxious to retain a Deaconess in a poor parish, was privately informed that her stay would depend on the appointment of a married clergyman to the vacant living. On the other hand, a married clergyman is as great a trial to the Sister of Mercy as an unmarried one to the Deaconess. The "Sister" idealizes the priesthood as she idealizes the poor. Their poverty is a misfortune; their improvidence an act of faith; their superstition the last ray of poetic religion lingering in this world of scepticism and commonplace. All the regularity and sense of order which exists in the Sister's mind is concentrated on her own life in the sisterhood; she is punctilious about her "hours," and lives in a perpetual tinkle of little bells. But in her work among the poor she revolts from system or organization. She hates the workhouse. She looks upon a guardian or an overseer as an oppressor of the poor. She regards theories of pauperism as something very wicked and irreligious, and lavishes her alms with a perfect faith that good must come of it. In a word, she is absolutely unwise, but there is a poetry in her unwisdom that contrasts strangely with the sensible prose of the Deaconess. While the one enters in her book of statistics the number of uneducated children, the other is trotting along the street with little Tommy in one hand and little Polly in the other on their way to the school. She has washed their faces and tidied their hair, and believes she has done service to little angels. Tommy and Polly are very far from being angels, but both sides are the happier for the romantic hypothesis. There is a good deal of romance and sentiment in the Sister's view of her work among the poor; but it is a romance that nerves her to a certain grandeur of soul. A London clergyman in whose district the black fever had broken out could get no nurses among the panic-stricken neighbours. He telegraphed to a "Home," and next morning he found a lady-like girl on her knees on the floor of the infected house, scrubbing, cleaning, putting the worn-out mother to bed, hushing the children, nursing quietly and thoroughly as few nurses could do. The fever was beaten, and the little heroine went off at the call of another telegram to charge another battery of death. It is this chivalrous poetic side that atones for the many follies of Sisterhoods; for the pauperism they introduce among the poor, the cliquism of their inner life, the absurdities of their "holy obedience." Each of these charitable agencies in fact has its work to do, and does it in its own way. On paper there can be no doubt that the Sister of Mercy is the more attractive figure of the three. The incumbent of a heavy parish will probably turn with a smile to the more methodical labours of the Deaconess. But those who shrink alike from the idealism of one and the system of the other, who feel that the poor are neither angels nor wheels in a machine, and that the chief work to be done among them is the diffusion of kindly feeling and the drawing of class nearer to class, will probably prefer to either the old-fashioned District Visitor.

THE EARLY HISTORY OF OXFORD

THE EARLY HISTORY OF OXFORD

To most Oxford men, indeed to the common visitor of Oxford, the town seems a mere offshoot of the University. Its appearance is altogether modern; it presents hardly any monument that can vie in antiquity with the venerable fronts of colleges and halls. An isolated church here and there tells a different tale; but the largest of its parish churches is best known as the church of the University, and the church of St. Frideswide, which might suggest even to a careless observer some idea of the town's greatness before University life began, is known to most visitors simply as Christchurch Chapel. In all outer seeming Oxford appears a mere assemblage of indifferent streets that have grown out of the needs of the University, and this impression is heightened by its commercial unimportance. The town has no manufacture or trade. It is not even, like Cambridge, a great agricultural centre. Whatever importance it derived from its position on the Thames has been done away with by the almost total cessation of river navigation. Its very soil is in large measure in academical hands. As a municipality it seems to exist only by grace or usurpation of prior University privileges. It is not long since Oxford gained control over its own markets or its own police. The peace of the town is still but partially in the hands of its magistrates, and the riotous student is amenable only to university jurisdiction. Within the memory of living men the chief magistrate of the city on his entrance into office was bound to swear in a humiliating ceremony not to violate the privileges of the great academical body which reigned supreme within its walls.

Historically the very reverse of all this is really the case. So far is the University from being older than the city, that Oxford had already seen five centuries of borough life before a student appeared within its streets. Instead of its prosperity being derived from its connection with the University, that connection has probably been its commercial ruin. The gradual subjection both of markets and trade to the arbitrary control of an ecclesiastical corporation was inevitably followed by their extinction. The University found Oxford a busy, prosperous borough, and reduced it to a cluster of lodging-houses. It found it among the first of English municipalities, and it so utterly crushed its freedom that the recovery of some of the commonest rights of self-government has only been brought about by recent legislation. Instead of the Mayor being a dependant on Chancellor or Vice-Chancellor,

Chancellor and Vice-Chancellor have simply usurped the far older authority of the Mayor.

The story of the struggle which ended in this usurpation is one of the most interesting in our municipal annals, and it is one which has left its mark not on the town only but on the very constitution and character of the conquering University. But to understand the struggle, we must first know something of the town itself. At the earliest moment, then, when its academic history can be said to open, at the arrival of the legist Vacarius in the reign of Stephen, Oxford stood in the first rank of English municipalities. In spite of antiquarian fancies, it is certain that no town had arisen on its site for centuries after the departure of the Roman legions from the isle of Britain. The little monastery of St. Frideswide rises in the turmoil of the eighth century only to fade out of sight again without giving us a glimpse of the borough which gathered probably beneath its walls. The first definite evidence for its existence lies in a brief entry of the English Chronicle which records its seizure by the successor of Ælfred. But though the form of this entry shows the town to have been already considerable, we hear nothing more of it till the last terrible wrestle of England with the Dane, when its position on the borders of the Mercian and West-Saxon realms seems for the moment to have given it a political importance under Æthelred and Cnut strikingly analogous to that which it acquired in the Great Rebellion. Of the life of its burgesses in this earlier period of Oxford life we know little or nothing. The names of its parishes, St. Aldate, St. Ebbe, St. Mildred, and St. Edmund, show how early church after church gathered round the earlier church of St. Martin. The minster of St. Frideswide, in becoming the later cathedral, has brought down to our own times the memory of the ecclesiastical origins to which the little borough owed its existence. But the men themselves are dim to us. Their town-meeting, their Portmannimote, still lives in shadowy fashion as the Freeman's Common Hall; their town-mead is still Port-meadow. But it is only by later charters or the record of Domesday that we see them going on pilgrimage to the shrines of Winchester, or chaffering in their market-place, or judging and law-making in their husting, their merchant guild regulating trade, their reeve gathering his king's dues of tax or honey or marshalling his troop of burghers for the king's wars, their boats floating down the Thames towards London and paying the toll of a hundred herrings in Lent-tide to the Abbot of Abingdon by the way.

Of the conquest of Oxford by William the Norman we know nothing, though the number of its houses marked "waste" in the Survey seems to point to a desperate resistance. But the ruin was soon repaired. No city better illustrates the transformation of the land in the hands of its new masters, the sudden outburst of industrial effort, the sudden expansion of commerce and accumulation of wealth which followed the Conquest. The architectural glory of the town in fact dates from the settlement of the Norman within its walls. To the west of the town rose one of the stateliest of English castles, and in the meadows beneath the hardly less stately Abbey of Osney. In the fields to the north the last of the Norman kings raised his palace of Beaumont. The canons of St. Frideswide reared the church which still exists as the diocesan cathedral: the piety of the Norman earls rebuilt almost all the parish churches of the city and founded within their new castle walls the church of the canons of St. George.

But Oxford does more than illustrate this outburst of industrial effort; it does something towards explaining its cause. The most characteristic result of the Conquest was planted in the very heart of the town in the settlement of the Jew. Here as elsewhere the Jewry was a town within a town, with its own language, its own religion and law, its peculiar commerce, its peculiar dress. The policy of our foreign kings secured each Hebrew settlement from the common taxation, the common justice, the common obligations of Englishmen. No city bailiff could penetrate into the square of little streets which lay behind the present Town-hall; the Church itself was powerless against the synagogue that rose in haughty rivalry beside the cloister of St. Frideswide. The picture which Scott has given us in 'Ivanhoe' of Isaac of York, timid, silent, crouching under oppression, accurately as it represents our modern notions of the position of his race during the Middle Ages, is far from being borne out by historical fact. In England at least the attitude of the Jew is almost to the end an attitude of proud and even insolent defiance. His extortion was sheltered from the common law. His bonds were kept under the royal seal. A royal commission visited with heavy penalties any outbreak of violence against these "chattels" of the king. The thunders of the Church broke vainly on the yellow gaberdine of the Jew. In a well-known story of Eadmer's the Red King actually forbids the conversion of a Jew to the Christian faith : it was a poor exchange which would have robbed him of a valuable property and given him only a subject.

At Oxford the attitude of the Jewry towards the national religion showed a marked consciousness of this royal protection. Prior Philip of St. Frideswide complains bitterly of a certain Hebrew with the odd name of "Deus-cum-crescat," who stood at his door as the procession of the saint passed by, mocking at the miracles wrought at her shrine. Halting and then walking firmly on his feet, showing his hands clenched as if with palsy and then flinging open his fingers, the mocking Jew claimed gifts and oblations from the crowd who flocked to St. Frideswide's on the ground that such recoveries of limb and strength were quite as real as any Frideswide had wrought. But though sickness and death, in the prior's story, avenge the insult to his shrine, no earthly power, ecclesiastical or civil, seems to have ventured to meddle with "Deus-cum-crescat." The feud between the priory and the Jewry went on unchecked for a century more, to culminate in a daring act of fanaticism on the Ascension-day of 1268. As the usual procession of scholars and citizens returned from St. Frideswide's, a Jew suddenly burst from the group of his comrades in front of the synagogue, and snatching the crucifix from its bearer trod it under foot. But even in presence of such an outrage as this the terror of the Crown shielded the Jewry from any burst of popular indignation. The sentence of the king condemned the Jews of Oxford to erect a cross of marble on the spot where the crime was committed; but even this was remitted in part, and a less offensive place was allotted for the cross in an open plot by Merton College.

With the Jewish settlement began the cultivation of physical science in Oxford. The Hebrew instruction, the Hebrew books which he found among its rabbis, were the means by which Roger Bacon penetrated to the older world of material research. A medical school which we find established there and in high repute during the twelfth century can hardly have been other than Jewish: in the operation for the stone, which one of the stories in the 'Miracles of

St. Frideswide' preserves for us, we trace the traditional surgery which is still common in the East. But it is perhaps in a more purely material way that the Jewry at Oxford most directly influenced our academical history. There as elsewhere the Jew brought with him something more than the art or science which he had gathered at Cordova or Bagdad; he brought with him the new power of wealth. The erection of stately castles, of yet statelier abbeys, which followed the Conquest, the rebuilding of almost every cathedral or conventual church, marks the advent of the Jewish capitalist. No one can study the earlier history of our great monastic houses without finding the secret of that sudden outburst of industrial activity to which we owe the noblest of our minsters in the loans of the Jew. The bonds of many a great baron, the relics of many an abbey, lay pledged for security in the "Star-chamber" of the Jew.

His arrival at Oxford is marked by the military and ecclesiastical erections of its Norman earls. But a result of his presence, which bore more directly on the future of the town, was seen in the remarkable development of its domestic architecture. To the wealth of the Jew, to his need of protection against sudden outbursts of popular passion, very probably to the greater refinement of his social life, England owes the introduction of stone houses. Tradition attributes almost every instance of the earliest stone buildings of a domestic character to the Jew; and where the tradition can be tested, as at Bury St. Edmunds or Lincoln, it has proved to be in accordance with the facts. In Oxford nearly all the larger dwelling-houses which were subsequently converted into halls bore traces of their Jewish origin in their names, such as Moysey's Hall, Lombards', Jacob's Hall. It is a striking proof of the superiority of the Hebrew dwellings to the Christian houses around them that each of the successive town-halls of the borough had, before their expulsion, been houses of Jews. Such houses were abundant in the town, not merely in the purely Jewish quarter on Carfax but in the lesser Jewry which was scattered over the parish of St. Aldate; and we can hardly doubt that this abundance of substantial buildings in the town was at least one of the causes which drew teachers and students within its walls.

The same great event which flung down the Jewish settlement in the very heart of the English town bounded it to the west by the castle and the abbey of the conquerors. Oxford stood first on the line of great fortresses which, passing by Wallingford and Windsor to the Tower of London, guarded the course of the Thames. Its castellan, Robert D'Oilly, had followed William from Normandy and had fought by his side at Senlac. Oxfordshire was committed by the Conqueror to his charge; and he seems to have ruled it in rude, soldierly fashion, enforcing order, heaping up riches, tripling the taxation of the town, pillaging without scruple the older religious houses of the neighbourhood. It was only by ruthless exaction such as this that the work which William had set him to do could be done. Money was needed above all for the great fortress which held the town. The new castle rose on the eastern bank of the Thames, broken here into a number of small streamlets, one of which served as the deep moat which encircled its walls. A well marked the centre of the wide castle-court; to the north of it on a lofty mound rose the great keep; to the west the one tower which remains, the tower of St. George, frowned over the river and the mill. Without the walls of the fortress lay the Bailly, a space cleared by the merciless policy of the castellan, with the church of St. Peter le Bailly which still marks its extent.

The hand of Robert D'Oilly fell as heavily on the Church as on the townsmen. Outside the town lay a meadow belonging to the Abbey of Abingdon, which seemed suitable for the exercise of the soldiers of his garrison. The earl was an old plunderer of the Abbey; he had wiled away one of its finest manors from its Abbot Athelm; but his seizure of the meadow beside Oxford drove the monks to despair. Night and day they threw themselves weeping before the altar of the two English saints whose names were linked to the older glories of their house. But while they invoked the vengeance of

Dunstan and Æthelwold on their plunderer, the earl, fallen sick, tossed fever-smitten on his bed. At last Robert dreamt that he stood in a vast court, one of a crowd of nobles gathered round a throne whereon sate a lady passing fair. Before her knelt two brethren of the abbey, weeping for the loss of their mead and pointing out the castellan as the robber. The lady bade Robert be seized, and two youths hurried him away to the field itself, seated him on the ground, piled burning hay around him, smoked him, tossed haybands in his face, and set fire to his beard. The earl woke trembling at the divine discipline; he at once took boat for Abingdon, and restored to the monks the meadow he had reft from them. His terror was not satisfied by the restitution of his plunder, and he returned to set about the restoration of the ruined churches within and without the walls of Oxford. The tower of St. Michael, the doorway of St. Ebbe, the chancel arch of Holywell, the crypt and chancel of St. Peter's-in-the-East, are fragments of the work done by Robert and his house. But the great monument of the devotion of the D'Oillys rose beneath the walls of their castle. Robert, a nephew of the first castellan, had wedded Edith, a concubine of Henry I. The rest of the story we may tell in the English of Leland. "Edith used to walke out of Oxford Castelle with her gentlewomen to solace, and that oftentymes where yn a certen place in a tree, as often as she cam, a certain pyes used to gather to it, and ther to chattre, and as

it were to spek on to her, Edyth much mervelyng at
this matter, and was sumtyme sore ferid by it as by
a wonder." Radulf, a canon of St. Frideswide's, was
consulted on the marvel, and his counsel ended in
the erection of the priory of Osney beneath the walls
of the castle. The foundation of the D'Oillys became one of the wealthiest and largest of the English
abbeys; but of its vast church and lordly abbot's
house, the great quadrangle of its cloisters, the alms-
houses without its gate, the pleasant walks shaded
with stately elms beside the river, not a trace remains. Its bells alone were saved at the Dissolution
by their transfer to Christchurch.

The military strength of the castle of the D'Oillys
was tested in the struggle between Stephen and the
Empress. Driven from London by a rising of its
burghers at the very moment when the crown seemed
within her grasp, Maud took refuge at Oxford. In
the succeeding year Stephen found himself strong
enough to attack his rival in her stronghold; his
knights swam the river, fell hotly on the garrison
which had sallied without the walls to meet them,
chased them through the gates, and rushed pell-mell
with the fugitives into the city. Houses were burnt
and the Jewry sacked; the Jews, if tradition is to
be trusted, were forced to raise against the castle
the work that still bears the name of "Jews' Mount";
but the strength of its walls foiled the efforts of the
besiegers, and the attack died into a close blockade.

Maud was however in Stephen's grasp, and neither the loss of other fortresses nor the rigour of the winter could tear the king from his prey. Despairing of relief, the Empress at last resolved to break through the enemy's lines. Every stream was frozen and the earth covered with snow, when clad in white and with three knights in white garments as her attendants Maud passed unobserved through the outposts, crossed the Thames upon the ice, and made her way to Abingdon and the fortress of Wallingford.

With the surrender which followed the military history of Oxford ceases till the Great Rebellion. Its political history had still to attain its highest reach in the Parliament of De Montfort. The great assemblies held at Oxford under Cnut, Stephen, and Henry III., are each memorable in their way. With the first closed the struggle between Englishman and Dane, with the second closed the conquest of the Norman, with the third began the regular progress of constitutional liberty. The position of the town, on the border between the England that remained to the West-Saxon kings and the England that had become the "Danelagh" of their northern assailants, had from the first pointed it out as the place where a union between Dane and Englishman could best be brought about. The first attempt was foiled by the savage treachery of Æthelred the Unready. The death of Swegen and the return of Cnut to Denmark left an opening for a reconciliation, and Englishmen

and Danes gathered at Oxford round the king. But
all hope was foiled by the assassination of the Law-
men of the Seven Danish Boroughs, Sigeferth and
Morcar, who fell at a banquet by the hand of the
minister Eadric, while their followers threw themselves into the tower of St. Frideswide and perished
in the flames that consumed it. The overthrow of
the English monarchy avenged the treason. But
Cnut was of nobler stuff than Æthelred, and his
conquest of the realm was followed by the gathering
of a new gemote at Oxford to resume the work of
reconciliation which Eadric had interrupted. Englishman and Dane agreed to live together as one people
under Eadgar's Law, and the wise government of
the King completed in the long years of his reign
the task of national fusion. The conquest of William
set two peoples a second time face to face upon the
same soil, and it was again at Oxford that by his
solemn acceptance and promulgation of the Charter
of Henry I. in solemn parliament Stephen closed the
period of military tyranny, and began the union of
Norman and Englishman into a single people. These
two great acts of national reconciliation were fit pre-
ludes for the work of the famous assembly which
has received from its enemies the name of "the Mad
Parliament." In the June of 1258 the barons met
at Oxford under earl Simon de Montfort to commence
the revolution to which we owe our national liberties.
Followed by long trains of men in arms and sworn
together by pledges of mutual fidelity, they wrested

from Henry III. the great reforms which, frustrated for the moment, have become the basis of our constitutional system. On the "Provisions of Oxford" followed the regular establishment of parliamentary representation and power, of a popular and responsible ministry, of the principle of local self-government.

From parliaments and sieges, from Jew and castellan, it is time to turn back to the humbler annals of the town itself. The first event that lifts it into historic prominence is its league with London. The "bargemen" of the borough seem to have already existed before the Conquest, and to have been closely united from the first with the more powerful guild, the "boatmen" or "merchants" of the capital. In both cases it is probable that the bodies bearing this name represented what in later language was known as the merchant guild of the town; the original association, that is, of its principal traders for purposes of mutual protection, of commerce, and of self-government. Royal recognition enables us to trace the merchant guild of Oxford from the time of Henry I.; even then indeed lands, islands, pastures already belonged to it, and amongst them the same "Port-meadow" or "Town-mead" so familiar to Oxford men pulling lazily on a summer's noon to Godstow, and which still remains the property of the freemen of the town. The connection between the two cities and their guilds was primarily one of traffic. Prior even to the Conquest, "in the time of King Eadward and Abbot Ordric," the channel of the river running beneath the walls of the Abbey of Abingdon became so blocked up "that boats could scarce pass as far as Oxford." It was at the joint prayer of the burgesses of London and Oxford that the abbot dug a new channel through the meadow to the south of his church, the two cities engaging that each barge should pay a toll of a hundred herrings on its passage during Lent. But the union soon took a constitutional form. The earliest charter of the capital which remains in detail is that of Henry I., and from the charter of his grandson we find a similar date assigned to the liberties of Oxford. The customs and exemptions of its burghers are granted by Henry II., "as ever they enjoyed them in the time of King Henry my grandfather, and in like manner as my citizens of London hold them." This identity of municipal privileges is of course common to many other boroughs, for the charter of London became the model for half the charters of the kingdom; what is peculiar to Oxford is the federal bond which in Henry II.'s time already linked the two cities together. In case of any doubt or contest about judgment in their own court the burgesses of Oxford were empowered to refer the matter to the decision of London, "and whatever the citizens of London shall adjudge in such cases shall be deemed right." The judicial usages, the municipal rights of each city were assimilated by Henry's charter. "Of whatever matter they shall be put in plea, they shall deraign themselves according to the law and customs of the city of London and not otherwise, because they and the citizens of London are of one and the same custom, law, and liberty."

In no two cities has municipal freedom experienced a more different fate than in the two that were so closely bound together. The liberties of London waxed greater and greater till they were lost in the general freedom of the realm: those of Oxford were trodden under foot till the city stood almost alone in its bondage among the cities of England. But it would have been hard for a burgher of the twelfth century, flushed with the pride of his new charter, or fresh from the scene of a coronation where he had stood side by side with the citizens of London and Winchester as representing one of the chief cities of the realm, to have dreaded any danger to the liberties of his borough from the mob of half-starved boys who were beginning to pour year after year into the town. The wealthy merchant who passed the group of shivering students huddled round a teacher as poor as themselves in porch and doorway, or dropped his alms into the cap of the mendicant scholar, could hardly discern that beneath rags and poverty lay a power greater than the power of kings, the power for which Becket had died and which bowed Henry to penance and humiliation. On all but its eastern side indeed the town was narrowly hemmed in by jurisdictions independent of its own. The precincts of the Abbey of Osney, the wide bailly of the castle, bounded it narrowly on the west. To the north, stretching away to the little church of St. Giles, lay the fields of the royal manor of Beaumont. The Abbot of Abingdon, whose woods of Cumnor and Bagley closed the southern horizon, held his leet court in the small hamlet of Grampound beyond the bridge. Nor was the whole space within its walls altogether subject to the self-government of the citizens. The Jewry, a town within a town, lay isolated and exempt from the common justice or law in the very heart of the borough. Scores of householders, dotted over the various streets, were tenants of abbey or castle, and paid neither suit nor service to the city court. But within these narrow bounds and amidst these various obstacles the spirit of municipal liberty lived a life the more intense that it was so closely cabined and confined.

It was in fact at the moment when the first Oxford students appeared within its walls that the city attained complete independence. The twelfth century, the age of the Crusades, of the rise of the scholastic philosophy, of the renewal of classical learning, was also the age of a great communal movement, that stretched from Italy along the Rhone and the Rhine, the Seine and the Somme, to England. The same great revival of individual, human life in the industrial masses of the feudal world that hurried half Christendom to the Holy Land, or gathered hundreds of eager faces round the lecture-stall of Abelard, beat back Barbarossa from the walls of Alessandria and nerved the burghers of Northern France to struggle as at Amiens for liberty. In England the same spirit took a milder and perhaps more practical form, from the different social and political conditions with which it had to deal. The quiet townships of Teutonic England had no traditions of a Roman past to lure them on, like the cities of Italy, into dreams of sovereignty. Their ruler was no foreign Cæsar, distant enough to give a chance for resistance, but a king near at hand and able to enforce obedience and law. The king's peace shielded them from that terrible oppression of the mediæval baronage which made liberty with the cities of Germany a matter of life or death. The peculiarity of municipal life in fact in England is that instead of standing apart from and in contrast with the general life around it the progress of the English town moved in perfect harmony with that of the nation at large. The earlier burgher was the freeman within the walls, as the peasant-ceorl was the freeman without. Freedom went with the possession of land in town as in country. The citizen held his burgher's rights by his tenure of the bit of ground on which his tenement stood. He was the king's free tenant, and like the rural tenants he owed his lord dues of money or kind. In township or manor alike the king's reeve gathered this rental, administered justice, commanded the little troop of soldiers that the spot was bound to furnish in time of war. The progress of municipal freedom, like that of national freedom, was wrought rather by the slow growth of wealth and of popular spirit, by the necessities of kings, by the policy of a few great statesmen, than by the sturdy revolts that wrested liberty from the French seigneur or the century of warfare that broke the power of the Cæsars in the plain of the Po.

Much indeed that Italy or France had to win by the sword was already the heritage of every English freeman within walls or without. The common assembly in which their own public affairs were discussed and decided, the borough-mote to which every burgher was summoned by the town-bell swinging out of the town-tower, had descended by traditional usage from the customs of the first English settlers in Britain. The close association of the burghers in the sworn brotherhood of the guild was a Teutonic custom of immemorial antiquity. Gathered at the guild supper round the common fire, sharing the common meal, and draining the guild cup, the burghers added to the tie of mere neighbourhood that of loyal association, of mutual counsel, of mutual aid. The regulation of internal trade, all lesser forms of civil jurisdiction, fell quietly and without a struggle into the hands of the merchant guild. The rest of their freedom was bought with honest cash. The sale of charters brought money to the royal treasury, exhausted by Norman wars, by the herd of mercenaries, by Crusades, by the struggle with France. The towns bought first the commutation of the uncertain charges to which they were subject at the royal will for a fixed annual rent. Their purchase of the right of internal justice followed. Last came the privilege of electing their own magistrates, of enjoying complete self-government. Oxford had already passed through the earlier steps of this emancipation before the conquest of the Norman. Her citizens assembled in their Portmannimote, their free self-ruling assembly. Their merchant-guild leagued with that of London. Their dues to the Crown are assessed in Domesday at a fixed sum of honey and coin. The charter of Henry II. marks the acquisition by Oxford, probably at a far earlier date, of judicial and commercial freedom. Liberty of external commerce was given by the exemption of its citizens from toll on the king's lands; the decision of either political or judicial affairs was left to their borough-mote. The highest point of municipal independence was reached when the Charter of John substituted a mayor of their own choosing for the mere bailiff of the Crown.

It is hard in dry constitutional details such as these to realize the quick pulse of popular life that stirred such a community as Oxford. Only a few names, of street and lane, a few hints gathered from obscure records, enable one to see the town of the twelfth or thirteenth century. The church of St. Martin in the very heart of it, at the "Quatrevoix" or Carfax where its four roads meet, was the centre of the city's life. The Town-mote was held in its churchyard. Justice was administered by mayor and bailiff sitting beneath the low shed, the "penniless bench" of later times, without its eastern wall. Its bell summoned the burghers to counsel or to arms. Around the church lay the trade-guilds, ranged as in some vast encampment; Spicery and Vintnery to the south, Fish Street falling noisily down to the Bridge, the corn market occupying then as now the street which led to Northgate, the stalls of the butchers ranged in their "Butcher-row" along the road to the castle. Close beneath the church to the south-east lay a nest of huddled lanes broken by a stately synagogue and traversed from time to time by the yellow gaberdine of the Jew, whose burying-place lay far away to the eastward on the site of the present Botanic Garden. Soldiers from the castle rode clashing through the narrow streets; the bells of Osney clanged from the swampy meadows; long processions of pilgrims wound past the Jewry to the shrine of Saint Frideswide. It was a rough time, and frays were common enough,—now the sack of a Jew's house, now burgher drawing knife on burgher, now an outbreak of the young student lads, who grew every day in numbers and audacity. But as yet the town seemed well in hand. The clang of the city bell called every citizen to his door, the summons of the mayor brought trade after trade with bow in hand and banners flying to enforce the king's peace. Order and freedom seemed absolutely secure, and there was no sign which threatened that century of disorder, of academical and ecclesiastical usurpation, which humbled the municipal freedom of Oxford to the dust.

THE HOME OF OUR ANGEVIN KINGS

THE HOME OF OUR ANGEVIN KINGS

FOR those who possess historic tastes, slender purses, and an exemption from Alpine mania, few holidays are more pleasant than a lounge along the Loire. There is always something refreshing in the companionship of a fine river, and whatever one may think of its summer sands Loire through the spring and the autumn is a very fine river indeed. There is, besides, the pleasantest variety of scenery as one wanders along from the sombre granite of Brittany to the volcanic cinder-heaps of Auvergne. There is the picturesque contrast between the vast dull corn-flats to the north of the great river and the vines and acacias to the south. There is the same contrast in an ethnological point of view, for one is traversing the watershed that parts two different races, and enough of difference still remains in dialect and manner to sever the Acquitanian from the Frank. And historically every day brings one across some castle or abbey or town that has been hitherto a mere name in the pages of Lingard or Sismondi, but which one actual glimpse changes into a living fact. There are few tracts of country indeed where the historical interest ranges equally over so long a space of time. The river which was the "revolutionary torrent" of Carrier had been the highway for the Northmen into the heart of Carolingian France. Saumur blends the tenth century and the sixteenth together in the names of Gelduin and Du Plessis; Chinon brings into contact the age of the Plantagenets and the age of Joan of Arc. From the mysterious dolmen and the legendary well to the stone that marks the fusillade of the heroes of La Vendée there is a continuous chain of historic event in these central provinces. Every land has its pet periods of history, and the brilliant chapters of M. Michelet are hardly needed to tell us how thoroughly France identifies the splendour and infamy of the Renascence with the Loire. Blois, Amboise, Chenonceaux, embody still in the magnificence of their ruin the very spirit of Catherine de Medicis, of Francis, of Diana of Poitiers. To Englishmen the relics of an earlier period have naturally a greater charm. Nothing clears one's ideas about the character of the Angevin rule, the rule of Henry II. or Richard or John, so thoroughly as a stroll through Anjou.

There the Angevin Counts are as vivid, as real, as the Angevin Kings are on English soil unreal and dim. Hardly a building in his realm preserves the memory of Henry II.; Richard is a mere visitor to English shores; Beaulieu alone and the graven tomb at Worcester enable us to realize John. But along the Loire these Angevin rulers meet us in river-bank and castle and bridge and town. Their names are familiar words still through the length and breadth of the land. At Angers men show you the vast hospital of Henry II., while the suburb around it is the creation of his son. And not only do the men come vividly before us, but they come before us in another and a fresher light. To us they are strangers and foreigners, stern administrators, exactors of treasure, tyrants to whose tyranny, sometimes just and sometimes unjust, England was destined to owe her freedom. But for Anjou the period of their rule was the period of a peace and fame and splendour that never came back save in the shadowy resurrection under King René. Her soil is covered with monuments of their munificence, of their genuine care for the land of their race. Nine-tenths of her great churches, in the stern grandeur of their vaulting, their massive pillars, their capitals breaking into the exquisite foliage of the close of the century, witness to the pious liberality of sovereigns who in England were the oppressors of the Church, and who when doomed to endow a religious house in their realm did it by turning its inhabitants out of an already existing one and giving it simply a new name. As one walks along the famous Levee, the gigantic embankment along the Loire by which Henry saved the valley from inundation, or as one looks at his hospitals at Angers or Le Mans, it is hard not to feel a sympathy and admiration for the man from whom one shrinks coldly under the Martyrdom at Canterbury. There is a French side to the character of these Kings which, though English historians have disregarded it, is worth regarding if only because it really gave the tone to their whole life and rule. But it is a side which can only be understood when we study these Angevins in Anjou.

To the English traveller Angers is in point of historic interest without a rival among the towns of France. Rouen indeed is the cradle of our Norman dynasty as Angers of our Plantagenet dynasty; but the Rouen of the Dukes has almost vanished while Angers remains the Angers of the Counts. The physiognomy of the place—if we may venture to use the term—has been singularly preserved. Few towns have it is true suffered more from the destructive frenzy of the Revolution; gay boulevards have replaced "the flinty ribs of this contemptuous city," the walls which play their part in Shakspere's 'King John'; the noblest of its abbeys has been swept away to make room for a Prefecture; four churches were demolished at a blow to be replaced by the dreariest of squares; the tombs of its later dukes have disappeared from the Cathedral. In spite however of new faubourgs, new bridges, and new squares, Angers still retains the impress of the middle ages; its steep and narrow streets, its dark tortuous alleys, the fantastic woodwork of its houses, the sombre grimness of the slate-rock out of which the city is built, defy even the gay audacity of Imperialist prefects to modernize them. One climbs up from the busy quay along the Mayenne into a city which is still the city of the Counts. From Geoffry Greygown to John Lackland there is hardly one who has not left his name stamped on church or cloister or bridge or hospital. The stern tower of St. Aubin recalls in its founder Geoffry himself; the nave of St. Maurice, the choir of St. Martin's, the walls of Roncevray, the bridge over Mayenne, proclaim the restless activity of Fulc Nerra; Geoffry Martel rests beneath the ruins of St. Nicholas on its height across the river; beyond the walls to the south is the site of the burial-place of Fulc Rechin; one can tread the very palace halls to which Geoffry Plantagenet led home his English bride; the suburb of Roncevray, studded with buildings of an exquisite beauty, is almost the creation of Henry Fitz-Empress and his sons.

But, apart from its historical interest, Angers is a mine of treasure to the archæologist or the artist. In the beauty and character of its site it strongly resembles Le Mans. The river Mayenne comes down from the north, from its junction with the Sarthe, edged on either side by low ranges of *coteaux* which approaching it nearly on the west leave room along its eastern bank for vast level flats of marshy meadow land, cut through by white roads and long poplar-rows—meadows which in reality represent the old river-bed in some remote geological age before it had shrunk to its present channel. Below Angers the valley widens, and as the Mayenne coils away to Ponts de Ce it throws out on either side broad flats, rich in grass and golden flowers, and scored with rhines as straight and choked with water-weeds as the rhines of Somersetshire. It is across these lower meadows, from the base of the abbey walls of St. Nicholas, that one gets the finest view of Angers, the colossal mass of its castle, the two delicate towers of the Cathedral rising sharp against the sky, the stern belfry of St. Aubin. Angers stands in fact on a huge block of slate-rock, thrown forward from one of the higher plateaux which edge the marshy meadows, and closing up to the river in what was once a cliff as abrupt as that of Le Mans. Pleasant boulevards curve away in a huge semicircle from the river, and between these boulevards and the Mayenne lies the dark old town pierced by steep lanes and break-neck alleys. On the highest point of the block and approached by the steepest lane of all stands the Cathedral of St. Maurice, the tall slender towers of its western front and the fantastic row of statues which fill the arcade between them contrasting picturesquely enough with the bare grandeur of its interior, where the broad, low vaulting reminds us that we are on the architectural border of northern and southern Europe. St. Maurice is in the strictest sense the mother church of the town. M. Michelet has with singular lucklessness selected Angers as the type of a feudal city; with the one exception of the Castle of St. Louis it is absolutely without a trace of the feudal impress. Up to the Revolution it remained the most ecclesiastical of French towns. Christianity found the small Roman borough covering little more than the space on the height above the river afterwards occupied by the Cathedral precincts, planted its church in the midst of it, buttressed it to north and south with the great Merovingian Abbeys of St. Aubin and St. Serge, and linked them together by a chain of inferior foundations that entirely covered its eastern side. From the river on the south to the river on the north Angers lay ringed in by a belt of priories and churches and abbeys. Of the greatest of these, that of St. Aubin, only one huge tower remains, but fragments of it are still to be seen embedded in the buildings of the Prefecture—above all a Romanesque arcade, fretted with tangled imagery and apocalyptic figures of the richest work of the eleventh century. The Abbey of St. Serge still stands to the north of Angers; its vast gardens and fishponds turned into the public gardens of the town, its church spacious and beautiful with a noble choir that may perhaps recall the munificence of Geoffry Martel. Of the rivals of these two great houses two only remain. Portions of the Carolingian Church of St. Martin, built by the wife of Emperor Louis le Debonnaire, are now in use as a tobacco warehouse; the pretty ruin of Toussaint, not at all unlike our own Tintern, stands well cared for in the gardens of the Museum.

But, interesting as these relics are, it is not ecclesiastical Angers that the English traveller instinctively looks for; it is the Angers of the Counts, the birthplace of the Plantagenets. It is only in their own capital indeed that we fully understand our Angevin Kings, that we fully realize that they were Angevins. To an English schoolboy Henry II. is little more than the murderer of Becket and the friend of Fair Rosamund. Even an English student finds it hard after all the labours of Professor Stubbs to lay hold of either Henry or his sons. In spite of their versatile ability and of the mark which they have left on our judicature, our municipal liberty, our political constitution, the first three Plantagenets are to most of us little more than dim shapes of strange manner and speech, hurrying to their island realm to extort money, to enforce good government, and then hurrying back to Anjou. But there is hardly a boy in the streets of Angers to whom the name of Henry Fitz-Empress is strange, who could not point to the ruins of his bridge or the halls of his Hospice, or tell of the great "Levee" by which the most beneficent of Angevin Counts saved the farmers' fields from the floods of the Loire. Strangers in England, the first three Plantagenets are at home in the sunny fields along the Mayenne. The history of Anjou, the character of the Counts, their forefathers, are the keys to the subtle policy, to the strangely-mingled temper of Henry and his sons. The countless robber-holds of the Angevin noblesse must have done much towards the steady resolve with which they bridled feudalism in their island realm. The crowd of ecclesiastical foundations that ringed in their Angevin capital hardly failed to embitter, if not to suggest, their jealousy of the Church.

Of the monuments of the Counts which illustrate our own history, the noblest, in spite of its name, is the Bishop's Palace to the north of the Cathedral. The residence of the Bishop was undoubtedly at first the residence of the Counts, and the tradition which places its transfer as far back as the days of Ingelger can hardly be traced to any earlier source than the local annalist of the seventeenth century. It is at least probable that the occupation of the Palace by the Bishop did not take place till after the erection of the Castle on the site of the original Evêché in the time of St. Louis; and this is confirmed by the fact that the well-known description of Angers by Ralph de Diceto places the Comitial Palace of the twelfth century in the north-east quarter of the town —on the exact site, that is, of the present episcopal residence. But if this identification be correct, there is no building in the town which can compare with it in historical interest for Englishmen. The chapel beneath, originally perhaps simply the substructure of the building, dates from the close of the eleventh century; the fine hall above, with its grand row of windows looking out upon the court, from the earlier half of the twelfth. It was to the building as it actually stands therefore that Geoffry Plantagenet must have brought home his English bride, Maud the Empress, the daughter of our Henry I., along the narrow streets hung with gorgeous tapestries and filled with long trains of priests and burghers. To Angers that day represented the triumphant close of a hundred years' struggle with Normandy; to England it gave the line of its Plantagenet Kings.

The proudest monuments of the sovereigns who sprang from this match, our Henry the Second and his sons, lie not in Angers itself but in the suburb across the river. The suburb seems to have originated in the chapel of Roncevray, the Roman-like masonry of whose exterior may date back as far as Fulc Nerra in the tenth century. But its real importance dates from Henry Fitz-Empress. It is characteristic of the temper and policy of the first of our Plantagenet Kings that in Anjou, as in England, no religious house claimed him as its founder. Here indeed the Papal sentence on his part in the murder of Archbishop Thomas compelled him to resort to the ridiculous trick of turning the canons out of Waltham to enable him to refound it as a priory of his own without cost to the royal exchequer. But in his Continental dominions he did not even stoop to the pretence of such a foundation. No abbey figured among the costly buildings with which he adorned his birth-place Le Mans. It was as if in direct opposition to the purely monastic feeling that he devoted his wealth to the erection of the Hospitals at Angers and Le Mans. It is a relief, as we have said —a relief which one can only get here—to see the softer side of Henry's nature represented in works of mercy and industrial utility. The bridge of Angers, like the bridges of Tours and Saumur, dates back to the first of the Count-Kings. Henry seems to have been the Pontifex Maximus of his day, while his care for the means of industrial communication points to that silent growth of the new mercantile class which the rule of the Angevins did so much to foster. But a memorial of him, hardly less universal, is the Lazar-house or hospital. One of the few poetic legends that break the stern story of the Angevins is the tale of Count Fulc the Good, how, journeying along Loire-side towards Tours, he saw just as the towers of St. Martin's rose before him in the distance a leper full of sores, who put by his offer of alms and desired to be borne to the sacred city. Amid the gibes of his courtiers the good count lifted him in his arms and carried him along bank and bridge. As they entered the town the leper vanished from their sight, and men told how Fulc had borne an angel unawares. Little of his ancestor's tenderness or poetry lingered in the practical utilitarian mind of Henry Fitz Empress; but the simple Hospice in the fields by Le Mans or the grand Hospital of St. John in the suburb

Y

of Angers displayed an enlightened care for the physical condition of his people which is all the more striking that in him and his sons it had probably little connexion with the usual motives of religious charity which made such works popular in the middle ages, but, like the rest of their administrative system, was a pure anticipation of modern feeling. There are few buildings more complete or more beautiful in their completeness than the Hospital of St. John; the vast hall with its double row of slender pillars, the exquisite chapel, trembling in the pure grace of its details on the very verge of Romanesque, the engaged shafts of the graceful cloister. The erection of these buildings probably went on through the whole reigns of our three Angevin sovereigns, but the sterner and simpler hall called the Lazar-house beside with its three aisles and noble sweep of wide arches is clearly of the date of Henry alone. It was occupied when I visited it some years ago as a brewery, but never was brewer more courteous, more genuinely archæological, than its occupant. Throughout these central provinces indeed, as throughout Normandy, the enlightened efforts of the Government have awakened a respect for and pride in their national monuments which extends even to the poorest of the population. Few buildings of a really high class are now left to ruin and desecration as they were twenty years ago; unfortunately their rescue from the destruction of time is too often followed by the more destructive attack of the restorer. And in almost every town of any provincial importance one may obtain what in England it is simply ridiculous to ask for, a really intelligent history of the place itself and a fair description of the objects of interest which it contains.

The broken ruins of the Pont de Treilles, the one low tower above the river Mayenne which remains of the walls around the suburb of Roncevray, show the price which Henry and his sons set on these costly buildings. They have a special interest in Angevin history, for they were the last legacy of the Counts to their capital. Across the river, at the south-west corner of the town itself, stands the huge fortress that commemorates the close of their rule, the castle begun by the French conqueror, Philip Augustus, and completed by his descendant St. Louis. From the wide flats below Angers, where Mayenne rolls lazily on to the Loire, one looks up awed at the colossal mass which seems to dwarf even the minster beside it, at its dark curtains, its fosse trenched deep in the rock, its huge bastions chequered with iron-like bands of slate and unrelieved by art of sculptor or architect. It is as if the conquerors of the Angevins had been driven to express in this huge monument the very temper of the men from whom they reft Anjou, their grand, repulsive isolation, their dark pitiless power.

It is a relief to turn from this castle to that southern fortress which the Counts made their home.

A glance at the flat tame expanse of Anjou northward of the Loire explains at once why its sovereigns made their favourite sojourn in the fairer districts south of the river. There are few drives more enjoyable than a drive along the Vienne to the royal retreat of Chinon. The country is rich and noble, deep in grass and maize and corn, with meadows set in low broad hedgerows, and bare scratchy vineyards along the slopes. The road is lined with acacias, Tennyson's "milk-white bloom" hanging from their tender feathery boughs, and here beneath the hot sun of the South the acacia is no mere garden shrub but one of the finest and most graceful of trees. Everywhere along the broad sunlit river of Vienne nature is rich and lavish, and nowhere richer or more lavish than where, towering high on the scarped face of its own grey cliff above the street of brown little houses edged narrowly in between river and rock, stands the favourite home of our Angevin Kings.

It is only in one or two points amidst the great mass of stately buildings which is known as the castle of Chinon that their hand can be traced now. The base of the Tour du Moulay, where tradition says the Grand Master of the Templars was imprisoned by Philippe le Bel, is a fine vault of twelfth-century date, which may have been the work of Henry II., and can hardly be later than his sons. But something of its original character as a luxurious retreat lingers still in the purpose to which the ground within the walls has been devoted; it serves as a garden for the townsfolk of Chinon, and is full of pleasant shadowy walks and flowers, and gay with children's games and laughter. And whatever else may have changed, the same rich landscape lies around that Henry must have looked on when he rode here to die, as we look on it now from the deep recessed windows of the later hall where Joan of Arc stood before the disguised Dauphin. Beneath is the broad bright Vienne coming down in great gleaming curves from Isle-Bouchard, and the pretty spire of St. Maurice, Henry's own handiwork perhaps, soaring lightly out of the tangled little town at our feet. Beyond, broken with copse and hedgerow and cleft by the white road to Loudun, rise the slopes of Pavilly leading the eye round, as it may have led the dying eye of the king, to the dim blue reaches of the west where Fontevraud awaited him.

No scene harmonizes more thoroughly than Fontevraud with the thoughts which its name suggests. A shallow valley which strikes away southward through a break in the long cliff-wall along the Loire narrows as it advances into a sterner gorge, rough with forest greenery. The grey escarpments of rock that jut from the sides of this gorge are pierced here and there with the peculiar cellars and cave-dwellings of the country, and a few rude huts which dot their base gather as the road mounts steeply through this wilder scenery into a little lane of cottages that forms the village of Fontevraud. But it is almost suddenly that the great abbey church round which the village grew up stands out in one colossal mass from the western hill-slope; and in its very solitude and the rock-like grandeur of its vast nave, its noble apse, its low central tower, there is something that marks it as a fit resting-place for kings. Nor does its present use as a prison-chapel jar much on those who have grown familiar with the temper of the early Plantagenets. At the moment of my visit the choir of convicts were practising the music of a mass in the eastern portion of the church, which with the transepts has now been set apart for divine service, and the wild grandeur of the music, unrelieved by any treble, seemed to express in a way that nothing else could the spirit of the Angevins. "From the devil we come, and to the devil we go," said Richard. In spite of the luckless restoration to which their effigies have been submitted—and no sight makes us long more ardently that the "Let it alone" of Lord Melbourne had wandered from politics into archæology—it is still easy to read in the faces of the two King-Counts the secret of their policy and their fall. That of Henry II. is clearly a portrait. Nothing could be less ideal than the narrow brow, the large prosaic eyes, the coarse full cheeks, the sensual dogged jaw, that combine somehow into a face far higher than its separate details, and which is marked by a certain sense of power and command. No countenance could be in stronger contrast with his son's, and yet in both there is the same look of repulsive isolation from men. Richard's is a face of cultivation and refinement, but there is a strange severity in the small delicate mouth and in the compact brow of the lion-hearted king which realizes the verdict of his day. To an historical student one glance at these faces as they lie here beneath the vault raised by their ancestor, the fifth Count Fulc, tells more than pages of chronicles; but Fontevraud is far from being of interest to historians alone. In its architectural detail, in its Romanesque work, and in its strangely beautiful cinque-cento revival of the Romanesque, in its cloister and Glastonbury kitchen, it is a grand study for the artist or the archæologist; but these are merits which it shares with other French minsters. To an English visitor it will ever find its chief attraction in the Tombs of the Kings.

CAPRI

I

CAPRI

WE can hardly wonder at the love of artists for Capri, for of all the winter resorts of the South Capri is beyond question the most beautiful. Physically indeed it is little more than a block of limestone which has been broken off by some natural convulsion from the promontory of Sorrento, and changed by the strait of blue water which now parts it from the mainland into the first of a chain of islands which stretch across the Bay of Naples. But the same forces which severed it from the continent have given a grandeur and variety to its scenery which contrast in a strangely picturesque way with the narrowness of its bounds. There are few coast-lines which can rival in sublimity the coast-line around Capri; the cliff wall of sheer rock broken only twice by little dips which serve as landing-places for the island, and pierced at its base by "blue grottoes" and "green grottoes" which have become famous from the strange play of light within their depths. The reader of Hans Andersen's 'Improvisatore' will remember one of these caverns as the scene of its closing adventure; but, strange as Andersen's description is, it is far less strange than the scene which he sketches, the deep blue light which turns the rocks into turquoise and emerald or the silvery look of the diver as he plunges into the waves. Twice in their course the cliffs reach a height of thirteen hundred feet above the sea, but their grandeur is never the barren grandeur of our Northern headlands: their sternest faces are softened with the vegetation of the South; the myrtle finds root in every cranny and the cactus clings to the bare rock front from summit to base. A cliff wall hardly inferior in grandeur to that of the coast runs across the midst of the island, dividing it into an upper and a lower plateau, with no means of communication save the famous rock stairs, the "Steps of Anacapri," now, alas, replaced by a daring road which has been driven along the face of the cliff.

The upper plateau of Anacapri is cold and without any striking points of scenery, but its huge mass serves as an admirable shelter to Capri below, and it is with Capri that the ordinary visitor is alone concerned. The first thing which strikes one is the smallness of the place. The whole island is only some four miles long and a mile and a half across, and, as we have seen, a good half of this space is practically inaccessible. But it is just the diminutive size of Capri which becomes one of its greatest charms. It would be hard in fact to find any part of the world where so much and such varied beauty is packed into so small a space. The visitor who lands from Naples or Sorrento mounts steeply up the slopes of a grand amphitheatre flanked on either side by the cliffs of St. Michael and Anacapri to the white line of the village on the central ridge with the strange Saracenic domes of its church lifted weirdly against the sky. Over the crest of this ridge a counter valley falls as steeply to the south till it reaches a plateau crowned with the grey mass of a convent, and then plunges over crag and cliff back again to the sea. To the east of these central valleys a steep rise of ground ends in the ruins of the Palace of Tiberius and the great headland which fronts the headland of Sorrento. Everywhere the forms of the scenery are on the largest and boldest scale. The great conical Tors, Tuorogrande and Tuoro-piccolo, the boldly scarped rock of Castiglione with its crown of mediæval towers, lead up the eye to the huge cliff wall of Anacapri, where, a thousand feet above, the white hermitage on Monte Solaro glimmers out fitfully from its screen of cloud.

Among the broken heights to the east or in the two central valleys there are scores of different walks and a hundred different nooks, and each walk and nook has its own independent charm. Steeps clothed from top to bottom in the thick greenery of the lemon or orange; sudden breaks like that of Metromania where a blue strip of sea seems to have been cunningly let in among the rocks; backgrounds of tumbled limestone; slopes dusty grey with wild cactus; thickets of delightful greenery where one lies hidden in the dense scrub of myrtle and arbutus; olive-yards creeping thriftily up the hill-sides and over the cliffs and down every slope and into every rock-corner where the Caprese peasant-farmer can find footing; homesteads of grey stone with low domed Oriental roofs on which women sit spinning, their figures etched out against the sky; gardens where the writhed fig-trees stand barely waiting for the foliage of the spring; nooks amidst broken boulders and vast fingers of rock with the dark mass of the carouba flinging its shade over them; heights from which one looks suddenly northward and southward over a hundred miles of sea—this is Capri. The sea is everywhere. At one turn its waters go flashing away unbroken by a single sail towards the far-off African coast where the Caprese boatmen are coral-fishing through the hot summer months; at another the eye ranges over the tumbled mountain masses above Amalfi to the dim sweep of coast where the haze hides the temples of Pæstum; at another the Bay of Naples opens suddenly before us, Vesuvius and the blue deep of Castellamare and the white city-line along the coast seen with a strange witchery across twenty miles of clear air.

The island is a paradise of silence for those to whom silence is a delight. One wanders about in the vineyards without a sound save the call of the vinedressers; one lies on the cliff and hears a thousand feet below the dreamy wash of the sea. There is hardly the cry of a bird to break the spell; even the girls who meet one with a smile on the hillside smile quietly and gravely in the Southern fashion as they pass by. It is the stillest place that the sun shines on; but with all its stillness it is far from being a home of boredom. There are in fact few places in the world so full of interest. The artist finds a world of "studies" in its rifts and cliff walls, in the sailor groups along its beach and the Greek faces of the girls in its vineyards. The geologist reads the secret of the past in its abruptly tilted strata, in a deposit of volcanic ash, in the fossils and bones which Augustus set the fashion of collecting before geology was thought of. The historian and the archæologist have a yet wider field. Capri is a perfect treasure-house of Roman remains, and though in later remains the island is far poorer, the ruins of mediæval castles crown the heights of Castiglione and Anacapri, and the mother church of San Costanzo with its central dome supported on marble shafts from the ruins hard by is an early specimen of Sicilian or Southern Italian architecture. Perhaps the most remarkable touch of the South is seen in the low stone vaults which form the roofs of all the older houses of Capri, and whose upper surface serves as a terrace where the women gather in the sunshine in a way which brings home to one oddly the recollections of Syria and Jerusalem.

For loungers of a steadily uninquiring order however there are plenty of amusements of a lighter sort. It is hard to spend a day more pleasantly than in boating beneath the cliffs of Capri, bobbing for "cardinals," cruising round the huge masses of the Faraglioni as they rise like giants out of the sea, dipping in and out of the little grottoes which stud the coast. On land there are climbs around headlands and "rock-work" for the adventurous, easy little walks with exquisite peeps of sea and cliff for the idle, sunny little nooks where the dreamer can lie buried in myrtle and arbutus. The life around one, simple as it is, has the colour and picturesqueness of the South. The girl faces which meet one on the hill-side are faces such as artists love. In the church the little children play about among the groups of mothers with orange kerchiefs on their heads and heavy silver rings on every finger. Strange processions with cowled faces and crucifix and banners borne aloft sweep into the piazza and up the church steps. Old women with Sibyl-like faces sit spinning at their doors. Maidens with water-jars on their heads which might have been dug up at Pompeii; priests with broad hats and huge cloaks; sailors with blue shirts and red girdles; urchins who almost instinctively cry for a "soldo" and break into the Tarantella if you look at them; quiet, grave, farmer-peasants with the Phrygian cap; coral-fishers fresh from the African coast with tales of storm and tempest and the Madonna's help—make up group after group of Caprese life as one looks idly on, a life not specially truthful perhaps or moral or high-minded, but sunny and pleasant and pretty enough, and harmonizing in its own genial way with the sunshine and beauty around.

Its rough inns, its want of English doctors, the difficulties of communication with the mainland from which its residents are utterly cut off in bad weather, make Capri an unsuitable resort for invalids in spite of a climate which if inferior to that of Catania is distinctly superior to that of either San Remo or Mentone. Those who remember the Riviera with no little gratitude may still shrink from the memory of its sharp transitions of temperature, the chill shade into which one plunges from the direct heat of its sun-rays, and the bitter cold of its winter nights. Out of the sun indeed the air of the Riviera towards Christmas is generally keen, and a cloudy day with an east wind sweeping along the shore will bring back unpleasant reminiscences of the England one has left behind. Capri is no hotter perhaps in the sunshine, but it is distinctly warmer in the shade. The wraps and shawls which are a necessity of health at San Remo or Mentone are far less necessary in the South. One may live frankly in the open air in a way which would hardly be safe elsewhere, and it is just life in the open air which is most beneficial to invalids. It is this natural warmth which tells on the temperature of the nights. The sudden change at sunset which is the terror of the Riviera is far less perceptible at Capri; indeed the average night temperature is but two degrees lower than that of the day. The air too is singularly pure and invigorating, for the village and its hotels stand some four or five hundred feet above the sea, and there are some fairly level and accessible walks along the hill-sides. At San Remo, or in the eastern bay of Mentone, one purchases shelter by living in a teacup and the only chance of exercise lies in climbing up its sides. But it must fairly be owned that these advantages are accompanied by some very serious drawbacks. If Capri is fairly free from the bitter east wind of the Riviera, the Riviera is free from the stifling scirocco of Capri. In the autumn and in the earlier part of the winter this is sometimes almost intolerable. The wind blows straight from Africa, hot, dusty, and oppressive in a strange and almost indescribable way. All the peculiar clearness of the atmosphere disappears; one sees every feature of the landscape as one would see them through a raw autumn day in England. The presence of fine dust in the air—the dust of the African desert to which this effect is said to be owing—may perhaps account for the peculiar oppressiveness of the scirocco; certain it is, that after two days of it every nerve in the body seems set ajar. Luckily however it only lasts for three days and dies down into rain as the wind veers round to the west.

II

CAPRI AND ITS ROMAN REMAINS

AMONG the many charms of Capri must be counted the number and interest of its Roman remains. The whole island is in fact a vast Roman wreck. Hillside and valley are filled with a mass of *débris* that brings home to one in a way which no detailed description can do the scale of the buildings with which it was crowded. At either landing-place huge substructures stretch away beneath the waves, the relics of moles, of arsenals, and of docks; a network of roads may still be traced which linked together the ruins of Imperial villas; every garden is watered from Roman cisterns; dig where he will, the excavator is rewarded by the discovery of vases, of urns, of fragments of sculpture, of mosaic pavements, of precious marbles. Every peasant has a handful of Roman coins to part with for a few soldi. The churches of the island and the royal palaces of the mainland are full of costly columns which have been removed from the ruins of Capri; and the Museum of Naples is largely indebted for its treasures of

statuary to the researches made here at the close of
the last century. The main archæological interest of
the island however lies not in fragments or "finds"
such as these but in the huge masses of ruin which
lie scattered so thickly over it. The Pharos which
guided the Alexandrian corn-ships to Puteoli stands
shattered on one of its headlands. The waves dash
idly against an enormous fragment of the sea-baths of
Tiberius. His palace-citadel still looks from the
summit of a mighty cliff across the Straits of Sorrento.
The Stairs of Anacapri, which in the absence of any
other date to which it is possible to assign them, we
are forced to refer to the same period of construction,
hewn as they were to the height of a thousand feet
in the solid rock, vied in boldness with almost any
achievement of Roman engineering. The smallness
of the space—for the lower part of the island within
which these relics are crowded is little more than a
mile and a half either way—adds to the sense of
wonder which the size and number of these creations
excite. All that remains too, it must be remembered,
is the work of but a few years. There is no ground
for believing that anything of importance was added
after the death of Tiberius or begun before the old
age of Augustus.

We catch glimpses indeed of the history of the
island long before its purchase by the aged Emperor.
Its commanding position at the mouth of the great
Campanian bay raised it into importance at a very

early period. The Teleboes whom tradition named as its first inhabitants have left only a trace of their existence in the verse of Vergil; but in the great strife between the Hellenic and Tyrrhenian races for the commercial monopoly of Southern Italy, Capri, like Sorrento, was seized as a naval station by the Etruscans, whose alliance with the Phœnicians in their common war against the Greeks may perhaps explain the vague legends of a Semitic settlement on the island. The Hellenic victory of Cumæ however settled the fate of Capri, as it settled the fate of the coast; and the island fell to the lot of Neapolis when the "new city" rose in the midst of the bay to which it has since given its name. The most enduring trace of its Greek colonization is to be found in the Greek type of countenance and form which endears Capri to artists; but like the cities of the mainland it preserved its Greek manners and speech long after it had passed with Neapolis into the grasp of Rome. The greater proportion of its inscriptions, even when dating from the Imperial period, are in Greek. Up to the time of Augustus however it played in Roman story but the humble part of lighting the great cornfleet from Egypt through the Strait of Sorrento. Statius tells us of the joy with which the sailors welcomed the glare of its Pharos as they neared the land, the greeting they addressed to its cliff, while on the other hand they poured their libations to the goddess whose white temple gleamed from the headland of Sorrento. Its higher destinies began with a chance visit of Augustus when age and weakness had driven him to seek a summer retreat on the Campanian shore. A happy omen, the revival of a withered ilex at his landing, as well as the temperate air of the place itself, so charmed the Emperor that he forced Naples to accept Ischia in exchange for it, and chose it as his favourite refuge from the excessive heat. Suetonius gives a pleasant gossiping picture of the old man's life in his short holidays there, his delight in idly listening to the prattle of his Moorish and Syrian slave-boys as they played knuckle-bones on the beach, his enjoyment of the cool breeze which swept through his villa even in summer or of the cool plash of water from the fountain in the peristyle, his curiosity about the big fossil bones dug up in the island which he sent to Rome to be placed in the galleries of his house on the Palatine, his fun in quizzing the pedants who followed him by Greek verses of his own making. But in the midst of his idleness the indefatigable energy which marked the man was seen in the buildings with which Suetonius tells us he furnished the island, and the progress of which after his death may possibly have been the inducement which drew his successor to its shores.

It is with the name of the second Cæsar rather than of the first that Capri is destined to be associated. While the jests and Greek verses of Augustus are forgotten the terrible invective of Tacitus and the sarcasm of Juvenal recall the cruelties and the terrors of Tiberius. His retirement to Capri, although as we have seen in form but a carrying out of the purpose of Augustus, marks a distinct stage in the development of the Empire. For ten years not Rome, but an obscure island off the Campanian coast became the centre of the government of the world. The spell of the Eternal City was suddenly broken, and it was never thoroughly restored. If Milan, Ravenna, Nicomedia, Constantinople, became afterwards her rivals or supplanters as the seat of empire, it was because Capri had led the way. For the first time too, as Dean Merivale has pointed out, the world was made to see in its bare nakedness the fact that it had a single master. All the disguises which Augustus had flung around his personal rule were cast aside; Senate, Consuls, the Roman people itself, were left contemptuously behind. A single senator, a few knights, a little group of Greek scholars, were all that accompanied Tiberius to Capri. The figure of the Emperor stood out bare and alone on its solitary rock. But, great as the change really was, the skill of Tacitus has thrown over the retirement of Tiberius a character of strangeness which, as we have said, hardly belongs to it. What in fact distinguished it from the retirement of Augustus to the same spot was simply the persistence of his successor in never returning to Rome.

Capri in itself was nothing but a part of the great pleasure resort which Roman luxury created round the shores of the Bay of Naples. From its cliffs the Emperor could see through the pure, transparent air the villas and watering-places which fringed the coast from Misenum to Sorrentum, the groves and lakes of Baiæ, the white line of Neapolis, Pompeii, and Herculaneum, the blue sea dappled with the painted sails of pleasure-boats as they wooed the summer air. The whole bay was a Roman Brighton, and the withdrawal of Tiberius from the world was much the same sort of withdrawal from the world as the seclusion of George IV. at the Pavilion. Of the viler pleasures which are commonly attributed to him in his retreat we need say nothing, for it is only by ingenious conjectures that any of the remains at Capri have been made to confirm them. The taste of Tiberius was as coarse as the taste of his fellow-Romans, and the scenes which were common at Baiæ —the drunkards wandering along the shore, the songs of the revellers, the drinking-toasts of the sailors, the boats with their gaudy cargo of noisy girls, the coarse jokes of the bathers among the rose-leaves which strewed the water—were probably as common in the revels at Capri. But for the more revolting details of the old man's life we have only the scandal of Rome to rely on, and scandal was easily quickened by the veil of solitude and secrecy which Tiberius flung around his retirement. The tale of his cruelties, of the fisherman tortured for having climbed the cliff which the Emperor deemed inaccessible, of criminals dashed into the sea down the steep of the "Salto di

Timberio," rest on the gossip of Suetonius alone. But in all this mass of gossip there is little that throws any real light on the character of the island or of the buildings whose remains excite our interest there; we can only guess at its far wilder condition from a story which shows us the Imperial litter fairly brought to a standstill by the thick brushwood, and the wrath of Tiberius venting itself in a ruthless thrashing of the centurion who served as his guide. The story is curious because it shows that, in spite of the rapidity with which the Imperial work had been carried on, the island when Tiberius arrived was still in many parts hidden with rough and impenetrable scrub, and that the wonderful series of hanging gardens which turned almost the whole of it into a vast pleasure-ground was mainly of his own creation.

It would of course be impossible to pass in review the numberless sites where either chance or research has detected traces of the work of Tiberius. "Duodecim villarum nominibus et molibus insederat," says Tacitus; and the sites of the twelve villas may in most cases be identified to-day, some basking in the sunshine by the shore, some placed in sheltered nooks where the cool sea-breeze tempered the summer heat, the grander ones crowning the summit of the hills. We can trace the docks of the Roman island, the grottoes still paved with mosaic which marks them as the scene of Imperial picnics, the terraces and arbours of the hanging gardens with the rock boldly cut away to make room for them, the system of roads which linked the villas together, the cisterns and aqueducts which supplied water, the buildings for the slaves of the household and for the legionaries who guarded the shore, the cemetery for the dead, the shrines and pavilions scattered about on the heights, and a small Mithraic temple hidden in the loveliest of the Caprese ravines. If we restore in fancy the scene to which these ruins belonged, fill the gardens with the fountains and statues whose fragments lie profusely scattered about, rear again the porticoes of marble columns, and restore the frescoes whose traces exist on the ruined walls, we shall form some inadequate conception of the luxury and grace which Tiberius flung around his retirement.

By a singular piece of good fortune the one great wreck which towers above all the rest is the spot with which the Emperor himself is historically associated. Through the nine terrible months during which the conspiracy of Sejanus was in progress, he never left, Seutonius tells us, the Villa Jovis; and the villa still stands on a huge promontory, fifteen hundred feet above the sea, from which his eye could watch every galley that brought its news of good or ill from Misenum and from Rome. Few landscapes can compare in extent or beauty with the view on which Tiberius looked. The promontory of Massa lies across the blue reach of sea, almost as it seems under one's hand yet really a few miles off, its northern side falling in brown slopes dotted with white villas to the orange gardens of Sorrento, its southern rushing steeply down to the hidden bays of Amalfi and Salerno. To the right the distant line of Apennine, broken by the shadowy dip that marks the plain of Pæstum, runs southward in a dim succession of capes and headlands; to the left the sunny bow of the Bay of Naples gleams clear and distinct through the brilliant air till Procida and Ischia lead the eye round again to the cliff of Anacapri with the busy little Marina at its feet. A tiny chapel in charge of a hermit now crowns the plateau which forms the highest point of the Villa Jovis; on three sides of the height the cliff falls in a sheer descent of more than a thousand feet to the sea, on the fourth the terrace walls are formed of fragments of brick and marble which recall the hanging gardens that swept downwards to the plain. The Villa itself lies partly hewn out of the sides of the steep rock, partly supported by a vast series of substructures whose arched vaults served as water-reservoirs and baths for the service of the house.

In strength of site and in the character of its defences the palace was strictly what Pliny calls it, "Tiberii principis arx," but this was no special characteristic of the Villa Jovis. "Scias non villas esse sed castra," said Seneca of the luxurious villas on the coast of Baiæ; it was as if the soldier element of the Roman nature broke out even amidst the patrician's idlest repose in the choice of a military site and the warlike strength of the buildings he erected on it. Within however life seems to have been luxurious enough. The ruins of a theatre, whose ground-plan remains perfect, show that Tiberius combined more elegant relaxations with the coarse revels which are laid to his charge. Each passage is paved with mosaic, the walls still retain in patches their coloured stucco, and here and there in the small chambers we find traces of the designs which adorned them. It is however rather by the vast extent and huge size of the substructures than by the remains of the house itself that we can estimate the grandeur of the Villa Jovis; for here, as at the Baths near the Marina, the ruins have served as quarries for chapels and forts and every farmhouse in the neighbourhood. The Baths stand only second in grandeur to the Villa itself. The fall of the cliff has torn down fragment after fragment, but the half of an immense calidarium still stands like an apse fronting the sea, a grand sea-wall juts out into the waves, and at its base, like a great ship of stone in the midst of the water, lies still unbroken after eighteen hundred years the sea-bath itself. The roof has fallen in, the pillars are tumbled from its front, but the high walls, though undermined by the tide, still stand erect. On the cliff above, a Roman fortress which must have resembled Burgh Castle in form and which has since served as a modern fort seems to have protected the Baths and the vast series of gardens which occupied the whole of the lower ground beneath the Stair of Anacapri, and whose boundary wall remains in a series of some twenty almost perfect arches.

The importance of these remains has long been understood by the archæologists of Italy, and something of their ruin may be attributed to the extensive excavations made by the Government of Naples a hundred years ago. But far more of the terrible wreck is owing to the ravages of time. With the death of Tiberius Capri sinks suddenly out of sight. Its name had in fact become associated with infamy, and there is no real ground for supposing that it remained as the pleasure-isle of later Emperors. But the vast buildings can only slowly have mouldered into decay; we find its Pharos flaming under Domitian, and the exile of two Roman princesses, Crispina and Lucilla, by Commodus, proves that Imperial villas still remained to shelter them. It is to the period which immediately follows the residence of Tiberius that we may refer one of the most curious among the existing monuments of Capri, the Mithraic temple of Metromania. Its situation is singularly picturesque. A stair cut in the rock leads steeply down a rift in the magnificent cliffs to the mouth of a little cave, once shrouded by a portico whose fragments lie scattered among the cacti and wild thyme. Within the walls are lined with the characteristic reticulated Roman masonry, broken chambers and doorways on either side are blocked by *débris*, and two semicircular

platforms rise one within the other to a niche in the
furthest recess of the cave where the bas-relief of
the Eastern deity which is now deposited in the
Museum at Naples was found by the excavators.
Beside it lay a stone with a Greek inscription so
strangely pathetic that it must tell its own tale :—
"Welcome into Hades, O noble deities—dwellers in
the Stygian land—welcome me too, most pitiful of
men, ravished from life by no judgment of the Fates,
but by a death sudden, violent, the death-stroke of a
wrath defiant of justice. But now I stood in the
first rank beside my lord! now he has reft me and
my parents alike of hope! I am not fifteen, I have
not reached my twentieth year, and—wretched I—I
see no more the light! My name is Hypatus; but I
pray my brother and my parents to weep for wretched
ones no more." Conjecture has coupled this wail of
a strange fate with the human sacrifices offered at
the shrine of Mithras, and has seen in Hypatus a
slave and favourite of Tiberius devoted by his master
to the Eastern deity; but there is no ground whatever for either of the guesses.

Such as it is however the death-cry of Hypatus
alone breaks the later silence of Capri. The introduction of Christianity was marked by the rise of the
mother church of San Costanzo, whose inner columns
of giallo antico and cipollino were torn from the ruins
of the Baths hard by, and from this moment we may
trace the progress of destruction in each monument of
the new faith. The sacrarium of San Stefano is paved

with a mosaic of marbles from the Villa Jovis, and the chapel of St. Michael is erected out of a Roman building which occupied its site. We do not know when the island ceased to form a part of the Imperial estate, but the evidence of a charter of Gregory II., overlooked by the local topographers, shows that at the opening of the eighth century the "Insula Capreæ cum monasterio St. Stefani" had passed like the rest of the Imperial property in the South to become part of the demesne of the Roman See. The change may have some relation to the subjection of Capri to the spiritual jurisdiction of Sorrento, of whose bishopric it formed a part till its own institution as a separate see in the tenth century. The name of the "Bishop of Quails," which attached itself to the prelate of Capri, points humorously to the chief source of his episcopal income, the revenue derived from the capture of the flocks of these birds which settle on the island in their two annual migrations in May and September. From the close of the ninth century, when the island passed out of the hands of Amalfi, it has followed the fortunes of the mainland; its ruin seems to have been completed by the raids of the Saracens from their neighbouring settlement on the coast of Lucania; and the two mediæval fortresses of Anacapri and Castiglione which bear the name of Barbarossa simply indicate that the Algerian pirate of the sixteenth century was the most dreaded of the long train of Moslem marauders who had made Capri their prey through the middle ages. Every raid and every fortress removed some monument of the Roman rule, and the fight which wrested the isle from Sir Hudson Lowe at the beginning of the present century put the coping-stone on the work of destruction. But in spite of the ravages of time and of man enough has been left to give a special archæological interest to the little rock-refuge of Capri.

III

THE FEAST OF THE CORAL-FISHERS

THE Caprese peasant has never had time to get the fact of winter fairly into his head. The cold comes year after year, but it comes in a brief and fitful way that sets our northern conceptions at defiance. The stranger who flies for refuge to the shores of the little island in November may find himself in a blaze of almost tropical sunshine. If a fortnight of dull weather at the opening of December raises hopes of an English Christmas they are likely to be swept away by a return of the summer glory for a month. Far away over the sea the crests of the Abruzzi range lift themselves white against the sky, but February has almost come before winter arrives, fitful, windy, rainy, but seldom cold, even when the mistral, so dreaded on the Riviera, comes sweeping down from the north. March ought by Caprese experience to be the difficult month; but "Marzo e pazzo," say the loungers in the little piazza, and sometimes even the "madness" of March takes the form of a delicious lunacy of unbroken sunshine. Corn is already rippling under the olives, leaf-buds run like little jets of green light along the brown vine-stems, the grey weird fig-branches are dotted with fruit, women are spinning again on the house-tops, boys are playing with the birds they have caught in the myrtles, the bright shore across the bay is veiled in a summer haze, and winter is gone. It is hard to provide in English fashion against such a winter as this, and the Capri fisherman prefers to regard it as something abnormal, exceptional, to be borne with "pazienza" and a shrug of the shoulders. When the storm-wind blows he lounges in the sunny corner of the Piazza; when the rain comes he smokes at home or mends his nets under the picture of the Madonna and the Bambino; when the cold comes he sits passive and numbed till the cold goes. But he knows that the cold will go, and that the rain will pass, and that peace will settle down again on the sunny bay; and so instead of making a fuss about winter he looks on it as a casual little parenthesis in the business of life, intensely disagreeable but luckily brief. He sees no poetry in it, no beauty of bare wold and folded mist; he hears no music in it like the music of tinkling icicles so dear to Cowper's heart. Christmas itself isn't much of a festa in the South, and has none of the mystery and home pathos which makes it dear to Englishmen. There is the "presepio" in the church, there is the procession of the Wise Men at Epiphany-tide, but the only real break to the winter's dulness is the Feast of the Coral-Fishers.

What with the poverty of the island and its big

families it is hard to see how Capri could get along at all if it were not for the extra employment and earnings which are afforded by the coral-fishery off the African coast. Some hundred or two hundred young fellows leave the island every spring to embark at Torre del Greco in a detachment of the great coral fleet which musters at that port, at Genoa, or at Leghorn; and the Sunday before they start—generally one of the last Sundays in January—serves as the Feast of the Coral-Fishers. Long before daybreak the banging of big crackers rouses the island from its slumbers, and high mass is hardly over when a procession of strange picturesqueness streams out of church into the sunshine. At its head come the "Daughters of Mary," some mere little trots, some girls of sixteen, but all clad in white, with garlands of flowers over their veils and girdles of red or blue. Behind come the fishermen, young sailor-boys followed by rough grizzled elders bearing candles like the girls before them, and then the village Brotherhood, fishers too, but clad in strange garments of grey, with black hoods covering their faces, and leaving nothing but the bright good-humoured eye to guide one under this sepulchral figure to the Giovanni or Beppino who was cracking jokes yesterday till the Blue Grotto rang again. Then beneath a great canopy upborne by the four elder fishers of the island, vested in gowns of "samite, mystic, wonderful"—somewhat like a doctor of music's gown in our unpoetic land—comes the Madonna herself, "La Madonna di Carmela," with a crown of gold on her head and a silver fish dangling from her fingers. It is the Madonna of Carmel who disputes with San Costanzo, the Saint of the mother-church below, the spiritual dominion of Capri. If he is the "Protector" of the island, she is its "Protectress." The older and graver sort indeed are faithful to their bishop-saint, and the loyalty of a vine-dresser in the Piazza remains unshaken even by the splendour of the procession. "Yes, signore!" he replies to a sceptical Englishman who presses him hard with the glory of "the Protectress," "yes, signore, the Madonna is great for the fisher-folk; she gives them fish. But fish are poor things after all and bring little money. It is San Costanzo who gives us the wine, the good red wine which is the wealth of the island. And so this winter feast of the fishermen is a poor little thing beside our festa of San Costanzo in the May-time. For the image of our Protector is all of silver, and sometimes the bishop comes over from Sorrento and walks behind it, and we go all the way through the vineyards, and he blesses them, and then at nightfall we have 'bombi' —not such as those of the Madonna," he adds with a quiet shrug of the shoulders, "but great bombi and great fireworks at the cost of the Municipio."

On the other hand, all the girls go with the fisher-folk in their love of the Madonna. "Ah yes, signore," laughs a maiden whose Greek face might have served Pheidias for a model, "San Costanzo is our protector, but he is old and the Madonna is young, so young and so pretty, signore, and she is *my* protectress." A fisherman backs up the feminine logic by a gird at the silver image which is evidently the strong point of the opposite party. The little commune is said to have borrowed a sum of money on the security of this work of art, and the fisherman is correspondingly scornful. "San Costanzo owes much, many danari, signore; and it is said," he whispers roguishly, "that if they don't pay pretty soon his creditors at Naples will send him to prison for the debt of the Municipio." But the Madonna has her troubles as well as the Saint. Her hair which has been dyed for the occasion has unhappily turned salmon colour by mistake; but the blunder has no sort of effect on the enthusiasm of her worshippers, on the canons who follow her in stiff copes, shouting lustily, or on the maidens and matrons who bring up the rear. Slowly the procession winds its way through the little town, now lengthening into a line of twinkling tapers as it passes through the narrow alleys which serve for streets, now widening out again on the hill-sides where the orange kerchiefs and silver ornaments of the Caprese women glow and flash into a grand background of colour in the sun. And then comes evening and benediction, and the fireworks, without which the procession would go for nothing, catherine-wheels spinning in the Piazza, and big crackers bursting amidst a chorus of pretty outcries of terror and delight.

Delight however ends with the festa, and the parting of the morning is a strange contrast in its sadness with this Sunday joy. The truth is that coral-fishing is a slavery to which nothing but sheer poverty drives the fishermen. From April to October their life is a life of ceaseless drudgery. Packed in a small boat without a deck, with no food but biscuit and foul water, touching land only at intervals of a month, and often deprived of sleep for days together through shortness of hands, the coral-fishers are exposed to a constant brutality from the masters of their vessels which is too horrible to bear description. Measured too by our English notions the pay of the men seems miserably inadequate to the toil and suffering which they undergo. Enough however remains to tempt the best of the Caprese fishermen to sea. Even a boy's earnings will pay his mother's rent. For a young man it is the only mode in which he can hope to gather a sum sufficient for marriage and his start in life. The early marriages so common at Naples and along the adjoining coast are unknown at Capri, where a girl seldom weds before twenty and where the poorest peasant refuses the hand of his daughter to a suitor who cannot furnish a wedding settlement of some twenty pounds. Even with the modern rise of wages it is almost impossible for a lover to accumulate such a sum from the produce of his ordinary toil, and his one resource is the coral-fishery.

The toil and suffering of the summer are soon forgotten when the young fisherman returns and adds his earnings to the little store of former years. When the store is complete, the ceremonial of a Caprese betrothal begins with "the embassy," as it is termed, of his mother to the parents of the future bride. Clad in her best array and holding in her hand the favourite nosegay of the island, a branch of sweet basil sprinkled with cinnamon powder and with a rose-coloured carnation in the midst of it, the old fishwife makes her way through the dark lanes to the vaulted room where her friends await her with a charming air of ignorance as to the errand on which she comes. Half an hour passes in diplomatic fence, in chat over the weather, the crops, or the price of maccaroni, till at a given signal the girl herself leaves the room, and the "ambassadress" breaks out in praise of her good looks, her industry, and her good repute. The parents retort by praise of the young fisherman, compliments pass quickly into business, and a vow of eternal friendship between the families is sworn over a bottle of rosolio. The priest is soon called in and the lovers are formally betrothed for six months, a ceremony which was followed in times past by a new appearance of the ambassadress with the customary offering of trinkets from the lover to his promised spouse. This old Caprese custom has disappeared, but the girls still pride themselves on the number and value of their ornaments — the "spadella," or stiletto which binds the elaborately braided mass of their ebon hair; the circular gold earrings with inner circles of pearls; the gold chain or lacétta, worn fold upon fold round the neck; the bunch of gold talismans suspended on the breast; the profusion of heavy silver rings which load every finger. The Sunday after her betrothal when she appears at

High Mass in all her finery is the proudest day of a Capri girl's life; but love has few of the tenderer incidents which make its poetry in the North. There is no "lover's lane" in Capri, for a maiden may not walk with her betrothed save in presence of witnesses; and a kiss before marriage is, as "Auld Robin Gray" calls it, "a sin" to which no modest girl stoops. The future husband is in fact busy with less romantic matters; it is his business to provide bed and bedding, table and chairs, drawers and looking-glass, and above all a dozen gaudy prints from Naples of the Madonna and the favourite saints of the day. The bride provides the rest, and on the eve of the marriage the families meet once more to take an inventory of her contributions which remain her own property till her death. The morning's sun streams in upon the lovers as they kneel at the close of mass before the priest in San Stefano; all the boyhood of Capri is waiting outside to pelt the bridal train with "confetti" as it hurries amidst blushes and laughter across the Piazza; a dinner of maccaroni and the island wine ends in a universal "tarantella," there is a final walk round the village at the close of the dance, and the coral-fisher reaps the prize of his toil as he leads his bride to her home.

THE END

www.ingramcontent.com/pod-product-compliance
Lightning Source LLC
Chambersburg PA
CBHW020224240426
43672CB00006B/410